C. J. Watson (1846–1927), lithograph after Thirtle's Self Portrait, No. 130

John Thirtle
1777-1839

Drawings in Norwich Castle Museum

Marjorie Allthorpe-Guyton

Norfolk Museums Service 1977
Francis Cheetham, Director

Permanent Collection Catalogues   Number 3

Previously published:

1   Henry Bright   1810–1873
    by Marjorie Allthorpe-Guyton   1973

2   John Sell Cotman   1782–1842
    by Miklos Rajnai assisted by Marjorie Allthorpe-Guyton   1975

Cover: detail from *View on the River near Cow's Tower, Norwich*, No. 15

ISBN 0 903101 23 8

Computer typeset and printed in Gt Britain by Page Bros (Norwich) Ltd,
Norwich

Contents

Foreword

Although John Thirtle is one of the best of the Norwich School artists, he has remained one of the least well known and his place among early English watercolourists has yet to be fully appreciated. There have been no papers published on him and only three exhibitions devoted to his work: the Norwich Art Circle Exhibition in 1886 and Centenary Exhibitions held by Messrs. Boswell & Sons and by Norwich Castle Museum in 1939. The latter created a ripple of surprise among connoisseurs of English watercolour:

'The delicate greens and silvery greys of some three or four landscape studies lent by Mr. Russell Colman . . . . . show the artist in an entirely fresh light . . . . . his Girtin-like breadth and simplicity of composition . . . . .' Paul Oppé 1939

Since the passing of critics such as Oppé, Binyon, Iolo Williams and latterly Martin Hardie, Thirtle's reputation, along with those of many other English watercolourists, has lapsed again into relative obscurity. A contributory factor has been of course the monopoly of the artist's work held by the Norwich Castle Museum: 169 drawings of which over 100, from the Colman Collection, have been kept in purpose-built cabinets and have seldom been exhibited. There was a revival of interest when Stephen Somerville included ten of the best in his East Anglian show at Colnaghi's in 1970. During Thirtle's bicentenary year it seemed more than appropriate that the Norfolk Museums Service should draw attention to him by publishing a catalogue of his work in the collection at Norwich Castle Museum.

This publication is the third in a series of biennially produced catalogues of the permanent collection; the two previous publications were *Henry Bright (1810–1873)*, published in 1973, and *John Sell Cotman, Drawings of Normandy in Norwich Castle Museum,* published in 1975. Much of the information used in this catalogue and the two preceding has accumulated as a result of Dr. Rajnai's research project on the History of the Norwich School sponsored by the Paul Mellon Centre and the City of Norwich. A reference work associated with this project on the Norwich Society of Artists has recently been published for the Centre by the Norfolk Museums Service.

Like the previous catalogues, this publication on John Thirtle is also marked by an exhibition which is being held from 18th June to 4th September 1977 in Norwich Castle Museum. All the drawings in the Catalogue are included in the exhibition as well as over forty items from public and private collections. I should like to extend my warmest thanks to those who have generously lent to the exhibition and to those who readily came forward with drawings both recorded and unrecorded. It is planned to show a selection from the exhibition at Eastbourne, at King's Lynn, at the Iveagh Bequest, Kenwood (in the Spring of 1978), and at the University Art Gallery, Nottingham. We have received substantial grants from the Paul Mellon Centre for Studies in British Art (London) Limited and the Arts Council towards the exhibition costs and a generous contribution has been made by the Eastern Arts Association. It is increasingly difficult for museums in the provinces to maintain a full publication and exhibition programme and it is to these organisations that we must look for continued support. We are gratified that it was forthcoming.

Francis W. Cheetham
Director
Norfolk Museums Service
May 1977

Acknowledgements

The compiler of any museum catalogue has a special debt to colleagues, both past and present. He has at his disposal the accumulated material of many contributors. Nothing could be more true of this publication.

Appreciation and gratitude is due above all to Dr. Miklós Rajnai: for giving unlimited access to the wealth of his material now being collated for his forthcoming publication on the History of the Norwich School; for offering much salient information; for his time and guidance in resolving the many problems of attribution, of chronology, of topography and for reading and correcting the manuscript; not forgetting an unsought for plunge into a dyke at Whitlingham in search of the site for *Trowse Meadows*. Warm thanks are extended also to Sheenah Smith for reading the manuscript and weeding out inconsistencies, for proof reading and helpful criticism; to Norma Watt for proof reading, for organising the plates for the catalogue, which were efficiently photographed by Peter Griffin of GGS Photography of Norwich, and for giving support by taking on extra work in the department; to other colleagues of the Norfolk Museums Service—Richard Malt for the design of the catalogue and exhibition publicity, Rosemary O'Donoghue for typing the drafts for the catalogue, Ken Heathcote and his department for work on the Thirtle Bicentenary Exhibition and Jane Porter for publicity work.

Special thanks are due to Mary Stevens for the arduous work of compiling, checking and typing indexes and for reading Cotman and Britton correspondence; to Gerald Chapman for work on auction records, for his transcriptions of Cotman family letters and for his good-humoured incredulity of the catalogue ever being finished; to Alec Cotman for many acts of kindness especially for passing on his notes on the fading of pigments; to Judy Hines for her invaluable work on the photographic archives of the Mellon project; to Philip Armes for his interest and his enthusiasm in undertaking the photography, in Norfolk wind and drizzle, of Thirtle's painting sites; to the University of East Anglia and the Norwich College of Art for help with the audio visual programme presented at the Thirtle Bicentenary Exhibition. Much of the information on Thirtle as a framemaker was contributed by Tessa Sidey who carried out this project with enthusiasm and efficiency. Barry Leveton kindly helped with this work. Likewise thanks are given: to Catherine Dinn, Diana Mawson, Helen Sutermeister and Charlotte Miller for archive and library searches; to Dr. Rosamund Harley who contributed her comments on Thirtle's manuscript; to Garry Thomson who offered advice on colour fading; to Michael Sheldon, Andrew Hemingway and Dr. Michael Pidgley for information and helpful conversations; to friends in the art trade for information always forthcoming and to many private owners for their help and hospitality.

Others who have freely given their time and help are: Francis Hawcroft, Timothy Clifford, Elizabeth Einberg, Philip Conisbee, Lindsay Stainton, Harley Preston, A. J. Stevens, Jane Grove, H. W. Earl, Andrew Stephenson, Peter Clayton and Mr. and Mrs. T. R. C. Blofeld. Colleagues in other institutions have been most co-operative: the staff of the Print Rooms of the British Museum (especially Reginald Williams), of the Victoria & Albert Museum, of the Ashmolean, and of the Fitzwilliam; of the Witt Library, the Warburg Institute and our colleagues in Norwich at the Norfolk and Norwich Record Office and the Norwich Reference and Colman & Rye Libraries.

Finally appreciation is extended to Francis Cheetham, Director of the Norfolk Museums Service, for his continued support and encouragement.

M.A-G.

Abbreviations

The following list does not include standard abbreviations which may be found in *The Concise Oxford Dictionary* nor does it include abbreviated information in the Provenance, Exhibitions and Reference Sections.

BM	British Museum
bt.	bought
c.	circa when before a date, otherwise centre
Cat.	Catalogue
CC	Colman Collection
EDP	*Eastern Daily Press*
EEN	*Eastern Evening News*
illus.	illustrated
l.	left or lower
l.l.	lower left
l.r.	lower right
litho.	lithograph
NCLN 1	Norfolk County Library: Norwich Division, Reference Library
NCLN2	Norfolk County Library: Norwich Division, Local History Library
NCM	Norwich Castle Museum
n.d.	no date
pub.	published
r.	right
repro.	reproduced
u.	upper
V & A	Victoria & Albert Museum
Witt	London, Courtauld Institute, Witt Library

Introduction

There is no more shadowy and elusive figure among the artists of the Norwich School than John Thirtle. He was, next to Crome and Cotman, the most talented watercolourist of his generation, yet little is known of his life, less even than that of John Crome's. Much of what is known is based on tradition and is undocumented. Of his birth, his setting up shop and subsequent business career, his marriage and his place within the Norwich Society of Artists, there exists today only the barest outline. Some reason for this lies in his apparent lack of success in attracting a wider than Norwich-based reputation during his lifetime. That this was also a root cause of Cotman's obscurity in the second half of the nineteenth century is expressed by Henry Ladbrooke (1800–1869) in a letter to his brother John Berney: . . . 'I am surprised that when men write upon Norwich Artists they should leave out, so much as they do the names of Cotman & Thirtle. As a man of genius Cotman was much Crome's superior & as a colorist Thirtle far surpassed them both—'[1]. Thirtle was Cotman's brother-in-law yet in the Cotman family correspondence there are only a few slight references to him. No letters to or from Thirtle have been traced[2]. However one important document has survived, his manuscript treatise on watercolour. This and the collection of his drawings in Norwich Castle Museum provide a firm basis for an appraisal of his achievement as a watercolourist, hitherto largely unappreciated and underestimated. This introduction sets down what is known of his life, his business and artistic contacts and attempts some analysis of his work.

Family

Thirtle, Thurtle or Thurtell as it is variously spelt, is a common enough Norfolk name and it occurs frequently in Norwich and Norfolk parish registers of the eighteenth and nineteenth centuries. John Thirtle was born into a Norwich family, he was baptised on 22nd June 1777, the son of John and Susanna Thurtle of St. Saviour's parish, Norwich[3]. His father, a shoemaker, may have been the brother of Thomas Thurtle of Norwich whose will is dated 30th March 1792[4]. He lists, as his beneficiaries, four sisters, a brother John Thurtle of Norwich (£5) and the widow of a late brother ?James Thurtle[5]. John Thirtle senior may have named his second son James, baptised 18th December 1785[3], after his brother. He seems to have had no other sons but a daughter Rachel was baptised 13th August 1780[3]. His wife Susanna Lincoln may have been a resident in St. Saviours as a widow Susanna Lincoln, probably her mother, was buried there 7th January 1791 aged 80 years[6].

Thirtle senior is traditionally said to have lived and carried on his shoemaking business in Elephant Yard, the picturesquely named alley which adjoined the Elephant Inn on the west side of Magdalen Street, south of Stump Cross. The inn was

---

1. ?1860. This date is in pencil at the head of the letter; Reeve Collection, Print Room, BM.
2. What are probably drafts of letters are on the *verso* of two drawings in the collection, Nos. 3, 21.
3. Norfolk and Norwich Record Office, register of baptisms, PD 33/6. I am grateful to Catherine Dinn for searches in the parish registers on my behalf.
4. Proved 3rd June 1801. Norfolk and Norwich Record Office, MC 2/7 450 × 7.
5. A James Thirtle, also a shoemaker, is given in the Norwich Poll Books for 1784 and 1799.
6. Norfolk and Norwich Record Office, register of burials, PD 33/6.

demolished in 1970 to make way for an 'elegant' freeway: 'the Magdalen Street Flyover'. Thirtle is said to have been born in Elephant Yard[1] but this was contested by a correspondent to *The Times* in 1886: 'he was born in the shop now occupied by myself, and known as the Magdalen Street Post-office. In fact, his widow lived there with me three years; and has not been long dead[2]. The Post Office adjoined the Elephant Inn to the north and it is possible that Thirtle's father took a shop and house in Elephant yard after his first child was born. As to the financial standing of the family, records examined so far[3] do not yield any precise information. A John Thirtle, presumably senior, is recorded in 1801–2 as the owner of a property in the occupation of Samuel Love, which was assessed at a rent of £14, 'others' £2.2.16. There are no entries for 'sums assessed on Personal Estates' or 'sums assessed on offices'. Tax paid was £2.16.0 per annum. There are further entries until 1804–5 when extra sums for 'stock' £40 and 'personal estate' £0.8.0 are given. Similar sums occur up to 1832–1833; but as the father did not die until 1825, it is not possible to distinguish between the property of father and son before that date. However, it is evident that John Thirtle senior owned and occupied his own property and ran a business from it. The assessed value is low to average for the parish so he does not seem to have been especially prosperous. Nevertheless he must have played a prominent role in the local community as he was both an overseer of the poor and a churchwarden in the parish, offices which Thirtle also held. On 20th February 1798 he is recorded as giving 6d, collected because of the 'severity of the winter and great hardship of the poor'[4]. James Reeve records an account of Benjamin Russell, watchmaker of Magdalen Street, Thirtle senior's nephew, which indicates that the business may have prospered later: 'speaks of his grandfather . . . as a well to do shoemaker & amusingly illustrates his position by telling one how he remembers his grandfather's customers coming down the yard in their carriages & that he has every reason to think well of him as he left his mother some 3 per cents which eventually came to him.'[5]

Whatever the exact nature of the family's financial position, it is clear that they were tradesmen with no private income.

London   Of Thirtle's boyhood we have no details, it is traditionally said that he was sent to London at an early age[6] to learn the business of a framemaker. He might well have gone to a Mr. Allwood to whom Jeremiah Freeman (1763–1823) went in 1784 and might have received the same sound advice as Freeman had from Benjamin Jagger (1723–1821) then the leading carver, gilder and framemaker of Norwich: 'am glad to hear you are at Mr. Alwoods—take Care to continue there, at least for 2 or 3 mths & part of time as a Carver—'tho you will, if in Gilding Shop see their Methods of Working & thereby practice on Evenings—that alone will not be sufficient you must Enquire ab[out] other shops—& where the best work is done—you sh*d* also see their Methods in the City, for there they work quick, cheap & shewy—This method you must also learn—don't forget the putty Work—your time is at present Very

1. James Reeve, Introduction to the Norwich Art Circle, Third Exhibition, *John Thirtle Catalogue* 1886 and subsequent biographers.

2. H. C. Thompson, 12th July 1886.

3. Norfolk and Norwich Record Office, Land and Window Tax Papers 1798–1832, St. Saviour's parish, Case 23(e) Box 4. I am grateful to Helen Sutermeister for carrying out this search on my behalf.

4. Norfolk and Norwich Record Office, St. Saviour's Parish Book, PD 33/37. I am grateful to Diana Mawson for carrying out this search on my behalf.

5. Manuscript note in the Reeve Collection, Print Room, BM.

6. James Reeve, Introduction to the Norwich Art Circle, Third Exhibition, *John Thirtle Catalogue* 1886 and subsequent biographers.

short—As to the Cannons Stannards & Cross & such like Gentry youll have nothing to do with, neither with their Methods or connections—they will all come to the D–gs—I never knew one of those people succeed—they are not fit for journeymen, therefore make Garrett Masters & Starve themselves & their familys. . .'[1] If Thirtle was apprenticed in London he must have gone at the age of twelve to fourteen, that is 1789–1791. If he served a full term of seven years he may have still been in London when Cotman left Norwich for the City in c. 1798. According to Reeve 'JJC [John Joseph Cotman] says that Thirtle was in the habit of going to the different shops his father [John Sell Cotman] had to do with to see whatever there might be new of his exhibiting in the windows'[2].

The Return to Norwich

Thirtle is presumed to have returned to Norwich in c. 1800 although the first documented record of his being there is in the catalogue of the first exhibition of the Norwich Society of Artists, in 1805, where he is listed simply as 'J. Thirtle, Norwich'. In 1806 he describes himself as a 'Miniature-Painter and Drawing Master' of St. Saviour's, Norwich. By this time he must have already 'opened a print shop not far from his father's residence this he altered and adapted to a Gilder's business which he carried on in conjunction with his profession as an artist and teacher of drawing.'[2] A natural inclination and his years in London may have led Thirtle to aspire to be a printseller but economic pressures in Norwich would have forced him to follow his early training into the more lucrative business of framemaking. He may have only rented premises for some time; he is not given in trade directories until 1822 when in Pigot's *National and Commercial Directory* he advertises as both a carver and gilder and a teacher of drawing. The earliest documented record of his occupying and possibly owning property[3], is in 1825, the year of his father's death, when he is entered in a Rate book[4] of that year as John Thirtle junior, a house and shop assessed at 5s. 10d.; his brother James is also given with property assessed at 4s. 10d. His shop, with living quarters above, was a three storied, double gabled building, probably dating from the sixteenth century and situated on the west side of Magdalen Street, south of Golden Dog Lane[5]. Unfortunately it has been replaced by a mean postwar building; the two gables are gone and the premises, nos. 26A and 26, are occupied respectively by a jeweller's shop and 'The Norwich Bargain Centre'.

The Norwich Society of Artists and Marriage

Thirtle's career was of necessity one of diversification, as a carver and gilder, a miniature painter, a drawing master and a landscape painter[6]. In view of the prominent role he later played, he was probably a founder member in 1803 of the Norwich Society of Artists, but his membership is not recorded until 1806 when members are first listed in the Society's catalogues. He remained a formal member of the Society and in 1812 he was chosen as Vice President by the President for that year, Francis Stone (1770–1835), an architect and the County Surveyor. For Thirtle 1812 was a signal year. At the mature age of thirty-five, on 2nd November in St. Saviour's Church he married Elizabeth Miles of Felbrigg, Norfolk. The witnesses

1. Freeman MSS, Bundle 1, NCM, Art Dept. archives. I am grateful to Tessa Sidey for bringing this letter to my attention during her research on Thirtle and framemaking carried out on my behalf.

2. Manuscript note in the Reeve Collection, Print Room, BM.

3. In the *Norwich Poll Book* of 1835 he is listed under 'Occupiers' not under 'Freeholders'.

4. Norfolk and Norwich Record Office, Rate Book N/T23/2 p. 169. I am grateful to Helen Sutermeister for this reference.

5. Dickes p. 219 reproduces a late nineteenth century/early twentieth century photograph showing the premises occupied by Breeze (No. 65: plumbers and glaziers; *Jarrolds' Norwich Directory* 1886).

6. Pigot's *National and Regional Trade Directory* 1830: 'landscape painter' and 'teacher of drawing'; White's *Norfolk Directory* 1836: 'Carver and Gilder'; the Norwich Society of Artists' exhibition catalogues 1806–1815 'Miniature Painter and Drawing Master'.

were John Hicks and Katherine Miles[1]. Three years earlier on 6th January 1809, in Felbrigg Church, John Sell Cotman had married Elizabeth's sister, Ann[2]. It must have been a happy period for both artists; Cotman writing to his wife from Normandy in 1820 reflects nostalgically when he saw 'three pretty farmers' daughters, well dressed and arm-in-arm; and I thought on Felbrigg and old times.'[3] Thirtle may have met his future wife through Cotman or through the Norwich Society as both Elizabeth and Katherine exhibited as Miss E. and Miss K. Miles in 1811. The girls were the daughters of Edmund Miles who was in Felbrigg by 1788, when the birth of Miles' children is first recorded in the parish registers of Felbrigg-with-Metton. A son Edmund was born that year, followed by Katherine in 1791, William in 1797 and Harriet in 1801. Elizabeth was born earlier, in 1787, probably in Yarmouth which may also have been the birthplace of Ann and another daughter Ann Maria[4].

In 1791 their father leased Swifts Grove Farm, Felbrigg, from William Windham of Felbrigg Hall, for a period of sixteen years from Michaelmas at a rent of £200 per annum. The land consisted of 348 acres and one rood, lying in Felbrigg, Roughton and Sustead[5]. Although a tenant-farmer at this period, Edmund Miles' will dated 8th February 1807[6] describes him as a 'Gentleman' and disposes of a considerable amount of property, both copyhold and freehold, as well as almost £5,000, and gives instructions for the sharing of rents and profits and the interest from securities. All the daughters received on their coming of age £500 each. His eldest son Edmund inherited all the estate and became a lieutenant in the Royal Navy[7]. It seems then that Cotman and Thirtle were married not to the daughters of a humble farmer but into a family of some means. Unlike Cotman and Ann, who had six, Thirtle and Elizabeth do not seem to have had any children.

In 1813 Thirtle was again chosen, by the President Elect Charles Hodgson (1769–1856), as Vice President of the Norwich Society. The following year he was himself elected President and selected James Sillett (1764–1840), the fruit, flower and architectural painter, as his Vice President. In 1816 Thirtle, Sillett and Robert Ladbrooke (1769–1842) seceded from the Society and formed a breakaway group which called itself the Norfolk and Norwich Society of Artists. The cause of the rift was a difference of opinion between Ladbrooke and John Crome. Henry Ladbrooke later wrote to his brother John Berney:

'after every exhibition there was a profit accruing to the Society he [Robert Ladbrooke] proposed that such profit should go to establish a fund for the purpose of purchasing casts, models or any other works of Art that might lay the foundation of an Academy for the members to study from—to make it a school for

<hr />

1. Copy of the marriage license by the Rev. R. J. Simpson in NCM, Art Dept. archives.

2. Kitson 1937 p. 127.

3. Kitson 1937 p. 231.

4. One of the entries, dated 13th October 1787, in the baptismal register of St. Nicholas Church, Yarmouth, records twins, daughter and son of Edmund and Mary (née Hancock), which could be proof of Edmund Miles' residence there but unfortunately no surname is given (Norfolk and Norwich Record Office, PD 28/16). Miles was however a common Yarmouth name; a James Miles sailed trading vessels from Yarmouth to London in 1790 (*The Universal British Directory*) and the talented miniaturist Edward Miles (1752–1828) was born in Yarmouth; he later moved to Norwich by 1775.

5. Norfolk and Norwich Record Office, WKC 5/122 400X4. I am grateful to Diana Mawson for researches into the Miles family.

6. Edmund Miles died by 11th April 1807 and his will was proved in Norwich on the 30th May and 29 July 1807. Norfolk and Norwich Record Office, NCC Wills 1807 no. 83.

7. A more elevated position than a press ganged sailor which Kitson 1937 suggests (p. 129). He died in 1855 'beloved, respected and lamented', as the inscription states on the substantial monument erected to him in the Rosary Cemetery, Norwich.

study and improvement—Crome differed from him and insisted that the members should meet once a month in the evening have a supper and chat of Art or anything else—Thirtle and Sillett I think were the only members who joined my father in the Secession, though Hodgson and one or two others, who advocated my father's opinions had not the moral courage to join him—Crome was certainly a more popular man than Ladbrooke and carried the motion for eating and drinking . . .'[1]

The three seceders had an exhibition room built on Theatre Plain where they and their associates held annual exhibitions for three consecutive years 1816–1818 after which their Society ceased. In the first year Thirtle showed fifteen works almost matching his highest contribution ever to the original Society, seventeen works in 1806. In 1817 he showed only six and none at all in 1818. A fact which was regretted by the local press 'We lament exceedingly that Mr. Thirtle, who made up the seceding triumvirate, should not have found time for a single drawing. His occupation is doubly to be regretted, because he stands highest and alone in the particular and beautiful department of watercolours, in which he has evinced so much decided excellence.'[2] That year the first volume of *Excursions through Norfolk* was published by Longman & Co., London. It included four engravings after drawings by Thirtle (a) *Bishop's Bridge, Norwich*, (b) *The City of Norwich*, (c) *Westwick House* and (d) *Bracondale*[3]. Another (e) *Costessey Park* appeared in volume two published in 1819[3]. According to Kitson[4] Thirtle was called on to help Cotman, who had been commissioned to produce almost a hundred drawings for the *Excursions*. This is a plausible explanation of how Thirtle's contribution to this publication came about.

Despite repeated requests for him to return Thirtle did not exhibit again with the original Society until 1828 and then he was an exhibitor only, he did not resume his membership. Sillett on the other hand returned straight away in 1819 and exhibited regularly thereafter, although not as a member. He became a subscriber in 1828. Ladbrooke returned, as an exhibitor only, in 1824. Thirtle's total contribution to the Norwich exhibitions, including the Secession, was 97 works, far short of Cotman's (344), Crome's (301), Sillett's (289) or Ladbrooke's (238). As contemporary reviewers and later biographers indicate the reasons were twofold: the demands of his business and his chronic illhealth.

John Thirtle suffered from that most notorious of diseases of the Romantic age: consumption. This was probably aggravated in his case, as it was in Girtin's, by his venturing forth in inclement weather in pursuit of his passion for effects of light and atmosphere 'Whenever a thunderstorm passed over the city the late Mrs. Thirtle used to say that it was her husband's wont to sally out upon the Castle Hill and watch its course as it journeyed over his head'.[5] He was probably always in delicate health and must have contracted consumption in later life as he lived to the age of sixty-three when he died "after a long and painful illness . . . . sincerely regretted by his relatives and friends."[6] Edmund Miles was in attendance. Thirtle left his not inconsiderable estate of £2,000 to his 'beloved wife Elizabeth'[7] who outlived her husband

1. ?1860. This date is in pencil at the head of the letter; Reeve Collection, Print Room, BM.

2. *Norwich Mercury* 1st August 1818.

3. (a) Bet. pp. 8 & 9. Engraved by W. Wallis, see the entry for No. 30; (b) Opp. p. 35. Engraved by J. Varrall, see the entry for No. 54; (c) Opp. p. 131. Engraved by T. Ranson, no drawing for this subject is known; (d) Opp. p. 155. Engraved by W. Wallis, see the entry for No. 5; (e) Opp. p. 50. Engraved by T. Higham, see the entry for No. 35.

4. pp. 184, 185. One other drawing by Thirtle, *Entrance to the Bishops Palace Norwich*, was engraved by Eastgate for Bell's *Antiquities of Norfolk*, of which only isolated impressions of the illustrations are known.

5. James Reeve Introduction to the Norwich Art Circle, *Third Exhibition Catalogue, John Thirtle* 1886.

6. *Norwich Mercury* 5th October 1939. His death certificate gives consumption as the cause of death (East Wymer Ward Book 2, Entry 203).

7. Will dated 31st July 1838, proved in London 3rd December 1839. Public Record Office, PROB 10 5897 X/K 4874.

by many years. She died in 1882 at the ripe old age of ninety-five and left an estate of just under £1,500 with several bequests; among them 19 guineas each to her nephews John Cotman (John Joseph Cotman) and John Kitton and 19 guineas each to the children of Miles Edmund Cotman[1]. Thirtle and his wife are buried in the Rosary Cemetery, Norwich[2].

Business Life

Thirtle's most formidable business competitors in Norwich were the Freemans father and son. Before them, in the second half of the eighteenth century, Benjamin Jagger had dominated the framing and printselling trade in Norwich. In 1795 his finished stock and his household were sold up[3] and he appears to have left the city and died in London in 1821[4]. His natural successor was his protegé Jeremiah Freeman who had set up shop as a carver, gilder and printseller of 9 London Lane by 1790[5]. In 1795 he moved to No. 2 London Lane 'nearer the market'[6] and by September 1806 he had acquired another property 'his Cabinet and upholstery Warehouse, No. 12 Upper-Market, Norwich'[7]. From 1790 Freeman regularly advertised as framemaker, picture restorer, colourman, printseller and gallery owner. At Knight's exhibition of Norwich shawl manufacturers in New Bond Street, London, he had the commission for 'the ornamental carving and gilding'[8]. By 1798 he was inviting subscriptions for 'prints now engraving' after portraits by Hoppner[9]; in 1800 he was selling Edmund Bartell's (1770–1855) *Cromer*[10] and prints after Keymer's portrait of Nelson. By 1804 he was both printseller and publisher.

His talents and influence extended to the Norwich Society of Artists with which he exibited from 1805[11]. During the Secession in 1817, he was chosen as Vice President under Michael Sharp and elected President in 1818 choosing John Berney Crome (1794–1842) as his Vice President. His son William Freeman (1784–1877) whom he had taken into partnership by 1809[12], married Elizabeth Barnes, sister of Philip Barnes (1792–1874), a Secretary of the Norwich Society from 1817–1821. It is not surprising therefore that the Freemans cornered both the framing and the printselling markets in the city. Their status is confirmed by the public patronage bestowed on them. In 1801 the Norwich City Committee ordered that 'Messrs. Cushing and Freeman [be] jointly appointed to make a frame for Lord Nelson's picture. Price must not exceed 27 gns.' In 1805 Freeman secured permission to publish Bell's mezzotint after the Nelson portrait by Beechey[13] which hangs in its magnificent frame in Blackfriars' Hall, Norwich[14]. Thereafter the Freemans and Cushing (fl. 1783–1836) were in sole charge of the repair of frames for the Civic Portrait collection[15].

1. Will dated 6th November 1875, proved in Norwich 4th May 1882, Somerset House, Probate 11, 1920.
2. Grave No. 1/759.
3. *Norfolk Chronicle* 14th March, 12th and 26th September 1795.
4. *Norwich Mercury* 10th March 1821.
5. *Norfolk Chronicle* 10th April 1790.
6. *Norfolk Chronicle* 10th Jan. 1795.
7. *Norfolk Chromicle* 15th Sept. 1806.
8. *Norwich Mercury* 6th April 1793, kindly communicated by Mr. Trevor Fawcett.
9. *Norwich Mercury* 16th June 1798.
10. *Observations upon the town of Cromer considered as a Watering Place and the Picturesque Scenery in its Neighbourhood* pub. London and Norwich 1800.
11. He had been first apprenticed to a painter, Robert Vandermyn of Norwich on 23rd May 1777.
12. *Norwich Mercury* 6th May 1809.
13. *Norwich Mercury* 30th November 1805.
14. He also executed in 1806 the monument to Nelson's victory at Cape St. Vincent in the Guildhall, Norwich.
15. City Committee Books 1801–1835, shelf 4 case 19, Norfolk and Norwich Record Office.

In the face of such rivals it is surprising that Thirtle survived in business at all. Especially as he does not seem to have advertised once in the local press, although he used trade directories from 1822. Freeman was the regular receiver for the Norwich Society exhibitions, but in 1815 Thirtle was also handling pictures, for the Dixon Memorial exhibition. However this contact would have been severed during the Secession of 1816–1818. By 1813 Thirtle was receiving subscriptions for Cotman's publications the *Antiquities of Norfolk* and *Sepulchral Brasses*[1], and in 1824 for Cotman's proposed etching of the Grand Musical Festival in St. Andrew's Hall[2]. Applications in 1830 for Stark's *Scenery of the Rivers of Norfolk* were invited by both Freeman and Thirtle[3]. In 1834 Thirtle was a purchaser at John Sell Cotman's sale[4] where he acquired three of this brother-in-law's oils for a total of £7.17s.

In 1823 Thirtle's mother died[5] and two years later he buried his father on 11th December 1825[6]. John Thirtle senior's will, proved 27th January 1826[7] allowed a third part of the sale of his property and effects to each of his three children. This benefit from his father's will may have given Thirtle some financial stability in the remaining thirteen years of his life.

It seems that much of Thirtle's work may have been through his fellow artists whose works he had to frame. He was closely acquainted with Joseph Clover (1779–1853), the Norfolk born portrait and genre painter of Newman Street, London. In the years of the Secession 1816 and 1817 he exhibited in Norwich and gave Thirtle as his address. Clover, a pupil and friend of Opie, painted many local dignitaries. He was commissioned to paint three of the Civic Portraits in 1809, 1813 and 1817 and was on social terms with two Norfolk families with whom Thirtle had contact[8]: the Prestons of Stanfield Hall, Wymondham and the Blofelds of Hoveton House, whose portraits he also painted. He may have directed clients to Thirtle and he certainly used Thirtle's services himself. In his account books[9] are payments to Thirtle for 28th April 1825 'Thirtle . . . £50', 13th December 1826 'paid to Thirtle £50.12.6' and in November 1828 for two threequarter frames £5.5.0, a large picture £6.16.0 and a case £2.4.6. The last payment is dated 19th May 1838, the year before Thirtle's death.

Clover was a friend of Stark and Vincent who both had Thirtle frame their work. He had Vincent's *Trowse Meadows* to frame and took the opportunity to copy it in watercolour, No. 110. Some of the scant references to Thirtle in the Cotman letters indicate that he occasionally received the family drawings to frame and sell; thus Miles Edmund Cotman writes to John Joseph, 3rd September 1835: 'I wish you would take two or three of the best you have of mine to Freeman's and hear if he will try to dispose of them. You might even try Thirtle . . .'[10] and John Sell writes to John Joseph, 14th December 1836, 'Ask Thirtle to lend Edmund the two Drawings I saw framed, opposite the Windows, if he will lend them send them up *without the Frames*

Framemaking

---

1. *Bury and Norwich Post* 26th May 1813.
2. *Norfolk Chronicle* 25th Sept. 1824.
3. *Norwich Mercury* 30th Jan. 1830.
4. Norwich, Spelman, Fri. 12th Sept. 1834, lots 114, 126, 127. See Kitson p. 116.
5. St. Saviour's Burials 30th May 1823, Norfolk and Norwich Record Office.
6. St. Saviour's Burials 11th December 1825, Norfolk and Norwich Record Office.
7. Dated 20th November 1820, Public Record Office, PROB 11/1707, 25815.
8. See Cat. Nos. 71, 153. There are references to Clover in the Blofield Diaries for 1831, in the collection of Mr. and Mrs. T. R. C. Blofield.
9. NMC, Art Dept. archives.
10. BM Add. MS 37029 p. 113. I am grateful to Andrew Hemingway for this and the following reference.

and thank him for the kindness from me.'[1] Thirtle evidently employed at least one craftsman, a Mr. Root[2], as a gilder.

There are several pictures by J. S. Cotman, J. B. Crome, Dixon, Lound, Sillett, Stannard and Vincent in the collection of Norwich Castle Museum whose frames bear Thirtle's trade labels of which there are three types. The earliest bears a simple caption only *J. THIRTLE, Magdalen Street, Norwich*. Another has in fine copperplate *Thirtle Carver Gilder Picture & Glass Frame Maker Magdalen Street Norwich* and the latest is embellished by a border design enclosing *JOHN THIRTLE CARVER, GILDER, PICTURE FRAME AND LOOKING GLASS MANUFACTURER, WHOLESALE AND RETAIL, MAGDALEN STREET NORWICH*. The frames, of fine but unexceptional contemporary designs, are moulded with corner and centre shell and scroll motifs with beading along the outer and inner edges of the frame. Some have sprig decoration covering the 'swept' band of the frame while one has a flattened infill design. On his death in 1839, Thirtle's shop was taken over by William Boswell, an apprentice to William Freeman[3]. The firm of Boswell flourished until 1948 when a collection of their framing moulds of box and fruit wood, which may include some early Thirtle moulds, was presented to the Bridewell Museum, Norwich.

The Drawing Master

From 1807–1817 Thirtle is described in the Norwich Society catalogues as a Drawing Master. There are a number of drawings in the collection whose attributions are under suspicion[4] but which are obviously influenced by Thirtle. Undoubtedly some of these are the work of pupils. However the only pupil for which there is a documented record is Mary Catherine Blofeld (1803–1851), the daughter of Thomas Calthorpe Blofeld (1777–1855) of Hoveton House, Norfolk, and his wife Mary Caroline Grose (1763–1852) who was the second daughter of Francis Grose, FSA, the antiquarian. By 1824[5] Thirtle was drawing master to Mary Blofeld; a watercolour study by him showing her seated beneath a tree in front of the house, is in the collection, No. 75. Perhaps Thirtle, like Miles Edmund Cotman, preferred ladies as pupils: *'nothing like Ladies they are* the things to teach—soft—ductile creatures!!'[6] A sketch-book and two watercolours by Mary Blofeld are still with the family. The watercolours are in Thirtle's manner but the drawing and palette are distinctly amateur. The Blofelds took a strong interest in artistic activities, apart from their dealings with Clover. Tom Blofeld enters in his diary for April 1819 'called on . . . the Artist Starke to see his Picture of Wroxham sailing Match with which I was much pleased tho' no portrait of the Country.'

The Blofelds were friends of the Prestons of Stanfield Hall, Wymondham, whose portraits Thirtle painted in 1819 and the Hall is the subject of a drawing in the collection, No. 71. Apart from these two families, Thirtle may have been acquainted and received work from the Burroughes of Burlingham St. Peter (see No. 141), from Peter le Neve-Foster (see No. 69) and Philip Martineau (see No. 5). He may have recruited pupils in this circle.

1. *op. cit.* p. 173.
2. See the entry for No. 110. Possibly the James Root given in Chase's *Norwich Directory* 1783 as 'Whitesmith' of 14 Red Lion Lane, and in Peck 1802 and Berry 1811 as of St. Saviours Church Lane.
3. Register of Admissions, Freemen's Books 1818–1937, Norfolk and Norwich Record Office.
4. See Works excluded from the Catalogue p. 77.
5. Thomas Blofeld's diary, April 1824 'Paid Thirtle DM [Drawing Master] in full £9. 16.9'. A further entry for Oct. 1831: 'Thirtle on Acc of his Bill . . . £5'; quoted by kind permission of Mr. and Mrs. T. R. C. Blofeld.
6. Miles Edmund Cotman to John Joseph Cotman, 14th Feb. 1834, BM Add. MS 37029 p. 32.

One of his more informal students was Henry Ladbrooke whose reminiscences were published posthumously in the *EDP* 1921: "As long as art is admired and studied, the water colour drawings of Thirtle must be held in the highest esteem . . . He was the most liberal man in imparting the knowledge of his art to any whom he took a liking for . . ."[1] He and Thirtle sketched together at Buckenham Ferry of which there is a drawing dated 1827 in the collection, No. 105, and at Dilham Staithe, see Nos. 115–118. They also visited Mundesley where 'seeing that the sun was just bursting out with a complete copper colour, he [Thirtle] made a sketch of the cliffs and a group of figures and boats.'[2] Other pupils may have included James Pattison Cockburn (1779–1847), the soldier and amateur artist, who was stationed in Norwich for a few years and who became one of the first honorary members of the Norwich Society with which he exhibited seventeen works in 1809. Cockburn was earlier a pupil of Paul Sandby, but his drawings of Norwich subjects in the museum's collection, such as *Cavalry Barracks*[3] and *Norwich Cathedral*[4], indicate some direct influence from Thirtle.

Thirtle's advice to his pupils and his own approach to watercolour is set down in his *Hints on Water-colour Painting*, the transcript of which is published in this catalogue. This treatise comes under discussion in the succeeding paragraphs.

Artistic Development

Thirtle is known only as a watercolourist although according to Henry Ladbrooke he attempted oil painting and took lessons from Robert Ladbrooke: 'He used to come on the Sunday morning for his lesson, but as he could not manage the 'pigments' and 'vehicles' he gave it up.'[5] Only one oil has ever been attributed to him, this is discussed in the entry for No. 113. Thirtle's decision was fortuitous, it gave him freedom to develop his extraordinary powers in the more fickle medium of watercolour.

'Mr. Thirtle's drawings in watercolour are certainly without rivals in either place. They have a warmth, a richness and a brilliancy that is very captivating.'

Richard Mackenzie Bacon 1817[6]

'. . . In the field of watercolour alone, Thirtle may well be considered a greater artist than Crome; the rarity of his known work is the reason for his relative neglect.'

Martin Hardie 1968[7]

The Manuscript Treatise on Watercolour

For a full understanding of Thirtle's achievement as a watercolourist much more work is required on his treatise *Hints on Water-colour Painting*. Indeed there is scope for a greater and more systematic study than has hitherto been attempted on the many drawing manuals and technical treatises published in the eighteenth and nineteenth centuries in England, and their relationship to the oeuvres of landscape painters of the period. This study is still in its infancy, a contributory factor being that collections of such works are scattered, the best is probably that from the Abbey Collection, now in the Yale Center for British Art, New Haven, USA[8].

Thirtle's manuscript is undated but he mentions Purple and Brown Madder which are not cited in eighteenth century sources and which were probably not available

1. *EDP* 22nd April 1921.

2. *EDP* 25th April 1921.

3. NCM, 29a.235.951, repro, Clifford pl. 60b.

4. NCM, 1134.76.94.

5. ?1860. This date is in pencil at the head of the letter; Reeve Collection, Print Room, BM.

6. *Norwich Mercury* 9th August 1817.

7. Hardie, vol. II, p. 66.

8. An article on this collection by Joan Friedman is published by *Apollo* April 1977, vol. CV, no. 182, pp. 262–267.

commercially until the early part of the nineteenth century[1]. It may be safe to tentatively date the manuscript as not earlier than 1810[1]. Therefore it is probably contemporary with such published works as Ackerman's *New Drawing Book of Light and Shadow*, London 1809, David Cox's *A Series of Progressive Lessons* 1811, W. H. Pyne's *Rudiments of Landscape Drawing* 1812, and John Hassell's *Aqua Pictura* of 1813. Thirtle's treatise differs in one fundamental aspect from those above in that it was probably not intended for publication and as a result it presents a disorganised stream of technical instructions alongside observations on optical phenomena. That some of these may be paraphrases of published works is more than likely. Thirtle writes on *Light and Shade:* 'the general Effect of the light & shade should be produced in the whole before any of the parts are begun to be finished' which reiterates Ackerman's *New Drawing Book* 1809 'the powerful relief that is produced by a just distribution of the lights and the shadows . . .'[2] In his instructions for clouds Thirtle writes 'Venetian Red & Indigo, the Red Predominating will do for the first wash of yrClouds as it will appear warm let yr next shadow have more Indigo making a Grey' and David Cox gives a similar instruction 'give depth of tone in the clouds by repeating with gray tints.'[3] Thirtle's list of colours is more extensive than that given by either Hassell or Pyne, neither of whom include Purple Madder. However Pyne gives a scheme for the colouring of clouds, skies, buildings, grounds, trees, etc. which is close to Thirtle's and both stress the usefulness of the notorious Indigo, for producing fine greys. That this was a root cause of the rapid deterioration of watercolours by several artists of the period, including Girtin, has been confirmed in recent publications[4]. The damage it caused is as widespread as its popularity was at the time. Nicholas Pococke (1741–1821) drew up 'a Sketch of Scales of tones produced with 3 Colours only which are sufficient to produce any colour or effect whatever'; each scale consists of a combination of Indigo with less or more red[5].

A closer examination of the relationship of Thirtle's text to these and other publications is required but two distinctive features are evident. He is deeply concerned with Nature, with optical phenomena, with the effect of atmosphere such as rainbows and storms, and he seems to have resisted any reference to contemporary notions of the Picturesque. Pyne, on the other hand, devotes a whole section to 'Observations on the Picturesque in Paintings' (pp. 5–6) and interestingly dismisses all modern structures as unfit subjects for the artist, having no picturesque qualities. Such a tenet would have been foreign to Thirtle since many of his subjects were new developments of a contemporary Norwich cityscape.

Thirtle's interest in technique, and in the theory of colour and in optics may have been stimulated by his friendship with Clover whose copies of Philip Otto Runge's colour diagrams are in one of his sketch books in the museum's collection[6]. Clover was friend of the colour-theorist George Field whose treatise on colour was owned by Thomas Lound and included in his sale of 1861[7]. Another colour theorist John

---

1. I am indebted to Dr. Rosamund Harley for her comments and this suggestion.

2. Text accompanying Pl. IX.

3. Friedman op. cit. p. 263.

4. e.g. N. S. Brommelle, 'The Russell and Abney Report on the Action of Light in Water Colours', *Studies in Conservation* vol. 9 1964. I am grateful to Garry Thomson for this reference.

5. Letter to Richard Bright 6th Feb. 1804, MS 9389, National Maritime Museum.

6. Inscribed 'Rugens (sic) System of Colours . . .', NCM 123 (27–31). 141.939. Noted by John Gage in his book review of J. Traegar, 'Philip Otto Runge und sein Werk', The *Burlington Magazine*, Jan. 1977, No. 886, vol. CXIX p. 49.

7. Norwich, Spelman, 6th March 1861 lot 309 Field. G. *Treatise on Colours and Pigments* 1835.

Burnet (1784–1868) was an honorary member of the Norwich Society from 1822–1833.

Portraits

Until 1815 Thirtle describes himself in the Norwich Society catalogues as a 'Miniature Painter'. His output in this genre must have been small as there is only one miniature in the collection, No. 123; another dated 1807 is in the Victoria and Albert Museum. The three other miniatures recorded[1] bear only tentative attributions to Thirtle. Most of Thirtle's portraits were exhibited between 1805 and 1808 and three of these were of his family[2]. The three later Miles family portraits in the collection[3] of small, but larger than miniature size, are nevertheless painted with a miniaturist technique of fine modelling to the face. The same sensitivity is found in the portrait of a small boy, No. 129, and in the self portrait and portrait of his wife in the collection, Nos. 130, 131. Thirtle's full length portraits of which there are five recorded are discussed in the entry for No. 132, *Portrait of Catherine Miles*, and the two other later portraits dated 1819 and 1820 of the Preston family, in the entry for No. 71. His early Cowper portrait, No. 124, which is markedly Cotmanesque in handling, is the only one in pencil recorded. What may be a family group portrait is the whimsical *Cottage Interior* of 1807 in the collection of J. H. Appleby[4]. The subject is believed traditionally to be the Miles family farmhouse. A similar theme is shown by Richard Westall in a pencil drawing called *Rustic Courtship*[5].

Thirtle was not a distinguished miniaturist or portraitist[6] but his work has sincerity, a clarity of handling and a charm which certainly places him on a level with the later and more prolific Norwich miniaturist, Horace Beevor Love (1800–1838), whose portrait of Thirtle was exhibited at the Norwich School exhibition 1927 (219)[7].

Figure Subjects

All Thirtle's known figure subjects are copies after other artists. At least three were after Richard Westall (1765–1836): 1805 (176) *Venus and Cupid, after Westall*[8], 1806 (127) *The mushroom gatherer* which may have been after Westall's *A girl gathering mushrooms* exhibited at the Royal Academy in 1798 (351), and No. 53 in the collection, *Harvest Scene*, which is copied from an engraving after Westall. Richard Westall was a leading genre and historical subject painter of the period and also had Norwich connections: he was baptised in Norwich in the church where his father was churchwarden[9]. He also exhibited a portrait with the Norwich Society in 1818. Thirtle's two other copies in the collection *Crossing the Brook*, No. 50, and *Dorothea*, No. 52, are based similarly on works by artists who were associated with Norwich. Although these two drawings, of similar size and date c. 1816, have suffered through fading, even so their overblown compositions and sentiment are not among the most successful in his oeuvre.

Thirtle's other exhibited figure subjects of 1806 *Nymph Bathing* and *Despairing Lover* and of 1808 *Walter and Jane* which was also shown at the Royal Academy in

---

1. Duleep Singh, ed. E. Farrer, *Portraits in Norfolk Houses,* 1927, Rainthorpe Hall 69, 70, and Tasburgh Hall, 46.

2. 1805 (166) *Portrait of his sister*, 1806 (56) *Portrait of Mr. James Thirtle* [his brother] and (112) *Portrait of his mother*.

3. Nos. 126, 127, 128.

4. See supplement of Loans to the Thirtle Bicentenary Exhibition no. L2.

5. Signed l.l. *RW*, H. Reitlinger coll. photo Witt.

6. He receives a consideration by Basil Long, *British Miniaturists*, 1929.

7. $6\frac{3}{4} \times 5\frac{1}{4}$ ins., lent by Charles R. Bignold; now untraced.

8. A 'Framed and Glazed' drawing, *Cupid*, was lot 55 in Mrs. Thirtle's sale, Norwich, Spelman 9th May 1882 bt. Thompson £1.10.0.

9. All Saints Church 13th Jan. 1765. Information from Mrs. Lindsay, great-great-niece of the artist, 1967.

1808 (642), his only exhibit outside Norwich, have not been traced. He evidently also made copies from Joshua Cristall (1767–1847) of which one example, dated 1815, is in the Victoria and Albert Museum (see the entry for No. 53) and another, *Girl Peeling Turnips*, was lent to the Norwich, Thirtle Centenary Exhibition 1939[1]. Thirtle probably saw the original Cristall in the collection of John Sell Cotman, as 'an upright drawing, outside measure 27 inches by 21', by Cristall, *Girl Paring Turnips*, was in Cotman's posthumous sale of 1861[2].

Landscape and Architecture

Of Thirtle's ninety-seven exhibits with the Norwich Society only five are non Norfolk subjects[3] and as there is no record of Thirtle travelling outside the county after his return from London in c. 1800, these may have been derived from other artists, such as John Varley[4]. Of his exhibited works almost half can be categorised as architectural subjects. The same pattern is found in the drawings in the museum's collection. Just as Crome found an inexhaustible source of subjects in the rutted lanes, the magnificent oaks and the time-worn fabric of cottages in Norwich and Norfolk, likewise Thirtle responded with an acute sensibility to the riverside cityscape of Norwich; to its warehouses and bridges and to the constant stream of waterborne traffic which plied the river between Whitlingham and New Mills. What de Wint was to Lincoln, John Thirtle was to Norwich.

Thirtle's work has been considered 'undated and undateable'[5] but his oeuvre reveals a clear stylistic development. There are dated drawings at regular intervals for the period 1803–1830, covering the artist's entire active life.

c. 1803–1808

The dominant influences on Thirtle's earliest drawings are the watercolours of Thomas Girtin (1775–1802), John Crome (1768–1821) and John Sell Cotman (1782–1842). The soft rounded forms and the spatial design, so typical of Girtin, of the watercolour *Farm Buildings near Norwich*, No. 2, are repeated in a number of monochrome drawings of this period. Apart from the early Cotman and from Girtin imitators such as Pearson, Thirtle at this period is closer to Girtin than most contemporary English watercolourists. At the same time the broad washes and muted greyish green, cream and grey palette of *Whitlingham Church*, No. 1, have qualities reminiscent of Crome.

Since Crome is almost as elusive a personality as Thirtle, there is no evidence of an early personal friendship between the two artists. However through his role in the Norwich Society and his business as a framemaker, Thirtle would have had Crome drawings through his hands[6]. Indeed a conviction of a direct and overriding influence on some of Thirtle's works has led Crome students to recognise that a problem of attribution exists between the two artists[7]. A watercolour, which is undoubtedly by

1. Watercolour, $19\frac{1}{2} \times 13\frac{3}{8}$ ins., lent ex catalogue by L. O'Malley, photo in NCM annotated copy of the catalogue; in the collection of V. A. Hutchins 1968; now untraced.

2. 'The Valuable and Genuine Cotman Collection, . . . late the property of John Sell Cotman Deceased', Norwich, Spelman Thurs. 16th May 1861 lot 179 bt. Hunt £6.16.6.

3. 1805 (180) *Welch Cottages*; Secession 1816 (7) *Croyland Abbey and Bridge, Lincolnshire*, (61, 62) two drawings with the same title *View on the Thames* and the Secession 1817 (57) *Drawing—Welch Scenery*.

4. Thirtle also showed two military subjects with the Norwich Society in 1812 (134, 151). These are unparalleled exceptions in his oeuvre. The first of these, watercolour $13\frac{1}{2} \times 20\frac{1}{2}$ ins., signed lower left *I THIRTLE* was with Walker's Gallery (photo Witt) and is now untraced.

5. Clifford p. 61, written at a time when the oeuvres of Norwich School artists, apart from Crome and Cotman were relatively uncharted.

6. Clifford, *John Crome* 1968, p. 110: D5 *Rocks near Matlock* bore Thirtle's trade label.

7. *op. cit.* D202 p. 159.

Crome, *Houses and Wherries on the Yare*, in the Whitworth Art Gallery, 'caused considerable argument whether it was by Crome or by Thirtle'[1]. Conversely *Old Waterside Cottages* which is undoubtedly by Thirtle, was suggested to be a Crome when it was exhibited at the Thirtle Centenary in 1939. This fine drawing is discussed in the entry for No. 42. The affinity with Crome is still felt in the subtle grey washes of later Thirtle monochromes of c. 1810–14 such as the haunting *Kirby Bedon Church Tower, Norfolk*, No. 33. However it is no longer discernible in *Norwich Cathedral, South Transept and Cloister*, No. 31, another drawing of exceptional quality.

Just as Crome and Cotman can be remarkably close stylistically in their simplification of forms and a subdued earthy palette, so Cotman and Thirtle can be related stylistically although not confused[2]. At the same time there is no denying that the early Thirtle drawings *Two Wherries by a Wharf*, No. 6, and *Boat House on the River*, No. 7, show Cotman's qualities of poise and an intuitive sense of substance and structure. This Thirtle expresses with even more effortless ease in later architectural subjects such as *Whitefriars Bridge*, No. 28 and *Fye Bridge*, No. 58.

1808–1813

Watercolours of the earlier years of this period are characterised by a restricted colour range of buffs, blues and grey browns, such as the *Interior of Binham Abbey*, in the Ashmolean Museum, Oxford, of which there is a version in the collection, No. 9. In the handling of the washes and in the subdued tonality an affinity with Girtin persists. Similarly in a later drawing of this period, *Bishopsgate Bridge, Norwich— Evening* dated 1813, No. 30, a strong Cotmanesque spirit pervades the colour and brushwork. A work of probably the same period, and one of the finest in Thirtle's oeuvre, is closer to Cotman than any other: *The River at King Street* in the Victoria and Albert Museum[3]. Even so the strong shape of the boat gliding in from the left is a compositional motif which is peculiar to Thirtle and occurs in other of his drawings. He employs it in the brilliantly fresh watercolour *Under Bishop Bridge* in the British Museum[4]. This independence of style is already formed in a drawing of c. 1809 *Devil's Tower near King Street Gates—Evening*, No. 13. The sobriety of mood, the all enveloping light and vigorous brushwork is entirely Thirtle's own. Likewise one of the most remarkable of the early drawings, *View on the river near Cow's Tower, Norwich*, No. 15, with its assured organisation of robust shapes and autumnal russet, cream and sage tones laid down in broad yet sensitive washes, is unmistakably Thirtle.

1814–1819

It is during this period that Thirtle perhaps reached his peak as a watercolourist. He can surely be included among those responsible for 'the great series of sketches which is perhaps the most fascinating of English visual achievements.'[5]

Watercolour studies of limpid, silvery tonality and broad assured washes such as *Scene at Costessey*, No. 35, and *Thorpe*, No. 39, were produced by the artist as

1. Iolo A. Williams, *Early English Watercolours*, London 1952, p. 156.

2. Nevertheless a watercolour, *Village Scene*, which is surely an early Cotman, in the collection of the Huntington Library, San Marino, USA, is attributed to Thirtle, $9\frac{1}{2} \times 12\frac{1}{4}$ ins., 59.55.126.

3. Pencil and watercolour, $15 \times 17\frac{3}{4}$ ins., P26–1926.

4. Pencil and watercolour, $11 \times 15\frac{1}{2}$ ins., 1902–5–14–478.

5. Joseph Burke, *English Art 1714–1800*, quoted by Hugh Honour 'A greatness of good taste', *The Times Literary Supplement*, 21st Jan. 1977.

preparatory sketches for more finished drawings. Five pairs of these studies and their worked up watercolours are discussed in the entry No. 38. They indicate the contemporary approach to an exhibition drawing to which incident and a fuller treatment is applied for a finished effect. The forward-looking quality of these sketches and of the studies of country houses discussed in the entry for No. 75, have led writers on Thirtle to group these mistakenly with his late work. Drawings such as *Hoveton House*, No. 75, and *Canal House, Ashwelthorpe*, No. 70, were undoubtedly sketched *en plein air* while Thirtle followed his own advice: '*Of Light & Shade* . . . to become a good Colourist you must Colour your sketches on the spot & grudge no time they may occupy it is no use to do it slightly by so doing youl observe how chaste & rich Nature is & it will enable you to discriminate between rich & gaudy colourg . . .'

The rich plummy tones of some of these sketches such as *Catton Church*, No. 36, are markedly like the vibrant watercolour sketches of Peter de Wint (1784–1849). De Wint visited the home of Colonel Greville Howard, Castle Rising, Norfolk, in 1824 and he exhibited Norfolk subjects with the Old Water Colour Society in 1828 (20, 87, 245). Thirtle may have known his earlier work but whether 'conscious influence is almost certain'[1] must remain open to debate. An artist who did have a direct influence on Thirtle at this period and later in the twenties was the prolific Samuel Prout (1783–1852). Thirtle evidently owned published works after Prout as *Twenty-six engravings* after him were included in Mrs. Thirtle's sale 1882 lot 90. Thirtle may have exhibited a faithful watercolour copy after Prout with the Norwich Society Secession in 1816 (96) *Fishing Boats—Storm coming on*. Thirtle's copy and the Prout original are discussed in the entry for No. 65.

This period also includes some of Thirtle's best cityscape subjects such as *The Haymarket*, No. 56, and the exceptionally fine panoramic views of Norwich, No. 54 and 55. The soft greens, purples and blond cream palette of these drawings bring to mind Girtin's germinal panoramic studies such as *Albion Mills after the fire* of c. 1797–8 in the British Museum.

The later work

From 1819 onwards Thirtle's work develops a higher pitch of colour with the use of a turquoise blue and of touches of white bodycolour and of a strong cobalt or ultramarine blue. These features are already evident in a work of 1817 *Rainbow Effect, on the River, King Street, Norwich*, No. 77. Characteristic late works, of 1827–1830, such as *The Devil's Tower and Carrow Bridge*, No. 107, and *Dilham Staithe*, No. 115, have a brilliancy of colour and an angularity of block-like forms. Thirtle's watercolour sketches of this period show a tendency to use tinted papers to add a depth and richness to the colour. One particularly successful example is *Sunset Landscape with Thorpe Hospital, Norwich*, No. 120. Finished drawings show a handling of skies which is probably influenced by Vincent's work in oil. Inevitably this is most obvious in No. 110, *Trowse near Norwich after Vincent*.

The quality of Thirtle's work always impressed contemporary reviewers but like many English watercolourists this reputation lapsed into comparative obscurity in the second half of the nineteenth century. Exhibitions devoted to his work in 1886 and 1939 brought his achievement briefly into the public eye but since it has been largely unrecognised. Thirtle's place in the school of English watercolour is in the move away from topographical drawing to greater spontaneity and atmosphere, at the

1. Clifford p. 79.

watershed created by Girtin and Turner, the 'sky sloppers and bush blotters' of Dr. Monro. The foremost artists of this revolution in English art are without doubt Cozens, Girtin, Turner, Constable and Cotman, with Cox and de Wint not far behind. John Thirtle has been considered hitherto only within the confines of the Norwich School. His right to independent membership of the wider circle has not yet been recognised.

While affinities exist with other artists because of contemporaneity, geographical and family relationships, the best watercolours of John Thirtle speak for themselves alone. More than most artists of the period, his works have suffered chromatic change through fading. The temperature of many drawings is distorted beyond a level for which the eye can compensate. Nevertheless sufficient survive in pristine condition to allow a just evaluation of his work.

The critical acclaim such as Thirtle has received has always been positive if muted. While Binyon could arguably say of Cotman's work 'the most perfect examples of pure watercolour ever made in Europe'[1], he only sensed the merits of Thirtle without becoming his protagonist, 'he has the touch of a born painter . . . an individual colourist with a distinctive feeling for his medium.'[2] Wider knowledge of Thirtle's watercolours cannot but increase the number of his enthusiasts, even if not necessarily all of them will go as far as Henry Ladbrooke, writing some twenty years after Thirtle's death:

> 'As a man of genius Cotman was much Crome's superior and as a colourist, Thirtle far surpassed them both . . .'

1. *cit*. Hardie vol. II, p. 96.
2. *EDP* 20th July 1939, 'Thirtle Centenary Exhibition, Mr. Laurence Binyon on the Norwich School.'

Exhibited Works

Thirtle exhibited only once outside Norwich: with the Royal Academy in 1808 (642) *Walter and Jane.*

The following list of his contributions to the Norwich Society of Artists is reproduced from Rajnai and Stevens, *The Norwich Society of Artists 1805–1833, a dictionary of contributors and their work* 1976.

In the original catalogues, an asterisk after the number of an exhibit, and sometimes after the title, indicates that it was for sale. This use of the asterisk has been retained here, but it is placed uniformly after the number.

Abbreviations

Io	initial only of christian name	*le*	list of exhibitors only
L	Ladbrooke led secession	m	member

1805   **Address:** Norwich
166   Portrait of his sister
171   Portrait of a lady
176   Venus and Cupid, after Westall
179   Cottages
180   Welch Cottages

1806 m   **Address:** Norwich, St. Saviour's. Miniature-Painter and Drawing-Master
2   Thorpe hall
56   Portrait of Mr. James Thirtle
85   A mill on Moushold heath
88   Mettingham castle
91   View on the river Wensum, St. George's, Norwich
101   Bishop-bridge, Norwich
111   Portrait
112   Portrait of his mother
113   Portrait of a lady
120   Nymph bathing
127   The mushroom gatherer
140   Portrait of a lady
143   Despairing lover
150   Portrait of a lady
163   Lakenham mills
167   The lime-kiln
178   The Font in Binham abbey, Norfolk
"In cloister'd solitude, she sits and sighs,
"While, from each shrine, still, small responses rise."
[untraced]

1807 m   **Address:** not given. Miniature-Painter and Drawing-Master
15   View on the [Wensum] river near the Devil's tower
36   Bishop-bridge
50   Fye-bridge

1808 m   **Address:** Norwich, Magdalen-street. Miniature-Painter and Drawing-Master
25   View on the River Wensum near King-street Gates
159   Part of the Interior of Binham Abbey
192   Walter and Jane [see RA 1808. 642]
"Jane has been weeping, Walter; prithee why?
"I have seen her laugh, and dance, but never cry,

"But I can guess; with her you should have been,
"When late I saw you loit'ring on the green.
"I'm an old woman, and the truth may tell;
"I say then, Boy, you have not us'd her well.
Bloomfield

206   Portrait of a Lady
248   Tan Yard, Thorpe near Norwich

1809 m   **Address:** Norwich, Magdalen-street. Miniature-Painter and Drawing-Master
17   Cottage
134   Mill and Cottage on Mousehold Heath
152   Devil's Tower, near King Street Gates— Evening
166   Cottages, Study from Nature
201   North-west View of Fyebridge, Norwich
202   View near Thorpe—Evening
205   Interior from part of Norwich Cathedral

1810 m   **Address:** Norwich, Magdalen-street. Miniature-Painter and Drawing-Master
2   Norwich, *evening*
3   View on the [Wensum] river looking from Carrow bridge, *evening*
125   Sketch on the [Wensum] river near Heigham
135   View on the [Wensum] river near Cow's tower, Norwich
148   Boat-builder's yard, Norwich
173   Cottage, Lakenham
181   South gates, Yarmouth

1811 m   **Address:** Norwich, Magdalen-street. Miniature-Painter and Drawing-Master
121*   Lakenham Mills
138*   View on the River from the Arch of Bishop's Bridge
141*   Sketch on the River Wensum
155*   Ferry Lane, Norwich
165*   Draining Mill, St. Bennett's Abbey, On the North [Bure] River

1812 m   **Address:** Norwich, Magdalen-street. Miniature-Painter and Drawing-Master. Vice-President
134   A View of the approach of the Troops under the command of Lieut.-Col. Smith, of his Majesty's 65th regt. on the 13th of Nov. 1809, to the attack of the Works and Town

of Rasil Kymer, situated on the Arabian side of the Gulf of Persia, from a sketch in the possession of Lieut. Taylor, of the 65th regt.

151 A view of the Bombarding Ford Shinaas, on the 1st of January, 1810, situated on the Arabian side of the Gulf of Persia, by the Gun Boats and Frigates, La Cliffone and Caloline, under the command of Capt. Wainwright, of the R.N. from a sketch in the possession of Lieut. Taylor, of the 65th regt. who was wounded at the storming of the above fort.

160 *See yonder hallowed tomb; the pious work Of names once famed, now dubious or forgot, And buried midst the work of things which were There lie interr'd, the more illustrious dead.*
                        Blair

169 Mill and Cottage—a Composition
190 Boat Builder's Yard, near the Cow's Tower, Norwich

1813 m **Address:** Norwich, Magdalen-street. Miniature-Painter and Drawing-Master. Vice-President
125 View on the River
136 Carrow Bridge—Evening
142 Portrait

1814 m **Address:** Norwich, Magdalen-street. Miniature-Painter and Drawing-Master. President
124 Horstead Mills, near Coltishall
127 A Drawing
136 Catton Church—a Sketch
138 Cottage at Thorpe
150 Scene at Costessey, the Seat of Sir G. Jerningham
152 Study of Dead Birds
154 Fish Market, Norwich

1815 m **Address:** Norwich, Magdalen-street. Miniature-Painter and Drawing-Master
135 Trowse Bridge, near Norwich
149 A View of Thorpe, with Steam Barge working up—Evening

156 A View of Fuller's Hole, near Norwich—Morning

L 1816 **Address:** not given
7 Croyland Abbey and Bridge, Lincolnshire
11 Drawing—Evening
56 Norwich, from Hellesdon—Morning
60 Sea Beach, Low Water
61 View on the Thames
62 Ditto
70 An Outlett, near Cossey [Costessey] Mills
78 View of Norwich from Mousehold Heath—Evening
91 Cottage Scene
96 Fishing Boats—Storm coming on
102 Portrait of Himself
110 A Portrait
116 Portrait
123 Fishing Boats—Calm
132 Landscape

L 1817 **Address:** Norwich, Magdalen-street. Drawing-Master
40 View near the Horse Barracks, Norwich
45 Part of the City Wall, Norwich, in 1809
51 Rainbow Effect, on the [Wensum] River, King-street, Norwich
57 Drawing—Welch Scenery
62 Bishopsgate Bridge, Norwich—Evening
73 View from Thorpe, looking towards Bracondale—Evening

1828 **Address:** Norwich   (*le: John Thirtle*)
176* St. Benet's Abbey
1829 **Address:** Norwich   (*John Thirtle*)
127* Boat Builders, Carrow
143* View Looking from Thorpe to Whitlingham—Evening   (*Io*)
180 Scene on the [Yare] River at Thorpe—Evening

1830 **Address:** not given
18* Dilham Staithe
25* Duke's Palace Bridge
45* Scene—Cromer
48* An East View of Norwich
53* Cromer Beach

Manuscript Treatise on Watercolour

Hints on Water-colour Painting by John Thirtle Artist

The following text by the artist is contained in a manuscript notebook of seventy-six pages of cream laid paper thread sewn and bound between marbled board covers 7 × 4¾ ins. The cover is inscribed in ink in an unknown hand as the title. The paper from page 41 bears a Strasburg lily watermark. The text is written mainly in brown ink both across and down the pages. There are indistinct inscriptions on pages 72, 73, 76 and pages 24, 50, 52–75 are free of text. There is a full watercolour study of a castle in a landscape on page 12 and there are pencil sketches of hot air balloons on p. 32 and landscape and boat sketches, some with colour notes, on pages 33, 34, 40, 41, 44, 50, 56, 62, 64, 65, 66. The book was owned by Minna Bolingbroke (1857–1939), the wife of C.J. Watson, and was lent by her executors to the Norwich Thirtle Centenary 1939 (133). It was presented by them to the museum in 1950 (183.950).

[Very faint pencil notes on inside cover] Cloud over the Sun of a Brown Purplish Hue with red Good Colord Edges—the Clouds as approach the Horison of A cool Grey & Pale Yellow Edges—Indigo Venetian Red. (or light Red) & Maddow Lake makes fine Greys

for a warm Sky the first wash of Yellow Ocre the second of Roman Ocre & light Red. . with Purple distanc.

[Very faint pencil notes] a drawg of Sun Sett—on the foot path to Thorpe of . . . .

The things to be attended to in Drawg. are a Correct outline a proper Distinction of Lights & Shadows, a harmony of Coloring, & the Giving of Objects their proper size & degree of distinctness According to their different distances, it is not sufficient that the parts of a Drawg. be correctly shewn & highly finished, it is necessary that they should produce a good effect when they are Combined together as forming a whole—there should be such a harmony of Colourg. as make the whole appear lighted up by the same Rays.—& to be seen through the same Medium, the lights should be so distributed & subordinate to each other that they may not distract the Eye nor Draw the attention from the Principal light by which it ought always to be first caught, & the size & distinctness of objects should always be such, & may Enable any one to determine at Once, the nearest parts from those that are most distant. *[p. 2 ... p. 3]*

Of Light & Shade

There should be in a Drawg. one great light Brighter than any other which should Generally be as in Nature in the sky which may be Called the great light of the Whole, there should be a principal light in the Landscape—this light may be in any part of the Drawg takg care that in Breath & Brightness it does not interfere with the sky, unless you make it your Principal light, then the sky of course must not interfere with it, the lights may be in any Part of where taste & Judgment direct. But perhaps the Effect is generally best when in the middle of the Drawg. there must be other lights all subordinate to the Principal light & some of them less Bright than others, which make a variety & by prope[r] Gradation Soften the principal light which without such subordinate lights would have a bad Effect. Drawgs that have more shade than light have a better Effect than those which light predominates the lights & shadows should be in large Masses the dividing them into small parts has a bad & Confused Effect the general Effect of the light & shade should be produced in the whole before any of the parts are begun to be finished. it is opposition of light & shade that Constitutes force & the Broader the light & shade the greater force you have, shadows are not so strong at Noon as they are Morng & Eveng. this is Occasioned by the atmosphere being more Enlightened, & the Reflection from all objects being stronger & Brighter—the atmosphere being the Medium through which all objects are seen, the Rays which comes from these Objects will have more or less of this to pass thro, as they are nearer or farther from the eye, & will consequently be more or less affected by it in proportion to their distance, the Colour of the atmosphere is light Blueish Grey. Objects which are of a Colour Brighter than this will loose their Brightness in *[p. 4 ... p. 5]*

p. 6 Proportion to the distance they are removed from the Eye for Example, those which are at a Greater Distance will have a Greyish tint as the rays Issuing from them will have a greater space of the atmosphere to pass thro—there are three different sorts of light in a Drawg. viz. direct secondary, and reflected when the sun shines every thing receivg his rays which pass without interruption, is the <u>direct light</u> & which must be the principal light of the Picture— Objects which receives ~~light~~ rays after they have passed through any transparent Medium such as the Clouds—is the secondary light of the Picture &c a ~~shadow~~ Red Blue & Yellow may be said to be the only Primitive Colours they Cannot be made by compoundg. of others whereas by different modes of mixg the Red Blue & Yellow almost Every tint is to be

p. 7 produced—to become a good Colourist you must Colour your sketches on the spot, & grudge no time they May Occupy it is no use to do it slightly by so doing youl observe how chaste & rich Nature is & it will Enable you to discriminate between Rich & Gaudy Colourg. thro you may be able to Colour well on the spot it by no means follows that you will be able to apply your knowledge of Colour so gained in making a picture, you must understand the Power of Contrast for Example if you have a Cool Greyish sky oppose it in the landscape by parts of warm Colourg. warm Greens opposed to Brown Banks Gray stones Buildgs &c &c Must

p. 8 Produce a good Effect You must not attempt to get force by Blackness but richness, & warm Colours tho ever so light in the foreground will answer the purpose of sending every object to a Distance, but in this you must be guided by Circumstances in Nature youl observe a great deal of Grey in Trees &c &c Stems of Trees ought ~~all~~ to be warm not forgetting a proper Mixture of Greys with them, if your sky is Yellow to the Horizon let your Distance be a Purple tint if you have a violent Green in trees &c this you want to rectify apply Purple shades & t'will bring them all right, figures ought allways to be a possitive or no Colour where there is a great deal of

p. 9 Coolness in a Drawg a figure Clothed in red have an Excellent Effect Produced by Contrast.—Purple tints upon Greens & Yellows becomes a fine Grey. in Mountain Scenery you may Put yr Dead Colours in with warm Grey Composed with light Red & Indigo with a little Gamboge, the Red Predominating. upon this tone yr Cooler Grey have a fine Aerial tint Im aware its impossible to give a Receipt for making Drawgs. but it is Absolutely necessary to have a plan to work upon & the above hints will Greatly facilitate yr work Youl avoid all manner by looking at Nature the lights you see in the Clouds & which appear White is Generally very warm—the undermentioned colours youl find sufficient to mix any that you

p. 10 may want. Occasionally you may use Black on the Sky. but do it with Care or you will make it Earthy—Venetian Red & Indigo, the Red Predominating will do for the first wash of yr Clouds as it will appear warm let yr next shadow have more Indigo making a Grey the 3rd make the Maddar Purple & Indigo when youl have a fine Tone in the Clouds

Indigo & Purple Madda
Pure Purple Madda
lamp Black & lake ⎫
for Buildgs & Stones ⎬
Indigo & light Red ⎭
Warm Gray Mountains
Indigo Bt Sienna
Do Gumboge & Do
Indigo Vandyke Brown

Indian Yellow Green ⎫
foregrounds used ⎬
sparingly———— ⎭

Indigo Roman Ocre
Black & Gumboge
Whitish Greens

light Red, Roman Ocre,
Yellow Ocre, are good
for lights Parts of Buildg

Madda Purple & light
Red for Bricks tyles

p. 11 Purple Black Greys in the foreground, when opposed to Warmer Colours will look as if it was Composed with Indigo owing to opposition—

For Skys

Indigo Venetian Red 1st Tone
Do Do More Indogo 2nd

Madda Purple Indigo 3rd
Light Red———————————
Roman Ocre———————————
Indigo———————————
Yellow Ocre———————————
Indian Yellow———————
Venetian Red———————————
Bt Sienna
Gumboge———————————
Vandyke Brown
Seppia for light & Shade
Ultramarine used very
sparingly in Sky & distances

the annexed Drawg shews the
Power of Contrast as the light
in the Windows & sky would
appear white, by the Opposition
of warm colours & Broad
light & shade if it was not
surrounded with White Paper.

p. 12

[Water colour drawing here, A Castle in a landscape, 3$\frac{1}{8}$ × 3$\frac{13}{16}$ ins.]

Water

Water when it does not Reflect a Dark object is always very light. a large smooth surface of p. 13
Water without shade, or reflection is Darkest at the farthest Extremity & Comes gradually
lighter as it approaches the Eye. but if any Object thows [sic] a shade over the water the
nearest part is then the darkest & it Grows gradually lighter as it retires for Water without
shade being Brighter then the Aerial tint will loose more of its brightness as it is seen thro a
greater Extent of atmosphere all the stokes or touches by which shades are made should be
perfectly horrizontal. the Reflection of Objects in the Clearest Water is not so strong or
distinct as the Objects themselves in Muddy or Rippled water still less so—when you have a
cool sky by making a warm strook of Colour in the Horrizon you will make it appear silvery p. 14
without destroying the Grey. there must be in a Picture some Principal Object—the distance
so managed that the Eye may range Pleasantly if it be a close subject then figures must supply
in the foreground the want of distanc[e] let your Compositions have angular forms avoiding
two [sic] many parrellel lines—where the rays of the three Primitive Colours intersect, Green
is between Blue & Yellow, Orange between Yellow & Red, & Purple or Violet between Red &
Blue

When you Draw from Nature, you must be at the distance of three times the height of the p. 15
Object; & when you begin to Draw, form in your own Mind a Certain Principal line (suppose
a Perpendicular) observe well the bearg of the parts towards that line; whether they Intersect
it, are parrellel to it. or oblique————If you mean that the Proximity of one Colour should
Give beaty [sic] to another that terminates near it observe the Rays of the Sun in the
Composition of the Rainbow, the Colours of which are Generated by the falling Rain, when
each drop in its descent. takes Every Colour of that Bow to Represent great darkness. it must p. 16
be with Contrast & light the same so a pale Yellow will make Red appear more Beatiful then
when opposed to Purple Colours may receive grace from Each other——as Green placed
near Red, while the effect would be totally Reverse if Placed near Blue, Harmony & Grace are
also produced by a Judicious arrangement of Colours such as Blue with Pale Yellow or White
& the like—the air participate less of the azure of Y the sky, in proportion as it comes nearer to
the Horizon Pure & subtil Bodies (such as compose the air) will be less Illuminated by the Sun
then those of thicker & Grosser Substances: & as it is certain that the air which is remote from p. 17
the Earth is thinner then that which is near it t'will follow that the latter will me more
Impregnated with the Rays of the Sun, which giving light at the same time to an Infinity of
Atoms floating in the Air, render it more sensible to the Eye, so that the air will appear lighter
towards the Horizon, & Darker as well as Blue in looking up to the sky, because there is more
of the thick Air between our Eyes & the horizon then from the Earth upwards—the azure of
the sky is Produced by the transparent Body of the air, Illuminated by the Sun, & Interposed p. 18
between the Darkness of the Expanse above, and the Earth below, the air in itself has no
Quality of smell, taste or Colour but is easily Impregnated with the Quality of other Matter
surrounding it; & will appear Blue in proportion to the darkness of space behind it, as may be
observed against the shady sides of Mountains, which are darker than any other Object—In

this Instance the Air appear of the most Beautiful Azure while on the other side that receives the light it shews through that more of the Colour of the Mountain—the Darker the Mountain is in itself the Bluer it will appear at a Great distance the highest part will be the darkest—as the air becomes Clear & fine.—there are situation where light appear dark & objects deprived of form & Colour this is caused by the Great light which pervades the intervening Air; as is observed at looking in at a Window at some distance from the Eye, but on Approachg we find

p. 20

the Room filld with light & can distinguish Every small object therein. A Fog in ye Morng or Eveng Buildgs seen afar off in the Morng or Eveng, when there is a fog, or thick air, shew only, those parts distinctly which are Enlightend by the sun toward the Horizon; and the parts of those Buildgs which are not turned towards the Sun remain confused & almost of the Colour of the Fog.

p. 21

Remember, that when you by the exercise of yr own Judgement, or the Observation of others, you discover any Errors in yr work, you Immediately sett about correcting them, lest in exposing them to the Public, you Expose yr Defects also. admit not any self Excuse by persuading yourself that you shall retrieve yr Character & that by some succeeding work you shall make amends for your negligence, for yr work does not perish as soon as it is out of yr

p. 22

Hands, like the sound of Music, but remains a standing Monument of your Ignorance, If you excuse yrself by saying that you have not time for the study Necessary to form a good painter. having to Struggle against Necessity, you yrself are only to blame; for the study of what is Excellent is good both for Mind & Body. how many Philosophers, born to great Riches, have given them away, that they might not be retarded in their Persuits—

a painter ought to study Universal Nature & Reason much within himself on all he sees

p. 23

Making use of the more excellent Parts that Compose the species of Every object before him his mind will by this Method be like a Mirror reflecting truly every Object placed before it, and become, as it were a second Nature Whoever flatters himself that he can retain in his mind memory all the Effects of Nature is deceived, for our Memory is not so capacious; therefore Consult Nature for Every thing—

p. 25

[Written in pencil]
Road Scene—
Catton Church
Isle of Wight
Sketch Back of Thorpe
Drawg after O [?wen]
Interior of Cathedral
View of Ferry
Sketch Scene River—
Large Drawg Cows & M . . . . .

p. 26

work yr Drawgs Particularly warm use Ocre, lay in yr Trees strong with warm Ocres—& yr colors of Greens & Grey over them—yr shadow Broad & warm & touch touched upon. with Green made of Lampblack & Ocre which Cause an Opeak Color—Use Gamboge with other warm Colors mix'd for Figures & Cattle—Yr Sky, should be worked. & the Broad Tones of Colors got in on yr Paper by being stretched on Frame Hollow at the back that may be

p. 27

Occasionally wetted at the back the Edges. of Clouds or other lights that want rubbing out in a soft & Pleasant Manner such as rays &c—& after the parts are moistend & remain so a little Time take the crum of Bread insted of rag—if you want a Greater warmth in sky than Can be got by orcre use raw Siennas—if at any Time yr Grey distance be two Dark—you may work it over with pipe Clay which will never Change & upon that you may tint with what Ever Color

p. 28

you please Turner has been known to use raw dry Ocres for Beach & rocks—& upon that work his Transparant Colors for Water &c

[Written in pencil]
Make yr Aerial & distant Greens with lamp Black Gumboge or Ocre Yr more Near Greens with Seppia Bt [?Umber] B Sienna & Indigo—or a little Rosa Madda
[Written in pencil]

p. 29

—it sometimes happens that yr light & shade of yr Picture is not right & frome the Effects of Colour you are not able to discover where it is. but by looking through a very Dark Green Glass which will neutrallize the Colour you may then discover the defect

if yr masses of shadow be two Bright pass a wash of lamp black over the whole—if its wanted

p. 30

more of a dullish Green use Seppia & Gamboge The best mode of using water colors is by a practice of always passing the Cooler tints over the warm ones. of always laying in with great boldness the general hues over the whole Drawg without mindg partial small lights they can be Easily restored Colors always look Dark while wet. but they dry much feinter because the gum is not abundant in them & is to a certain degree absorbed into the paper if you are pleased with the richness or Depth of any color you are spreadg & wish it to Dry as you then see it. Immediately add more color of the same hue & it will dry nearly as you wish though at the same it is wet it will appear two strong

Remark will what Effects are produced by wetting yr Drawg as you may often get a good hint p. 31 from it to add Depth of Color or richness of hue. warm Colors generally speaking consist of all Yellows that approach the golden & straw color & all Browns that have more of Yellow in their composition (technically speakg.) than of Red—Yellow or Yellow Green. Yellow Purple Yellow Brown Yellow Grey will be absolutely more warm than their component parts such as Red purples Red Browns—&c therefore where warmth of color is desired much Yellow must be Introduced & opposed by pure Grey Colors & something that might be Calld purple or Purply brown & Grey—I say might be calld, because I do not mean crude possitive colors of p. 32 such hues but by Comparison they should appear so—this nicety divides divides a fine work from a bad or Vulgar One—one would be Crude & Common & disgustg to the Eye, while the other will give the greatest pleasure. for Instance do not put in a color of gamboge alone. Ocre. Red. blue or absolute Green—but pass some thin purply Grey over the Yellows some lake like hue over Green tints or a Brown one—& some Indian Red or light Red or Venetian Red or a Composition of lake & one of these Colors Either in yr Blues or Over the blue Colors or let yr Blue be passed over some such preparation—Cold colors first Blue purple the next—black p. 33 Grey composed of those—possitive Green blue Green. Green Grey & purply Red—& all such hues. therefore when you have got yr Color two vivid remember that possitive grey which is neither purple or Blue but a negative tint will for the backgrounds & foregrounds & all Intermediate distances reducd the brilliancy Purples over a strong Yellow if it is a red purple. makes brown because its composition is of more red & yellow than of Blue. Red lake & Blue make the deepest purple Indian Red & Blue next Venetian or light Red & Blue the next gradation—Maddow brown lake & Blue another sort of Purple—Maddow lake over Seppia & p. 34 Bt Sienna makes a powerful rich Brown leave out the Seppia & the hue will be two rich for anything but Cattle or men & womens dresses lamp black over Yellows dirty them & reduce the hue to a pale sort of Green Yellow lamp black over Green deepends it & makes it more subdued the same black over blue of course makes a blue slate Color & will do for hues in water. & seppia or Vandyke Brown over Green Composed of lamp Black or Blue & Gumboge turns it to a Brown dark dull colord Green—Purple over Green will destroy it Quite p. 35 if strong Enough & Black is produced Red & Yellow makes Orange Colors—Blue over Bt Sienna make a fine Green. so will the union of the two—whatever color is uppermost that will command the hue & there is a great difference between Blue over Yellow or Red—or Red & Yellow over Blue. Owing to the light Catchg the particles of color that are uppermost—if in your Picture you are two Yellow Red or Brown or Green will be Render'd right by Purple. purply Greys—or possitive Greys—on the Other Hand a Color two Blue—According to its p. 36 place may be Improved by passing red over it not lake or some brown or Yellows but not Gamboge the whole mystery lays in the knowledge of the Combinations of the three primitive Colors viz—Red Yellow & Blue the three compose together a Black or Grey. Red— perfect symetry in Colorg is harmony Consequently it Implies a Judicious admixture of Warm & Cold Colors of a proper proportion & balance of yellow brown Red Green purple & Blue & their Intermediate Colors. if Possible no parts of the Picture should strike the Eye predominantly the whole alone should Impress you with pleasure—Red can be least tolerated p. 37 & it requires a large portion of Blue & Yellow or Grey Colors to ballance it—Yellow is so agreable that very little Red & Green & Grey will adorn it Green is Easily beautified by Red Greys & warm purple colors behind it or adjoining it—purples & their varieties are adorned best by rich Yellows & Browns & retired by Green Hues & the Green by Browns up to the darkest tints. Red opposed well by Grey & Pearl Colors & purples into Blue Carries off the Gradation. Yellow or some such hue must come next to the Blue. then a warm Color again p. 38 Each color being a regular change from cold to warm lighter or Darker as required but Green Trees upon Blue Mountgs or Blue skies should be avoided as bad. unless they are Yellow Green or Brown Green of course Red Trees upon Browns & Reds appear appear well against blues & Greens—Ocre's Blue & Black are excellent Colors they are strong rich & aeriall. while the foreground Greens keep them back by their superior strength when Colors appear in Nature to their greatest advantage & Certain Hues of the brightest & most Captivating p. 39 Quality write down their assosiations Also be careful to Observe the pressence of Cool tints & of Absolute Aerial Colors round these tints it will be found Invariably that the greatest beauty proceeds from Yellow Combined with green & purply grey. & Deep Orange red somewhere if the Yellow is Broad & large so will the opposition of Grey be found to make the Effect Captivating Hence the Famed Combination of a Golden Harvest & Glowing Green Woods— but the Poet Omits the Great help in this Essemblage the Assosiate of Grey. dont forget p. 40

Nature; she must be courted & wooed; Nor is there any dame that demands & Requires so much Eternale attention & persevering Adoration—once yr Eyes are opened to the beauties of a finished work & to the Everlastg delight of Followg. nature in all her simplest minutive—you will despise hasty sketches. if the Mind is not made rich by a store of long continued study of all & Every variety a sketch become of little use. you will find Embarrasment at Every step

p. 41

you take & wonder what Each touch and dab did mean—toutches & dabs become in Consequence their Representatives in the Finished work which will Ever leave the Eye & mind unsatisfied—but if you make Every touch of yr Pencil describe a Certain something you will wonder how & where yr dabs are to stand. Claude delights Every Cultivated & Common Eye. because he Enforces his subjects by every poetical Excellance, by chusing the nicest

p. 42

beauties to Embellish a decided time of Day—you cannot do better then regularly both Cattle & the human figure you must begin with the bones & know how many parts of the figure present the bone & skin only to our view. the skull collerbones Elbows knees shinns all the way down to the ankle the rest is muscle & tendon. & sinews—of a Cow find how many bones appear rude & bare discover in yourself you will then know what you see & what you draw & will give a proper meang to your forms Assertain by measurements in proportional parts, what

p. 43

are the proportions of the Human form & the same of the Animal learn where the greatest Projections come & where the greatest hollows half yr work is done—follow the animal walking & learn the Motion of the muscles in the shouldr one does for both as the Rigging of one mast in a ship does for the other two or nearly so observe then the Muscles of the neck Erect & stooping. . the hind Quarter will come next for the body remains nearly the same at all Times if you attempt the whole together you will find it like the Bundle of sticks not to be

p. 44

conqured but piece meal you may subdue it—in yr walks observe the variety of Plants their shapes & colors alongside of Ditches or Ponds of Water they are Excellent studies for foregrounds—Even in a Road the Infinite variety of stones—watch the rolling of the waves on the beach, the order of them & how they break the different shades of the Sea ocasioned by Clouds or shallow sands—

Eveng distances accordg to their Height situation or nature will vary We see them a warm

p. 45

Yellow Grey, sometimes a pure Grey. sometimes & Indeed very often of a Blue Color, the Red is then above in the sky & below on the Earth, which gives to the blue a purplish hue as the objects advance near to us, when the Sun sets of an Orange color yellow, then the distances are hot & Purple combined, the Yellow & the red mix'd with it overpowering the Blue, but the blue helps to dirty the hue & prevents its two accute purity, when the sun sets Red then the Yellow is thrown above in the sky & the distance is sure to be Blue as it is the Original Principal in

p. 46

Nature & arrises in a great Measure from the Abundance of vapor then rising or falling to the Earth. I have alway observed that Vapors being damp necessarily it gives a blue color under every circumstanc but dust such as we see near large Cities or Towns in the summer Time, produce in the Even'g rich yellow hues—so that the red seen arises from thickness of vapor & by that means produces the blue & not purple under ~~near the~~ & near the Sun. but to the North

p. 47

South & East a rich purple hue prevail over Mountgs & Elevated distances. Orange & Red & Brown Colord clouds can then be the only hues. though we see sometimes Yellow & Even Whitish Clouds with this hue. but they are so high above the region tinged with Red as to Escape being effectd untill the Sun is set. & then we see them Red & Rose colord.

Observe that deep blue grey objects, oppose the purple produced by the Orange & yellow sky—when the sun sets of any powerful color rather have the <u>other</u> hues both primitive &

p. 48

compound, if a possitive hue) it is when the Sun setts of a Modest & Concealed Color that the hues are most Difficult to ~~optain~~ ^{attain} rely upon it that cullg philosophy to yr aid. you will unfold the difficult Knots Nature is simple though so unceasingly varied, she is goven'd by laws & may be read by the Accurate Observer

p. 49

Yellow Ocre & Indigo make a beautiful tint on a Warm Purplish Ground

Naples Yellow & Vermillio [n] a Delicate Tone for Flesh

Vermillion & Ultramarine a Beautiful Grey.

Yellow Ocre & Maddow Brown for reflected lights on shadows.

p. 51

Hints from Clover

Burnt Brown from <u>Ivory Shavings</u>—A Beautiful Brown & mixed with Vermillion used by Westall—the Ivory shavings is Burnt in a crucible & kept repeating stiring untill it is the tint wanted it may be burnt untill it become a Beautiful Black—

Ultramarine Ground with great care on a Pollished porphery with a little Maddow lake gives it Beautiful Tone for faces & likewise fixes it

Catalogue

The catalogue is arranged in three sections: landscapes Nos. 1–122, portraits Nos. 123–133, pencil sketches No. 134–169, in a suggested chronological order. Related drawings in other collections are listed in the main body of the entries or in a note to them.

Titles

When it can be established with reasonable certainty that the museum's drawing was exhibited by the artist the exhibition title is used. Otherwise the title recorded when the picture entered the museum's collection is retained unless it is incorrect.

Sizes

Height is given before width in centimetres followed by inches in brackets.

Inscriptions

All inscriptions are in the artist's hand unless stated otherwise. When the inscription of the artist's name is accepted as a signature it is preceded with the word 'signed'. Mounters notes and suchlike are not included.

Condition

Most of the drawings in the Colman Bequest were treated by S. Kennedy North between 1939 and 1940. A few appear to have been cut down slightly during restoration, some unfaded areas may have been trimmed. Many of the drawings were mounted and framed up in cabinets especially designed by Kennedy North to accommodate these and the large collection of Norwich School watercolours acquired by R. J. Colman from the Bulwer Collection.

Provenance

When a group of drawings has the same provenance, it is given only in the entry of the first one and the others are referred to it. Sales are given in full if a copy of the catalogue has been located otherwise the source referring to the sale is given. Further information about previous owners and donors is given on p. 85.

Exhibitions

All exhibitions have been abbreviated. Full details may be found on p. 90.

References

This section includes published references only. A concordance of Museum and Colman Collection Catalogues and another of Museum accession numbers is given on pp. 79. Full titles and a key to abbreviations may be found in the bibliography on pp. 94.

Catalogues

Catalogue references are given in this section only if the title differs substantially from that recorded when the picture entered the collection.

1 Whitlingham Church, Norfolk   Pl. 6

Pencil and watercolour on cream laid paper with watermark along upper edge (paper cut) *PORTAL & BRIDGES/1795*[1]; 24.5 × 33.9 ($9\frac{5}{8}$ × $13\frac{5}{16}$).

COND: Cleaned and ? cut down by Kennedy North, Nov. 1939[2]. Removed from Bulwer cabinet, March 1976. Mounted Royal.

PROV: Mrs. Thirtle sale, Norwich, Spelman Tues. 9th May 1882 bt. for J. J. Colman[3]; his bequest to R. J. Colman 1898; R. J. Colman Bequest 1946, registered 1951.

This drawing may have been dated *September 18th 1803*[2] and if so, may be the earliest work by Thirtle recorded[4]. Although it is much faded both the monochrome palette and the handling is reminiscent of Crome and it also seems to indicate some knowledge of Girtin.

The church of St. Andrews, Whitlingham, stands on a ridge above the river Yare. Today only 'the round tower, one window with cusped Y-tracery and the E. window remain.'[5] Other Whitlingham subjects in the collection are referred to in No. 38[6].

1. Churchill records (p. 52) *1780 Portal, J. Laverstoke mill; 1796 Portal & Co.*

2. In the typescript of Colman collection pictures and drawings with dates ascribed by Percy Moore Turner, this drawing is listed with a pencil note *Dated 1803*. Similar notes refer to drawings which are still inscribed. Also in the entry for this drawing in the CC MS vol. I (p. 119 no. 454) is recorded 'Drawing Made September 18th 1803.'

3. CC records. Very few of the titles in this sale are specific.

4. A drawing catalogued as by Thirtle was sold at Christie's, English Drawings 17th April 1973 lot 150 *The Bull Inn at Little Thurock, near Grays in Essex dated June 25 1803 on reverse*, pencil and watercolour, $4\frac{5}{8}$ × $10\frac{3}{8}$ ins.

5. Pevsner p. 293.

6. Thirtle made at least one other drawing of the church which was in the Rev. John Bailey sale, Norwich, Spelman Tues., Wed. 4th, 5th March 1884 first day *Water Colour Drawings, framed and glazed* lot 30 *Whitlingham Church*.

2 Farm Buildings near Norwich   Pl. 6

Pencil and watercolour with slight scraping out on cream laid paper; 27.1 × 39.7 ($10\frac{11}{16}$ × $15\frac{5}{8}$).

COND: Cleaned and laid by D. Lewisohn, Sept. 1976. Mounted Royal.

PROV: James Reeve Bequest, with a collection of pictures and applied art, 1921.

EXH: Tate 1922 (239); Norwich, Thirtle Centenary 1939 (42); Lowestoft 1948 (66); Leeuwarden 1948 (46); Kettering 1952 (26); Harrogate 1953 (49); Stoke-on-Trent 1953; Nottingham, Portsmouth and Bolton 1953–54 (34); Kidderminster 1954 (38).

A student of English water colour visiting the collection has suggested that this drawing should be ascribed to a Girtin follower, which is an obvious choice in view of the spatial design of the composition, with its typically Girtinesque diagonal lines, and the rounded forms of the foliage. However when compared with Nos. 1, 3 and 4, which have a provenance from Mrs. Thirtle, it is obvious that the same hand is responsible for all four drawings. The treatment of foliage is especially similar in them and the sky in this watercolour is echoed by that of later

Thirtle watercolours such as *View on the river near Cow's tower, Norwich*, No. 15.

3 Gothic Barn, Castle Acre, Norfolk   Pl. 7

Pencil and brown wash on cream laid paper with watermark upper centre, (inverted) ? *P* (paper cut); 24.7 × 34 ($9\frac{3}{4}$ × $13\frac{3}{8}$).
Verso, Studies of Cows
brown wash

INSCR: Dated in pencil in an unknown hand l.r. *Oct 23–1803*; verso, a long inscription—presumably a letter—in pencil (inverted; mostly erased) across page (paper cut) *. . . Friend Britton . . .*

COND: Cleaned and ? cut down by Kennedy North, Nov. 1939. Removed from Bulwer cabinet, March 1976. Mounted Royal. *Verso*, gum along u. & r. edge, paper stained.

PROV: C. C. R. Spelman sale[1], Norwich, Spelman Tues.–Thurs. 17th–19th March 1914 second day lot 466 *Two—Castleacre, An Interior* bt. Walker 28s. or lot 502 *Three—Norwich Cathedral and Castleacre* bt. Ada $6\frac{1}{2}$ gns. for R. J. Colman[1]; R. J. Colman Bequest 1946, registered 1951.

The broad washes applied with a full brush and the horizontal composition of this drawing are very close to its companion No. 4. Their markedly Girtinesque handling in turn is similar to the watercolour of the previous entry. Unfortunately the most important document on the *verso* was virtually erased during conservation in 1939. This letter, in Thirtle's hand, is probably addressed to John Britton (1777–1857), the antiquary and an honorary member of the Norwich Society of Artists from 1811–1833. No other documentary evidence has come to light of Thirtle's contact with Britton, who was a friend of John Sell Cotman and corresponded with at least one other Norwich artist, David Hodgson.

Castle Acre is situated in West Norfolk, four miles north of Swaffham. There are two other drawings of Castle Acre subjects attributed to Thirtle, one in the collection of the Yale Center for British Art and British Studies, New Haven, USA[2], and the other in the Huntington Library, San Marino, California[3].

1. CC records.

2. *Castle Acre Priory*, watercolour 15 × $11\frac{1}{2}$ ins., exh. Norwich, Thirtle Centenary 1939 (1), lent by the Royal Institute of British Architects.

3. *Castle Acre*, monochrome, $8\frac{1}{4}$ × 13 ins., exh. Norwich, Thirtle Centenary 1939 (118), lent by Sir Michael Sadler.

4 Tudor House, Castle Acre, Norfolk   Pl. 7

Pencil and greyish-brown wash on cream laid paper with water mark lower edge (cut) *PORTAL & BRIDGES*[1]; 24.5 × 33.8 ($9\frac{5}{8}$ × $13\frac{5}{16}$).

INSCR: Inscribed in pencil, slightly erased, l.l. *Oct 23–182* (sic) and below, in an unknown hand, *Oct 23–1803*[2]; verso, inscribed in pencil u.l., in an unknown hand, *Tudor House*.

COND: Cleaned by Kennedy North, Nov. 1939. Mounted Royal.—Staining u.r.; *verso*, staining and bleached foxing marks.

PROV: See No. 3.

It is a companion drawing to No. 3 and is discussed in that entry. The building represented has not been identified.

See the entry for No. 3 for details of other Castle Acre subjects, attributed to Thirtle, recorded.

1. Same as No. 1; see Note 1 of that entry.

2. Same hand as the inscription of No. 3.

3. Pevsner, *North-West and South Norfolk* p. 114.

5 Carrow Abbey, Norwich   Pl. 9

Pencil and grey wash on cream laid paper with watermark lower centre edge, a Strasburg lily[1]; $22 \cdot 5 \times 30 \cdot 8$ ($8\frac{7}{8} \times 12\frac{1}{8}$).

COND: Cleaned by Kennedy North, Nov. 1939. Removed from Bulwer cabinet, March 1976. Mounted Royal.

PROV: See No. 1.

EXH: Norwich, Art Circle 1886 (51) lent by J. J. Colman.

REF: Dickes p. 233.

An early drawing which can be grouped with those of the preceding entries but the handling is more robust, the use of reserved spaces more assured and the contrast between light and shade is more sharply defined.

Carrow Abbey is a misnomer as the house is in fact the sixteenth century Prioress lodging of Carrow Priory which was founded by Benedictine nuns in 1146 and which stood on a site, now occupied by Reckitt & Colman's Carrow works, at the lower end of King Street: '. . . . the last Prioress Isabel Wygun, had built herself a house to the W of the cloister which, in its sumptuousness and wordliness, almost seems to justify the Dissolution.'[2] Carrow Abbey was acquired by the Colman family in 1878 and survives intact. In the early nineteenth century it was owned by Philip Meadows Martineau (?1752–1829)[3] surgeon, whose seat in Bracondale was also drawn by Thirtle and engraved by W. Wallis for *Excursions through Norfolk* 1818. Martineau owned Crome's painting of Carrow Abbey, which was exhibited in 1805, and his daughter Frances Anne (1812–1877) was a pupil and copyist of John Sell Cotman.

1. Watermark of *KORFF & DE VRIES* recorded with a date of 1788 by Churchill (p. 84 fig. 416).

2. Pevsner p. 286.

3. F. R. Beecheno, *Notes on Carrow Priory* 1886, p. 5; the frontispiece is a lithograph of the Abbey, also from the back, by C. J. Watson (1846–1927).

6 Two Wherries by a Wharf with a Figure unloading   Pl. 8

Pencil and brown wash on cream wove paper; $22 \cdot 3 \times 34 \cdot 1$ ($8\frac{3}{4} \times 13\frac{7}{16}$) subject, $24 \cdot 2 \times 34 \cdot 1$ ($9\frac{1}{2} \times 13\frac{7}{16}$) paper *Verso* undefined sketches in pencil and brown wash of ? barrels, a pole and ? two figures.

INSCR: Dated in pencil u.r. *Sept. 3rd 1805*; *verso*, numbered in pencil u.c. *No 10.*

COND: Mounted Royal.—*Recto*, gum and remains of old mount along lower l. & r. edges; *verso*, staining. Edge of paper ragged along lower l. and r. edges.

PROV: See No. 1.

Although a less assured drawing than *Boat House on the*

River, No. 7, the handling of the washes conveys a sense of spatial repose which is distinctly Cotmanesque.

7 Boat House on the River   Pl. 8

Pencil and grey wash on cream laid paper; $11 \cdot 7 \times 18 \cdot 5$ ($4\frac{9}{16} \times 7\frac{1}{4}$).

COND: Unmounted.—Small tear l.c.r. Slight foxing. *Verso*, gum at corners.

PROV: One of fifty-eight drawings presented by Robert Fitch, F.S.A., in 1894 as part of a large collection of antiquities, archaeological and geological material, manuscripts and books, and etchings and drawings by Norwich School artists. A selection was exhibited at the Thirtle Centenary in 1939 (131) and reviewed in the *EEN*, 20th July 1939, where it was stated that the drawings were 'taken from one of Thirtle's sketch books belonging to the Robert Fitch collection.' The drawings may have come from an album (not a sketchbook) but they were presented to the museum on separate card mounts inscribed in pencil, in two different hands, *J. Thirtle* and they were placed in a Fitch Collection folder. All fifty-eight drawings were remounted in 1966 and some have since been cleaned.

Of eight others one is now attributed to James Pattison Cockburn (1134.76.94) and seven other drawings cannot now be accepted either as by Thirtle's hand: 1143, 1148, 1156, 1157, 1158, 1169, 1184.76.94. One drawing, *Three figures in costume with a dog* (1186) was unfortunately lost while away in the conservation studio, 1976.

This is an early drawing of c. 1803–1806. With its delicate but confidently placed washes it brings to mind Cotman's pre Greta monochrome drawings.

8 Courtyard and Archway   Pl. 9

Pencil and watercolour on cream laid paper; $16 \cdot 5 \times 24 \cdot 1$ ($6\frac{1}{2} \times 9\frac{1}{2}$) *Verso*, sketch in pencil of chimney stack l.l.

COND: Cleaned by Kennedy North between 1939–1940. Removed from Bulwer cabinet, March 1976. Mounted Royal.—Foxing.

PROV: See No. 1.

This is an early drawing; the washes, applied sparingly, of colour restricted to a range of buffs, blues and grey browns characteristic of the group of watercolours Nos. 9, 10, 11.

The identity of the early buildings shown in the drawing has not been established. In the Colman Collection Catalogue[1] the drawing is described with the title above, but by 1940[2] it was called *Old Houses, Great Walsingham*. There is an inscribed early grey wash drawing of a Walsingham subject[3] by Thirtle in a private collection, giving firm evidence that he visited either or both Great and Little Walsingham, adjoining villages in north-east Norfolk, four and a half miles south of Wells. Both villages have a number of important buildings and remains dating from the twelfth century onwards.

1. CC MS vol. 1 p. 117 no. 434.

2. This title is inscribed on the backing paper attached during Kennedy North's conservation of 1939–1940.

3. Pencil and grey wash, $10 \times 14\frac{3}{4}$ ins., inscribed in pencil l.r. *West Window/ . . atton* [indistinct] *Hall/Walsingham*; exh. Norwich, Thirtle Centenary 1939 (119) as *Walsingham*, lent by C. B. Bolingbroke. The subject is not identified.

9 Interior of Binham Priory   **Pl. 10**

Pencil and watercolour on buff wove paper; 27·1 × 36 ($10\frac{11}{16}$ × $14\frac{1}{8}$).

INSCR: Inscribed in pencil l.r. *J. Thirtle.*

COND: Cleaned by Kennedy North, Nov. 1939. Removed from Bulwer cabinet, Aug. 1976. Mounted Royal.—Hole l.c.l.

PROV: See No. 1.

Binham is situated five miles south of Wells, North Norfolk. The extensive remains of Binham Priory Church include the present church of St. Mary. Thirtle's drawing shows part of the nave viewed from the east end looking north-west. Another version of similar size, in the Ashmolean Museum, Oxford[1], has a palette of predominantly blueish-grey with touches of pink. When compared with this, the museum's drawing appears coarser, the details less finished and although it does not seem to be a copy, the attribution should be viewed with caution. The Ashmolean version may have been that Thirtle exhibited with the Norwich Society in 1808 (159) *Part of the Interior of Binham Abbey.* He had also shown in 1806 (178) *The Font in Binham Abbey, Norfolk.*

The composition of both these versions is very close to a Cotman watercolour in the collection. Thirtle's figure group differs and while the light is directed from the left there is no attempt at expressing the sunbeams which stream across the Cotman drawing. However the similarity of the two compositions suggests that one may have been drawn with a knowledge of the other. Stylistically Thirtle's drawing can be placed with Nos. 10 and 11 which date from c. 1809. Cotman was at Binham in 1811 when he sketched the exterior north-west view[2]. The Priory was also drawn by John Britton and Frederick Mackenzie.

1. Pencil, watercolour with some white bodycolour, $10\frac{3}{4}$ × $14\frac{5}{16}$ ins., Pierrepont Barnard Collection 1934.

2. Pencil, $7\frac{3}{4}$ × $10\frac{11}{16}$ ins., inscribed, signed and dated l.r. *Sketched July 17 1811—Drawn 1816 J. S. Cotman,* in the Glasgow Art Gallery. See Kitson 1937 p. 149. The same view was drawn by Thirtle and exhibited at the Norwich, Thirtle Centenary 1939 (124), monochrome, 10 × 15 ins., lent by the Royal Institute of British Architects and now in the collection of the Yale Center for British Art and British Studies, New Haven, USA. A *Binham Abbey,* attributed to Thirtle was in the C. C. R. Spelman sale, Norwich, Spelman Tues.–Thurs. 17th–19th March 1914, second day bt. Wilton 16s.

10 Triforium, Norwich Cathedral   **Pl. 10**

Pencil, watercolour and some white bodycolour on cream wove paper; 30·3 × 37·7 ($11\frac{15}{16}$ × $14\frac{13}{16}$).

COND: Cleaned by Kennedy North, Nov. 1939. Removed from Bulwer cabinet, Aug. 1976. Mounted Royal.—*Verso,* paper stained.

PROV: James Reeve; bt. from him by H. S. Theobald[1]; bt. from him Feb. 1910 by R. J. Colman; his bequest 1946, registered 1951.

The fine pencil work and subdued tonal range of this drawing compares with the *Interior of Binham Priory* in the Ashmolean Museum, Oxford (see the entry for No. 9). The drawing is an interior view of the Cathedral from the north triforium of the chancel over the transept crossing to the north triforium of the nave. The organ wall is shown in

the background and also indicated is the catwalk which then spanned the north transept at the crossing[2]. A monochrome sketch of the same composition without the figure, is in a private collection[3].

The museum's drawing may have been that which Thirtle exhibited with the Norwich Society in 1809 (205) *Interior from part of Norwich Cathedral.* There are three drawings of two other compositions recorded of the Cathedral interior, which show the vault of Bishop Goldwell (1472–99) in the north chancel[4].

1. CC records.

2. The catwalk is also shown in a drawing by David Hodgson in the collection, 157.41.98.

3. Monochrome wash, $10\frac{7}{16}$ × $15\frac{1}{8}$ ins; exh. Norwich, Thirtle Centenary 1939 (110), lent by Sir Michael Sadler.

4. (a) Watercolour, $5\frac{1}{2}$ × $6\frac{1}{2}$ ins., Leeds City Art Gallery, 5.242/52, a sketch taken from the first pillar from the crossing, north side of the chancel.—(b) watercolour, 21 × $25\frac{3}{4}$ ins. (sight measurement), in the Russell-Cotes Art Gallery and Museum, Bournemouth, of which there is a facsimile version of similar size in a private collection. They were taken from the north side of the chancel, west of the present Cathedral Treasury. Both versions are close to Cotman in their palette and handling. Either version could have been exhibited with the Norwich Society in 1812 (160) *See yonder hallowed tomb . . .* [Blair].

11 View on the River Wensum, Norwich   **Pl. 11**

Pencil, watercolour and some white bodycolour on buff wove paper; 26·5 × 38·9 ($10\frac{7}{16}$ × $15\frac{5}{16}$).

COND: Cleaned by Kennedy North, Nov. 1939. Removed from Bulwer cabinet, March 1976. Mounted Royal.

PROV: ? James Mill's sale Norwich, Spelman Wed. 14th June 1865, Water colour drawings in gilt frames and glazed, lot 186 *VIEW on the NORWICH RIVER: the Duke's Palace previous to the erection of the Bridge, Early drawing—very fine Painted for his friend James Stark* bt. Dalrymple £4.14.6; Charles Thompson[1]; bt. from him by James Reeve[1] by 1903[2]; bt. from him by H. S. Theobald; bt. from him by R. J. Colman Feb. 1910; R. J. Colman Bequest 1946, registered 1951.

EXH: Norwich 1903 (95) as *Duke's Palace Norwich,* $10\frac{1}{2}$ × $18\frac{1}{2}$ ins. (sic), lent by James Reeve.

The colours of this early drawing are remarkably unfaded. The subject was described by Reeve[1] as *Dukes' Palace—previous to the erection of the bridge Stark's Dye houses on right, wherries on left, river in foreground St. Giles Church in the distance.* The church in the drawing is shown with a cupola similar to that of St. Giles'. However it is not possible any more to confirm that the warehouses and buildings on the right show the dye works of Michael Stark (the father of James) which were situated on the left bank of the river, or that this drawing shows the site of the Duke's Palace Bridge, which adjoined the dye works up river. The bridge is the subject of a later drawing, No. 92.

1. Reeve Coll. MS p. 35 no. 43.

2. See EXH.

12 The Devil's Tower, Norwich   **Pl. 11**

Pencil and watercolour on cream wove paper; 21·5 × 34·9 ($8\frac{7}{16}$ × $13\frac{3}{4}$).

COND: Treated with Chloramine T, Sept. 1948. Cleaned by J. MacColum, 1967. Mounted Royal.—Repairs u.c.l., u.l. corner and l.r.; small tears along edges. *Verso,* paper surface grazed.

PROV: Presented with a collection of Norwich School drawings, under the terms of the Sydney Kitson Bequest, through Sir Henry Hake, 1938.

EXH: Worthing 1957 (43); University of East Anglia 1964 (6); Bedford and Cambridge 1966 (61).

With blocks of masonry in the foreground, locking the lower edge of the picture, this is an unusual composition for Thirtle. The Devil's Tower is viewed from down river possibly where Old Carrow Bridge and its successor of 1833 spanned it from 1810 until it was replaced by a new bridge on the present site. As the river is straight after the Tower, a plausible explanation for the masonry and wooden bulwarks, seemingly jutting out from the bank, is that the drawing, an early one, shows the old bridge being built.

13 Devil's Tower near King Street Gates—Evening
Pl. 12

Pencil, watercolour and some white bodycolour on cream wove paper; 33·3 × 43·8 (13⅛ × 17¼).

COND: Treated with Chloramine T, Sept. 1948. Laid. Mounted Imperial.—Backing paper foxed.—Colour faded.

PROV: William Bircham sale, 'The Ollands', Reepham, Norfolk, 4th and 5th Oct. 1883 first day lot 44 as *The River with the Devil's Tower & shipping Norfolk* bt. for J. J. Colman with two others 13 gns.[1]; J. J. Colman Bequest 1898, registered 1899.

EXH: ? Norwich Society of Artists 1809 (152) as *Devil's Tower near King Street Gates—Evening*; Norwich 1885 (351) lent by J. J. Colman; Norwich, Art Circle 1886 (62); R.A. Winter Exhibition, 1892 (27); Norwich 1894 (64); London 1897 (27); Tate 1922 (244); Norwich, Thirtle Centenary 1939 (84); Arts Council, Norwich 1947 (54); Lowestoft 1948 (65); Leeuwarden 1948 (45); Kidderminster 1954 (37); Derby and Nottingham 1959 (63); Manchester, Whitworth 1961 (41); China 1963 and Berlin 1964 (61); Bedford and Cambridge 1966 (60); Rouen 1967 (55); Kenwood 1969 (71); The Hague 1977 (57).

REF: *EDP* 3rd Feb. 1885, 'The Art Loan Exhibition, fourth notice'; *Norwich Mercury* 7th July 1886 'The John Thirtle Exhibition'; *Norfolk Chronicle* 10th July 1886 'The Norwich Art Circle'; Norwich Art Circle, *Third exhibition catalogue, John Thirtle* 1886 illus. in litho by C. J. Watson (1846—1927) p. 7[2]; *Norwich Mercury* 13th Feb. 1899 'Mr. J. J. Colman's gift to the museum'; Dickes p. 222 repro. p. 223; Cotman and Hawcroft p. 17 repro. pl. 11; Hardie p. 67; Mallalieu repro. p. 46 pl. 34.

The Devil's Tower, part of the medieval fortifications of Norwich, became so called in the romantic ambience of the early nineteenth century. One of the two boom towers on the River Wensum at the foot of Butter Hills, south of King Street, it stands on the left of the river. In 1833 one of its three turrets and much of the western wall fell[3] and since then the fabric has further deteriorated.

A date of c. 1809 is proposed for this drawing, as it seems reasonable to assume that it relates to the Norwich Society drawing of that date[4] when Thirtle's exhibited works prompted acclaim from the *Norwich Mercury* 29th

July 1809: 'Messrs. Ladbrooke, Crome, Dixon & Thurtle (sic) have also some more excellent proofs of their improving science, particularly the latter gentleman.' It is one of the most powerful compositions in Thirtle's oeuvre and aptly illustrates some of the ideas in his 'hints': 'Of Light & Shade There should be in a Drawg. one great light Brighter than any other which should generally be as in Nature in the sky which may be called the great light of the whole, there should be a principal light in the Landscape . . . But perhaps the Effect is generally best when in the middle of the Drawg . . . shadows are not so strong at Noon as they are morng & eveng . . .'[5] The present warm colouring is misleading. The tonal values are probably unaltered but the original overall colour must have been a dark greyish-blue of which a narrow band remains on the right edge, under the mount. It seems that an injudicious use of fugitive indigo has resulted in a total loss of the blueish tones of the sky and buildings and of the green in the water and foreground foliage. The original colour, although here much darker for an evening effect, may have approached the palette of a larger drawing of c. 1810 *View on the river near Cow's tower* in the collection, No. 15. In these two early drawings Thirtle comes close to Crome in the massy, monumental forms, the strong structural composition and almost monochromatic colour. Stylistically they can be loosely grouped with a number of large drawings such as *The Boatyard* 1812 (No. 29), *Bishop Bridge*, dated 1813 (No. 30), and the Mackintosh collection *Costessey Weir*, dated 1814[6]. There is a smaller version of the Devil's Tower in the collection, No. 14[7], and two other drawings from a more distant viewpoint, Nos. 12 and 106. The Devil's Tower appears also in two later drawings, but this time viewed from the right bank looking down river, Nos. 107 and 108[8].

The Devil's Tower was a strikingly picturesque motif and the subject was much favoured by many of the Norwich artists: by John Sell Cotman, J. J. Cotman, James Stark, Thomas Lound and by the soldier and amateur artist James Pattison Cockburn.

1. MS note in James Reeve's hand, Art Dept. archives, and annotated catalogue from the library of R. J. Colman in NCLN2.

2. Compiler's pagination.

3. Stark's *Scenery of the Rivers of Norfolk* 1834, text to pl. 15.

4. Thirtle also exhibited in 1807 (15) *View on the* [Wensum] *River near the Devil's Tower.*

5. *Hints on Water-colour Painting* p. 3 ff.; compiler's pagination.

6. Pencil, watercolour, some white bodycolour and slight scraping out, 19¼ × 26⅝ ins. (sight measurement).

7. There is a very similar composition by Peter de Wint (1784—1849), *Near Norwich*, black and white chalk on grey paper, 12⅞ × 20¾ ins., in the Fitzwilliam Museum, Cambridge, 3412. An early watercolour by him of the Devil's Tower looking down river, 17¼ × 25¼ ins., is in the Usher Gallery. Lincoln, 1511.

8. Other Devil's Tower subjects, attributed to Thirtle, are:
   (1) *Watercolour—View of the Yare & Devil's tower, Norwich*, Richard Ferrier sale, Gt. Yarmouth, Samuel Aldred Thurs., Fri., 17th, 18th June 1869 second day lot 98.
   (2) *The Devil Tower and Carrow Bridge*, exh. Norwich 1878 (425), lent by Mr. Wm. Runacres. William Runacres was the purchaser of two lots in the Thirtle Sale 1882: lot 34 *Old Houses* £3 and lot 57 *Old Houses* £5.5.0.
   (3) *The Devil's Tower, Norwich*, watercolour, 7¼ × 10⅛ ins., Manning Galleries Exhibition June 1968 (51). See No. 107.
   (4) *Norwich, King Street*, monochrome wash, 5½ × 8 ins., Huntington Library, San Marino, California, USA.

14 Devil's Tower, Norwich   **Pl. 12**

Pencil and watercolour on buff laid paper; 23 × 30 ($9\frac{1}{16}$ × $11\frac{13}{16}$).

INSCR: Inscribed in pencil with colour note u.c.l. *Silvery/Yellow* and l.c.l. *?Graysh* (indistinct).

COND: Cleaned by Kennedy North, March 1940. Removed from Bulwer cabinet, Aug. 1976. Mounted Royal.—Corner torn l.r. *Verso*, remains of old backing paper.—? Colour faded.

PROV: F. T. Keith sale, Agricultural Hall, Norwich, Keith & Smith Thurs. 19th Feb. 1903 lot 287 as *Large water-colour drawing, River Yare and Boom Tower, Norwich* bt. North for T. H. Keith £2–3?[1]; bt. from him for R. J. Colman £5[2]; R. J. Colman Bequest 1946, registered 1951.

EXH: RA 1934 (800) lent by R. J. Colman; Norwich, Boswell Centenary 1939 (10) lent by R. J. Colman.

This drawing is a close version of, or study for, No. 13. It differs in that there is only one wherry to the left and no sailing boat or cows under the tower. There is reason to believe that the present colour in both is misleading. In this one there are traces of blue and pink in the figures and a greenish tinge in the river bank on the right. The inscribed colour notes of silvery yellow and greyish indicate that some blue-grey has faded, leaving an overall appearance of brown wash. It is also possible that the drawing was cut down, removing any unfaded area, by Kennedy North, in 1940.

1. According to CC records T. H. Keith was the purchaser at his father's, F. T. Keith, sale.

2. CC records.

15 View on the river near Cow's Tower, Norwich   **Pl. 1**

Pencil and watercolour on cream wove paper; 40·5 × 54·8 ($15\frac{15}{16}$ × $21\frac{5}{8}$).

COND: Cleaned by Kennedy North, Nov. 1939. Removed from Bulwer cabinet, Sept. 1976. Cleaned and laid by D. Lewisohn, Feb. 1977. Mounted Imperial.—Paper surface grazed. Repair u.l. corner.

PROV: ? Francis Stone sale[1], Norwich, Spelman Mon.–Fri. 19th–23rd Oct. 1835 fifth day lot 120 *Water-colour Drawings . . . Thirtle Scene on the River Wensum, near Cow Tower, in Norwich;* A. J. Chambers[2]; bt. from him by J. J. Colman[2]; his bequest to R. J. Colman 1898; R. J. Colman Bequest 1946, registered 1951.

EXH: ? Norwich Society 1810(135).

Cow Tower stands at the north-east corner of the city on the right bank of the River Wensum: 'the last and most spectacular tower, 50 ft high and 36 ft thick, with a strong batter and remains of battlements. This is an early example of the use of brick in Norwich. Bills exist of 1378 for the purchase of the brick and the making of the stone arrow slits. The bricks are 9 by $9\frac{1}{4}$ by 2 in. in size'[3]

Thirtle showed two Cow Tower subjects with the Norwich Society in 1810(135) *View on the river near Cow's tower, Norwich,* possibly the museum's drawing although there is another version of similar size in a private collection, and 1812 (190) *Boat Builder's Yard, near the Cow's Tower, Norwich,* probably No. 29[4].

40

In 1810 Thirtle along with his fellow artists received an encouraging review from the *Norfolk Chronicle* of 25th August '. . . In the landscape and View department we have the greatest number of competitors and if we may presume to decide the most masterly performances, the names of Crome, Dixon, Ladbrooke, Thirtle and Cotman will naturally occur to our readers all of whom appear to have gained professional strength since the former exhibition. . .'

One of four exhibition pieces discussed in the entry for No. 30, this drawing with its silvery tonality and simple forms is one of the most forward looking in the collection: the mid-distance is almost proto-impressionist in feeling.

1. Francis Stone (1770–1835), Norfolk County Surveyor, President of the Norwich Society of Artists in 1812 and 1822. Unfortunately the NCM copy of his sale catalogue is not annotated.

2. CC records.

3. Pevsner p. 259.

4. There are three other Cow Tower drawings, attributed to Thirtle (1) NCM 1352.B33.235.951, doubtful and consequently not included in this catalogue, (2) No. 26 and (3) *View of Norwich with Cow Tower,* watercolour, $6\frac{1}{4}$ × $13\frac{1}{4}$ ins., exh. Norwich School Exhibition 1927(273), lent by C. R. Bignold, poor photo in NCM annotated copy of the catalogue.

16 Castle on a Hill   **Pl. 16**

Pencil and watercolour on buff wove paper; 13·2 × 20 ($5\frac{3}{16}$ × $7\frac{7}{8}$).

COND: Mounted Royal.—*Verso*, gum at corners.

PROV: See No. 7.

EXH: Rouen 1967 (53c); Kenwood 1969 (68c).

This is a very Cotmanesque drawing on the type of thick rough wove paper which Cotman used especially in the period c. 1808–11. However the attribution to Thirtle is confirmed by its closeness to No. 18, which has a similar paper, and to the little watercolour sketch illustrating *Light and Shade* in his MS p. 12.

17 A Castle   **Pl. 17**

Pencil, watercolour and white bodycolour on cream wove paper; 11·7 × 14·6 ($4\frac{5}{8}$ × $5\frac{3}{4}$).

Verso, cloud study in pencil.

COND: Mounted Royal with Nos. 92 and 93.—*Verso*, gum at corners.

PROV: See No. 7.

EXH: Rouen 1967 (54a).

As an ideal landscape, Cotmanesque in feeling, this drawing is untypical of Thirtle.

18 Sky Study with Trees and Rooftop   **Pl. 19**

Pencil and watercolour on buff wove paper; 8·6 × 19·1 ($3\frac{3}{8}$ × $7\frac{1}{2}$). *Verso*, sketch in pencil of wherry and figures.

INSCR: Inscribed in pencil with colour notes.

COND: Mounted Royal with Nos. 90 and 91.—*Verso*, gum at corners.

PROV: See No. 7.

This drawing is close to No. 16 and is discussed in that entry.

19 River Scene   Pl. 16

Pencil and watercolour on cream wove paper with watermark upper centre [?WHATMA]N; 10·2 × 15·3 (4 × 6).

COND: Mounted Royal with Nos. 16 and 20.—*Verso*, gum at corners.

PROV: See No. 7.

EXH: Rouen 1967 (53b); Kenwood 1969 (68b).

20 Rainbow   Pl. 17

Pencil and watercolour on cream wove paper; 8·8 × 18·2 ($3\frac{7}{16}$ × $7\frac{3}{16}$). *Verso*, slight sketches of geometric shapes.

INSCR: Colour notes in pencil u.l. *Purple/Red/Yellow/Green/Purple/Yellow*.

COND: Mounted Royal with Nos. 16 and 19.—*Verso*, gum at corners.

PROV: See No. 7.

EXH: Rouen 1967 (53a).

This is one of several sketches in the Fitch collection which can be directly related to Thirtle's MS, where his preoccupation with colour and its relationship to light is expressed in his analogy of colour in pigments and of the colour of light in the rainbow: '. . . . If you mean that the Proximity of one Colour should Give beaty (sic) to another that terminates near it observe the Rays of the Sun in the Composition of the Rainbow, the Colours of which are Generated by the falling Rain, when each drop in its descent takes Every Colour of that Bow . . .'.

It was natural enough that Thirtle should refer to the rainbow. In the early nineteenth century the manifestations of light became a preoccupation of artists and theorists, above all J. M. W. Turner[1]. Also in Constable's oil sketches of 1812 and in the later large canvases such as *Salisbury Cathedral* the rainbow is a central theme[2]. The remarkable sketch books of the Norfolk born librarian of Cambridge University and amateur artist, Thomas Kerrich (1748–1828) show an overriding interest in light phenomena[3]. Nearer home, John Sell Cotman sketched 'A Representation of that curious and beautiful phenomena the Parthelion, as seen from the cliffs at Hunstanton Norfolk . . . . . . July 6 1815'[4] and in 1841 he commented on 'a remarkable and beautiful coincidence a fine rainbow appearing at the very moment we alighted under the Portico of Wolterton to see the glorious one painted by Rubens'[5].

1. See John Gage *Colour in Turner*, especially ch. 6 'Colour in the perspective lectures'.

2. See Leslie Parris and Ian Fleming Williams, *Constable*, exhibition catalogue 1976.

3. Photos, Witt.

4. Sepia, $11\frac{1}{4}$ × $7\frac{1}{2}$ ins., BM Dept. MSS.

5. Cotman's drawing of the rainbow, $7\frac{1}{4}$ × $10\frac{1}{2}$ ins., is in the BM, 1902–5–14–158. Rubens' famous *Rainbow Landscape* came to England in 1802 and was bought by Lord Orford of Wolterton in 1823; it is now in the Wallace Collection, London, P 63.

21 St. Benets Abbey   Pl. 14

Pencil and grey wash with some white bodycolour on cream laid paper with watermark lower centre right, a Strasburg lily over *GR*; 25 × 34·5 ($9\frac{13}{16}$ × $13\frac{9}{16}$).

Verso, sketch in pencil of a female figure u.c.l.; a head u.c.r.; a badge u.c.r.

INSCR: Inscribed and signed in pencil along lower edge (inverted) *Friend/I having been some time out of Town I did not receive yr letters til yesterd/yesterday* (sic) *Rec'd both letters having out of Town/I am sorry its not in my Power to fulfil yr Request having at Presend* (sic) *no Ti*[me] (paper cut)/*I being now totally out of My Way therfore hope youl Excuse/I Remain Yrs/John Thirtle*[1]

COND: Cleaned and cut down[2] by Kennedy North, Nov. 1939. Removed from Bulwer cabinet, March 1976. Mounted Royal.

PROV: Mrs. Thirtle sale, Norwich, Spelman Tues. 9th May 1882 bt. for J. J. Colman[3]; his bequest to R. J. Colman 1898; R. J. Colman Bequest 1946, registered 1951.

EXH: Norwich, Art Circle 1886 (24) lent by J. J. Colman.

For notes on St. Benets Abbey, see the entry for No. 23. This is an early drawing of c. 1811; stylistically it relates closely to another monochrome study of the Abbey in the collection, No. 22. Like the pencil drawing No. 137, a north-east aspect of the gateway, it is an unusual view but this time it is taken from the north-west. With the ragged light of the sky, it is perhaps one of the strongest of the monochrome drawings in the collection.

1. Unfortunately the identity of Thirtle's client, addressed here, is not indicated.

2. See INSCR.

3. There were two lots called St. Benet's Abbey: lot 39 bt. Hansell £1.17.6 and lot 48 bt. Thompson £1.15.0.

22 St. Benedict's Abbey North Bure   Pl. 14

Pencil and grey wash on white laid paper with watermark upper edge *EDMEADS & PINE*[1] 26·7 × 37 ($10\frac{1}{2}$ × $14\frac{1}{2}$).

INSCR: Inscribed in pencil l.c.l. *St Benndict Abbey North* B[ure]; numbered in pencil in an unknown hand l.l. *775*.

COND: Deframed and treated with Thymol Vapour Sept. 1960. Cleaned and laid by D. Lewisohn, Sept. 1976. Mounted Royal.—Paper surface grazed l.l.

PROV: F. R. Beecheno; his bequest, with a collection of pictures, furniture and books, 1935.

REF: *EDP* 5th Dec. 1935 'The Beecheno Bequest'.

This is an early drawing and may be a study for Thirtle's exhibit with the Norwich Society of 1811, which has a title similar to the inscription of this sketch (165*)[2] *Draining Mill, St. Bennett's Abbey, on the North* [Bure] *River*. Other compositions of this subject are discussed in the entry for No. 23.

1. Churchill records (p. 50) *1801 Edmonds & Pine*.

2. Pictures asterisked in the catalogue were for sale.

23 St. Benet's Abbey, Norfolk   Pl. 15

Pencil, watercolour, some white bodycolour with slight scraping out on cream wove paper with watermark upper left (inverted) *J WHATMAN/1811*; 50·5 × 73·5 ($19\frac{7}{8}$ × $28\frac{15}{16}$).

COND: Cleaned by D. Lewisohn, Feb. 1977. Mounted Atlas.—Bleached foxing stains.—Colour faded.

PROV: Thomas Agnew & Sons; James Worthington; Robert Worthington; bt. from him by Percy Moore Turner £37 5th July 1939[1]; bt. from him out of the Southwell Bequest Fund £125 1940.

EXH: ? Royal Manchester Institution as by J. S. Cotman, lent by James Worthington[2]; Norwich, Thirtle Centenary 1939 (62) lent by Percy Moore Turner; Harrogate 1953 (50); Worthing 1957 (21); Derby and Nottingham 1959 (60).

REF: Norwich, Thirtle Centenary Catalogue 1939, repro.; *EDP* 21st July 1939, repro; Paul Oppé, 'The Thirtle Centenary Exhibition at Norwich', *Country Life*, 5th Aug. 1939 p. 115, repro.; Day III repro. p. 95.

A south-east view of St. Benet's Abbey which is situated close to the north bank of the River Bure, about three miles south of Horning, Norfolk. By the early nineteenth century only a portion of its gateway remained and this was partly obscured by the tower draining mill built inside it. This curious and highly picturesque subject was painted, drawn or etched by almost every Norwich School artist. When—before 1939—it was in the collection of James Worthington this drawing was attributed to John Sell Cotman[3], no doubt because of its resemblance to the composition of Cotman's etching *East view of the Gateway of St. Bennet's Abbey* published in 1813 as pl. 25 of his *Architectural Antiquities of Norfolk 1818*[4]. The broad washes of the sky are close to Cotman but overall the drawing is stylistically far removed from him.

Thirtle exhibited two St. Benet's Abbey subjects with the Norwich Society: in 1811(165*)[5] *Draining Mill; St. Bennett's Abbey on the North* [Bure] *River* and in 1828, his only exhibit that year and the first since the Secession of 1816–18, (176*)[5] *St. Benet's Abbey*. The museum drawing is certainly an exhibition piece but stylistic and other evidence call for caution in identifying it as either the 1811 or 1828 exhibit. It might seem significant that it bears a watermark of 1811, but it is usually wise to ascribe to a drawing a somewhat later date, at least 2–3 years later than its watermark. The drawing has certain features, such as the treatment of the sky and foreground foliage which are close to, for example, *Bishop Bridge*, dated August 1813, No. 30, but the fluid, creamy handling of the Abbey is unlike the solid, monumental buildings in the latter and points to a later date. There are two smaller studies of *St. Benet's Abbey*: one in the collection, No. 24, and the other in the BM[6]. In both the treatment of the sky is close to that in *Bishop Bridge*. It would seem safe to date the subject of this entry to c. 1813–1816: it postdates *Bishop Bridge*, the composition may have been influenced by the Cotman etching of 1813 and Thirtle's treatment of skies and foliage seems to have altered at about 1816, see for example *River Scene*, No. 47.

There is in the collection an early monochrome drawing No. 22, which is possibly a study for the 1811 exhibited work[7] as it is inscribed with a similar title.

1. Percy Moore Turner Stock Book, entry No. 2565 Art Dept. archives.

2. Typescript of 'Labels etc. on inside of backboard' removed from old mount; no date for the Manchester exhibition is given.

3. Labels removed from old mount.

4. Mrs. Thirtle's sale 1882 included two lots of Cotman etchings, lot 84 *Seven etchings* and lot 86 *Twelve etchings, Architectural views.*

5. Pictures asterisked in the catalogue were for sale.

6. See the entry for No. 24.

7. J. N. Waite lent *St. Benet's Abbey*, watercolour, 17 × 23¾ ins. to the Norwich Art Circle Exhibition 1886 (31) which was described as *The remains of the Abbey and the windmill in centre, with a group of horses and a pool of water in the foreground.* It was still in his collection in 1889 when he lent it to Great Yarmouth 1889 (86). A large drawing, this could be either the 1811 or 1828 Norwich Society exhibit.

24 St. Benet's Abbey, Norfolk   Pl. 15

Pencil and watercolour on buff wove paper; 23·2 × 32·3 (9⅛ × 12¾).

COND: Cleaned by Kennedy North, April 1940. Removed from Bulwer cabinet, Dec. 1969. Cleaned and inlaid by J. Skillen 1972. Mounted Royal.—*Verso*, foxing.—Colour faded.

PROV: See No. 21.

EXH: Norwich, Art Circle 1886 (56) lent by J. J. Colman; Norwich 1903 (92) lent by R. J. Colman.

REF: Norwich Art Circle, *Third Exhibition Catalogue, John Thirtle* 1886 illus. in litho by Robert Bagge Scott (1849–1925) p. 4; Dickes p. 224.

This drawing has faded to its present dusky pink from original greens and blues which must have approached the fresh palette of another version of this composition, of similar size, in the BM[2]. Both drawings may be studies for the large watercolour, possibly of c. 1813–16, No. 23.

1. Compiler's pagination.

2. Pencil and watercolour, 9½ × 13¾ ins., 1902–5–14–483.

25 St. Benet's Abbey, Norfolk   Pl. 13

Pencil and watercolour on grey-buff wove paper; 21·8 × 30·4 (8 9/16 × 11 15/16).

INSCR: *Verso*, inscribed in pencil c. *J Thirtle* and in an unknown hand l.r. *Sketch by John Thirtle*.

COND: Cleaned by Kennedy North, Nov. 1939. Removed from Bulwer cabinet, March 1976. Mounted Royal.—*Verso*, paper stained left & r. edges.

PROV: H. S. Theobald; bt. from him by R. J. Colman Feb. 1910; R. J. Colman Bequest 1946, registered 1951.

This is probably an early drawing of c. 1811–16 in common with the other drawings of the subject in the collection which are discussed in the entry for No. 23. It is rather weak in execution, but the pencil work is characteristic and the palette and washes compare well with No. 26.

26 Bishopgate Bridge and Cow Tower, Norwich   Pl. 13

Pencil, watercolour and some white bodycolour on blue-grey wove paper; 17·4 × 30·2 (6⅞ × 11⅞).

COND: Cleaned by Kennedy North, March 1940. Removed from Bulwer cabinet, March 1976. Mounted Royal.

PROV: Mrs. Thirtle sale, Norwich, Spelman Tues. 9th May 1882 bt. for J. J. Colman[1]; his bequest to R. J. Colman 1898; R. J. Colman Bequest 1946, registered 1951.

This drawing shows Bishop Bridge and the Cow Tower from the left bank of the river Wensum. The recently demolished Cavalry Barracks, erected in 1792 half a mile north-west of the city near Pockthorpe, are shown in the right distance. There is a larger but similarly unfinished watercolour version of this composition in the Whitworth Art Gallery[2].

Thirtle exhibited with the Norwich Society Secession in 1817 (40) *View near the Horse Barracks, Norwich,* for which the museum's drawing and/or the Whitworth version may be studies[3]. The Cavalry Barracks were also painted by Thirtle's contemporary, the soldier and amateur artist James Pattison Cockburn (1778–1849) whose panoramic watercolour is in the collection[4]. Other drawings of Bishop Bridge and the Cow Tower are discussed in the entries for Nos. 30 and 15.

1. CC records. See No. 30 Note 10.

2. Pencil and watercolour, $11\frac{1}{8} \times 26\frac{1}{4}$ ins., D.13. 1923, previously attributed to Thomas Lound.

3. P. E. Hansell lent to the Norwich 1874 Exhibition J. Thirtle (98) *Near the Barracks, Norwich* which may be the exhibited work or the Whitworth version.

4. Watercolour and bodycolour, $9\frac{9}{16} \times 18\frac{3}{16}$ ins., 29a.235.951. Repro. Clifford 1965 p. 47 pl. 60b, wrongly captioned Lound.

27 Lakenham Mills   Pl. 19

Pencil and watercolour on buff wove paper; $19 \cdot 8 \times 25 \cdot 1$ ($7\frac{3}{4} \times 9\frac{7}{8}$).

COND: Cleaned by Kennedy North, April 1940. Removed from Bulwer cabinet, March 1976. Mounted Royal.—Slight foxing.—Colour faded.

PROV: J. J. Colman by 1886[1]; his bequest to R. J. Colman 1898; R. J. Colman Bequest 1946, registered 1951.

EXH: Norwich, Art Circle 1886 (46) lent by J. J. Colman; Norwich 1903 (84) lent by R. J. Colman.

REF: Norwich Art Circle, *Third Exhibition Catalogue, John Thirtle* 1886 illus. in litho by C. J. Watson (1846–1927) p. 9; *Norwich Mercury* 7th July 1886 'John Thirtle Exhibition'; Dickes p. 225.

Thirtle exhibited three Lakenham subjects with the Norwich Society: in 1806 (163) *Lakenham Mills,* in 1810 (173) *Cottage, Lakenham* and in 1811 (121*)[2] *Lakenham Mills.* The museum's drawing is possibly a study for the 1811 exhibit. A band of the original fresh blue remains along the top edge of the drawing. The palette when still unfaded and deepened by the ground of a buff tinted paper, places this drawing with works of c. 1811 such as Nos. 25 and 26. There is a pencil sketch for the museum's watercolour in the BM[3]. Both are pleasingly sensitive drawings and far surpass a monochrome 'study' which entered the collection as by John Thirtle, but whose attribution cannot be accepted. The underlying pencil drawing is perhaps characteristic, but the shapeless and flabby washes are not[4].

Lakenham in the nineteenth century was a small hamlet with a hall, some cottages, a watermill, and an inn at the bottom of the steep slope of Long John Hill, south of Norwich. Thirtle's drawing shows the old watermill on the left and the post office on the right. The mill became a yarn factory and was destroyed by fire in 1908. It was also drawn by Robert Dixon[5] and Henry Ninham[6].

A drawing by Thirtle of the Hall at Lakenham is in the collection, No. 74[7].

1. See EXH. No provenance is given in the CC records but the drawing may have been in John Wodderspoon sale, Norwich, Murrell Thurs. Fri. 15th, 16th Jan. 1863 second day lot 329 *"Old Lakenham Mill"* by John Thirtle 23s.

2. Pictures asterisked in the catalogue were for sale.

3. $7\frac{3}{16} \times 9\frac{7}{8}$ ins., 1902–5–14–488.

4. $9\frac{7}{16} \times 12\frac{7}{16}$ ins., Kitson Bequest 1938, 60.155.938.

5. Pencil, $9\frac{3}{8} \times 11\frac{5}{8}$ ins. (paper), inscribed in pencil l.r. *Lakenham Mill,* in the museum's collection, 40.59.935.

6. Watercolour, $4\frac{1}{2} \times 6$ ins., BM, 1902–5–14–447.

7. Another subject *Holl's Lane, Lakenham,* $8\frac{1}{2} \times 13\frac{1}{2}$ ins., was lent by W. Boswell & Son to the Norwich, Thirtle Centenary 1939 (61); poor photo in NCM annotated catalogue.

28 Whitefriars Bridge, Norwich   Pl. 2a

Pencil and watercolour on buff laid paper; $23 \cdot 1 \times 32$ ($9\frac{1}{8} \times 12\frac{5}{8}$).

COND: Cleaned by Kennedy North, April 1940. Removed from Bulwer cabinet, Dec. 1969. Mounted Royal.—*Verso,* gum at left & r. edges.—Colour faded.

PROV: See No. 1.

EXH: Norwich, Art Circle 1886 (49) lent by J. J. Colman; RA 1934 (799) lent by R. J. Colman; Colnaghi 1970 (117).

REF: Norwich Art Circle, *Third Exhibition Catalogue, John Thirtle* 1886 illus. in litho by Charles Clowes (fl. 1871–1898) p. 7[1]; Dickes p. 240.

Although much faded[2] this is one of the finest drawings in the collection. The structure of the bridge and buildings and their reflections in the water, is expressed with a clarity and an economy of washes which bear comparison with the best of Cotman[3].

Whitefriars Bridge spans the River Wensum between St. Martin's Palace Plain and Cowgate Street, to the north of the Cathedral. Originally of timber it was rebuilt in stone in 1591 and again virtually rebuilt in 1835.

1. Compiler's pagination.

2. A band of unfaded colour under the mount shows that the drawing was predominantly blue and grey with touches of green and brown.

3. The museum's drawing may be a study for another drawing of Whitefriars Bridge which was in the William Dixon sale, Norwich, Spelman Thurs. 30th Nov. 1871 lot 183 *View on the Norwich River, looking towards White Friars' Bridge with boats and figures. A fine drawing.* £6.6.0; now untraced.

29 Boat Builder's Yard, near the Cow's Tower, Norwich
Pl. 18

Pencil and watercolour with slight scraping out on cream wove paper; $44 \cdot 5 \times 65 \cdot 4$ ($17\frac{1}{2} \times 25\frac{3}{4}$).

COND: Cleaned and laid by D. Lewisohn, Aug. 1974. Mounted Atlas.—Corners creased and rubbed.

PROV: See No. 30.

EXH: ? Norwich Society 1812 (190).

REF: *On View* 1975 p. 52.

This drawing is a view of Cow Tower, which is discussed in the entry for No. 15, from the left bank of the River

Wensum. The ruins of St. Leonard's Priory are on the centre left horizon: 'All that remains of this once noble building is an old piece of stone wall, in which is an arch and adjoining it a small farm-house, the site of the original buildings being ploughed over'.[1]

Thirtle exhibited two other boat builders subjects with the Norwich Society; in 1810 (148) *Boat-builder's yard, Norwich* which is probably the drawing now in the collection of Mr. John Allen[2] and in 1829 (127*) *Boat Builders, Carrow.*

Of the four major exhibition pieces in the collection (see No. 30) only this watercolour and No. 15 have retained most of their original colour. They are among the few drawings whose present condition can show Thirtle's fondness for soft greys, greyish-blues and sage greens heightened by the contrast of cream, buff and brown. These two drawings, in spite of their probable identity with Thirtle's exhibits with the Norwich Society in 1810 and 1812, seem less Cotmanesque and much less solid than *Boat-builder's yard, Norwich* dated 1810[2] and the later *Bishop Bridge* dated 1813, No. 30, and stylistically would better fit a later date.

1. P. Browne, *History of Norwich*, 1814 p. 308.

2. See No. 30 Note 3.

30 Bishopsgate Bridge, Norwich—Evening Pl. 2b

Pencil and watercolour on cream wove paper; 49·2 × 71·9 (19$\frac{3}{8}$ × 28$\frac{5}{16}$).

INSCR: *Verso*, dated in brown ink c. *Norwich Augst 1813.*

COND: Mounted Imperial.—Foxing and staining. Crease across u.l. & u.r. corner, l.r. corner torn.—Colour faded.

PROV: Rev. G. H. K. Sherlock; bt. from him with No. 29 with the aid of a 50% grant from the V & A, 1974.

EXH: ? Norwich Society Secession 1817 (62).

REF: ? *Norfolk Chronicle* 2nd Aug. 1817; *On View* 1975 p. 52.

View on the river near Cow's tower, Norwich 1810, No. 15, *Boat Builder's Yard near the Cow's Tower, Norwich* 1812, No. 29, *Bishop Bridge*, the subject of this entry, dated 1813, and *A View of Thorpe, with Steam Barge Working up—Evening* 1815 No. 38, are the four major exhibition pieces by the artist in the collection.

Thirtle exhibited four Bishop Bridge subjects with the Norwich Society: in 1806 (101) *Bishop-Bridge, Norwich*, in 1807 (36) *Bishop Bridge*, in 1811 (138*) *View on the River from the Arch of Bishop's Bridge* and with the Secession in 1817 (62) *Bishopsgate Bridge, Norwich—Evening.* The latter, reviewed in the *Norfolk Chronicle* 2nd August as 'a bold and masterly effort of his pencil', may be the museum's drawing. This composition or a version of it, as there are variations in the wherries, was engraved by W. Wallis for *Excursions through Norfolk* published 1818[1].

Bishop Bridge built c. 1340 is the only remaining medieval bridge in Norwich; it adjoined the east side of Bishop's Gate of c. 1436 'a neat gothic building, (by far the lightest and handsomest of any of the city gates)'[2] which was demolished in 1791. In Thirtle's drawing the bridge is viewed up river from the right bank. The city arms are visible over the centre arch. The bridge is small,

compact and picturesque but Thirtle has dramatically enlarged it, an effect given further emphasis by the hills of Mousehold in the distance. The fine range of early gabled buildings to the north of the bridge were demolished in 1878; the Red Lion public house stands on the site today. The drawing has qualities such as the almost abstract shapes of colour filled areas and the buff, green and blue palette of the hills and foreground on the right, which are strongly reminiscent of Cotman's post Greta period. A similar affinity with Cotman is seen in *The Boatyard* dated 1810 in Mr. John Allen's collection[3].

Bishop Bridge was the subject of at least five other compositions by Thirtle: (1) A view from the left bank, looking up river, a pencil sketch in the museum's collection, No. 140.—(2) A view from the water looking up river, the most accomplished rendering of which is a drawing of c. 1816–19 in the collection of Rowntree Mackintosh Ltd[4]. A version or copy is in a Norfolk private collection[5], another was lent by Miss Burleigh to the Art Circle Exhibition 1886 (16)[6] and yet another, smaller and elaborated by the addition of a wherry on the right, was lent by Mr. Geoffrey Buxton to the Norwich, Thirtle Centenary 1939 (265)[7].—(3) A view from the road on the high left bank to the north, which is known in a grey wash drawing lent by Charles Bolingbroke to the Norwich, Thirtle Centenary 1939 (115)[8] and in a finished watercolour which was sold at Christie's, as by J. Crome, in 1924[9]. While the watercolour can be confidently ascribed to Thirtle, the grey wash drawing seems to point in Crome's direction without allowing a firm reattribution to him.—(4) A view which includes the Cow Tower, as it appears in the museum's collection No. 26 and its larger version in the Whitworth Art Gallery.—(5) A view looking through the arches of the bridge, a fresh watercolour study in the BM[10], which in consequence of its subject, may be related to the 1811 Norwich Society exhibit, although it seems later in date as it is close to the watercolour studies in the museum's collection discussed in the entry for No. 38.

1. Vol. 2 between pp. 8 and 9.

2. P. Browne *History of Norwich* 1814, p. 265.

3. Pencil and watercolour, 12$\frac{1}{8}$ × 19$\frac{1}{16}$ ins. (sight measurement), signed and dated l.l. *J. Thirtle/1810*, exh. Norwich, Thirtle Centenary 1939 (29), lent by W. Boswell & Son.

4. Pencil, watercolour, some white bodycolour and slight scraping out, 19$\frac{7}{8}$ × 26$\frac{7}{8}$ ins. (sight measurement), exh. Norwich, Thirtle Centenary 1939 (36), lent by Sir Robert Bignold.

5. Watercolour, 19$\frac{3}{4}$ × 27 ins., exh. Norwich, Thirtle Centenary 1939 (23), lent by A. T. Chittock.

6. 10$\frac{1}{4}$ × 16$\frac{3}{4}$ ins., previously lent by R. W. Burleigh to the Norwich 1878 exhibition (450), when the reviewer of the *EDP* 13th Dec. 1878 suggested that the Bignold drawing (419) 'should be compared with No. 450, the same subject, but with better tone and finish'.

7. 13 × 16$\frac{1}{2}$ ins., poor photograph in NCM annotated catalogue. Major G. C. Buxton's sale, Cromer, Allman & Co. Wed.—Fri. 15th–17th Jan. 1941 second day lot 387.

8. Pencil and grey wash, 10$\frac{1}{4}$ × 15$\frac{1}{16}$ ins. (sight measurement), in the collection of H. Bolingbroke 1972.

9. ? watercolour, 12$\frac{1}{2}$ × 17 ins., Nesham sale, Christie's 30th July 1924 lot 43 bt. Agnew's, sold by them shortly afterwards to Vickers Bros., now untraced.

The relationship between these two drawings is not clear. The grey wash drawing could be regarded as a Thirtle study for the watercolour, but whilst the washes are characteristic of Thirtle's early monochromes of c. 1803–1808, the pencil work is not. However he did exhibit two drawings of the subject with the Norwich Society in this period: in 1806 and 1808. Crome also showed with the Society in 1805 (98) *Bishop-gate Bridge, Norwich* and in 1807 (75) *View near Bishop-gate*, the title of which would fit well this drawing. It is tempting to attribute it to Crome and to conclude that Thirtle later made a watercolour version from it, but the sharp, hatched pencil work is not typical of Crome either. The fact remains that there is a date gap between the two, as the watercolour, stylistically close to the museum's *Bishop Bridge*, must date from c. 1810–1813.

10. *Under Bishop Bridge, Norwich*, watercolour, 11 × 15½ ins., 1902–5–14–478, ex. coll. J. J. Colman (Reeve coll. MS Print Room BM), possibly bt. at Mrs. Thirtle's sale 1882 lot 46 *Under Bishop Bridge* bt. Thompson £5.15.6. Other Bishop Bridge subjects recorded with a Thirtle attribution in posthumous sales and exhibitions are: Thomas Lound sale 1861 (103); Rev. Samuel Titlow sale, Norwich, Spelman Tues.–Fri. 13th–16th June 1871 first day lot 183 £5.10.0; Mrs. Thirtle sale 1882 lot 44 bt. Edwards £2.0.0; Norwich 1885 exhibition (657), lent by Mr. W. Rupert; I. B. Coaks sale, Norwich Spelman Tues.–Fri. 8th–11th, and Mon. 14th March 1910 second day lot 479 17 gns.

An early watercolour, 17 × 23½ ins., in the collection of Rhode Island School of Design, USA, attributed to Thirtle is unlikely to be by him.

11. n.d. NCM Todd coll. vol. 2 Box 6 p. 293.

31 Norwich Cathedral, South Transept and Cloister
Pl. 22b

Pencil and grey wash on buff laid paper; 33·2 × 25·1 (13$\frac{1}{16}$ × 9$\frac{7}{8}$).

COND: ? Cleaned by Kennedy North between 1939–1940[1]. Removed from Bulwer cabinet, March 1975. Mounted Royal.—Tear l.l. edge.

PROV: C. C. R. Spelman sale Norwich, Spelman Tues.–Thurs. 17th–19th March 1914 lot 502 *Three—Norwich Cathedral and Castle acre* bt. Ada 6½ gns. for R. J. Colman[2]; R. J. Colman Bequest 1946, registered 1951.

REF: Cotman and Hawcroft repro. p. 48 pl. 16.

Of the monochrome drawings in the collection this is one of the most successful. The light and shadow of the façade of the cloister is perfectly balanced by the assured washes of the sky.

The drawing shows the south transept of the Cathedral and the east range of the cloister from the second opening. The early gabled buildings perched picturesquely on the top of the cloister were still in existence in 1828 when they appear in a lithograph of the Cathedral and cloister by James Sillett (1764–1840)[3].

1. The drawing is not listed in any of the restoration typescripts in the CC records except one where it is an addition in manuscript with a question mark.

2. CC records.

3. *Views of the Churches, Chapels, and other Public Edifices in the City of Norwich by J. Sillett* 1828 pl. 1.

32 St. Ethelbert's Gate, Norwich Cathedral
Pl. 22a

Pencil and grey wash on cream laid paper; 33·8 × 28·4 (13$\frac{5}{16}$ × 11$\frac{3}{16}$).

COND: Cleaned by Kennedy North, Nov. 1939. Removed from Bulwer cabinet, Jan. 1976. Mounted Royal.—*Recto*, paper from old mount u.r.

PROV: See No. 1[1].

EXH: Norwich, Art Circle 1889 (54) lent by J. J. Colman.

REF: Cotman and Hawcroft repro. p. 38 pl. 4.

Presumably a companion drawing to No. 31. The composition is a view taken from east of the north cluster of columns beneath the vaulting of St. Ethelbert's Gate, looking west across Tombland to Queens Street and Redwell Street. The houses, in Tombland, to the left beyond the arch, have since been altered and the earlier gabled house opposite has gone.

1. The only Norwich Cathedral subject specified in Mrs. Thirtle's sale was a watercolour lot 10. *Two water colours—Norwich Cathedral and Trimingham* bt. Hansell £2.10.0.

33 Kirby Bedon Church Tower, Norfolk
Pl. 21

Pencil and grey wash on buff laid paper; 32·6 × 24·3 (12$\frac{13}{16}$ × 9$\frac{9}{16}$).

Verso, slight sketch in pencil of a landscape with gate u.l.

COND: Cleaned by Kennedy North, March 1940. Removed from Bulwer cabinet ? Dec. 1969. Cleaned and inlaid by J. Skillen, Nov. 1972. Mounted Royal.

PROV: C. C. R. Spelman sale, Norwich, Spelman Tues.–Thurs. 17th–19th March 1914 lot 485 *Kirby Church* bt. Mase for R. J. Colman 30s; R. J. Colman Bequest 1946, registered 1951.

EXH: Norwich, Thirtle Centenary 1939 (120) lent by R. J. Colman.

An unusually low angle of viewpoint in this drawing emphasises the majestic monumentality of the ruined tower. The time-worn fabric of the building is sensitively expressed by subtle tones of grey wash. The drawing shows Thirtle at his best and it is one of the finest of his works in the collection.

Kirby Bedon is situated three miles south-east of Norwich. Of the ruined church of St. Mary, opposite the mainly nineteenth century church of St. Andrew, only the round tower and parts of the walls of the nave and chancel remain.

34 Broken Ground in Thorpe
Pl. 20

Pencil and grey wash on cream laid paper; 20·8 × 29·4 (8$\frac{3}{16}$ × 11$\frac{9}{16}$).

INSCR: Inscribed in pencil with colour notes.

COND: Cleaned by Kennedy North, Nov. 1939. Removed from Bulwer cabinet, March 1976. Mounted Royal.

PROV: See No. 1.

The robust handling of the grey wash conveys with ease the rough broken ground. The site has not been identified: the title is that given in the Colman Catalogue[1].

1. CC MS vol. 1 p. 117 no. 438.

35 Scene at Costessey, the Seat of Sir G. Jerningham
Pl. 3a

Pencil and watercolour on cream wove paper; 26·4 × 41·9 (10$\frac{3}{8}$ × 16$\frac{1}{2}$).

Verso, slight sketch in pencil of a figure right.

INSCR: Inscribed in pencil with colour notes in sky and water. *Verso*, inscribed in pencil lower c. *J. Thirtle* (faint).

COND: Cleaned and ? cut down by Kennedy North, Nov. 1939[1]. Removed from Bulwer cabinet, Dec. 1969. Mounted Royal.—Inlaid.

PROV: H. S. Theobald; bt. from him by R. J. Colman, Feb. 1910; R. J. Colman Bequest 1946, registered 1951.

EXH: Colnaghi 1970 (110) repro. pl. XXVI.

This drawing is a study for the larger finished work, dated 1814, formerly in the collection of Sir Robert Bignold and now one of a group in the collection of Rowntree Mackintosh Ltd. The two drawings are one of five pairs recorded which are discussed in the entry for No. 38. There are only slight variations between the study and the final work but as in Nos. 38, 39, 47 and 48 Thirtle adds incident to the latter by the little figure of a boy carrying a child, and a rock breaking the reflections in the foreground.

Thirtle drew Costessey church in 1816, see No. 59, and exhibited one Costessey subject with the Norwich Society in 1814 (150) *Scene at Costessey, the Seat of Sir G. Jerningham* and another one with the Secession in 1816 (70) *An Outlett, near Cossey* (sic) *Mills*. In view of the date and the subject—the aggrandised River Tud with the weir near Longwater Lane in the foreground and Costessey Old Hall, the Jerninghams' seat, in the distance—it is most likely that the museum's watercolour is a study for the first of these two exhibits. The subject was engraved, with two figures added on the footbridge, by T. Higham for *Excursions through Norfolk* and published in 1818[3]. There is no known connection between Thirtle and the Jerninghams, but he may have known them through Crome who was drawing master to the family.

1. CC records. The colour notes u. and l.c. are cut.

2. Pencil, watercolour, some white bodycolour, with touches of blue crayon and slight scraping out, 19¼ × 26⅝ ins. (sight measurement), *verso*, signed and dated *J. Thirtle 1814/Costessey Park*, exh. Norwich, Thirtle Centenary 1939 (39), lent by Sir Robert Bignold.

3. Vol. II opp. p. 50.

36 Catton Church—a Sketch Pl. 23

Pencil and watercolour on cream wove paper; 24·3 × 34 (9⁹⁄₁₆ × 13⅜).

COND: Cleaned by Kennedy North, Nov. 1939. Removed from Bulwer cabinet, March 1976. Mounted Royal.

PROV: See No. 1.

EXH: ? Norwich Society 1814 (136) as *Catton Church— a Sketch*.

If this drawing is that which Thirtle exhibited in 1814 it is of particular importance as it is one of three exhibited works which he describes as a sketch. It gives a clear idea of what was not then accepted as a finished drawing. The rich dark purple brown hues of the church, contrasted to the dark green foliage, are close to de Wint.

St. Margaret's Church, Catton, is situated two miles north of Norwich. Catton was the home of Thomas Harvey (1748–1819), the patron of Crome.

37 St Mary's Church, Wroxham, Norfolk Pl. 23

A sketch in pencil of a stained glass window, parallel with

upper edge. Pencil and watercolour on cream wove paper with watermark parallel with right edge [W] *HATMAN/1811*; 21·6 × 31·7 (8½ × 12½). *Verso*, St. Andrew's Church, Thorpe, Norwich (inverted). Pencil and brown wash.

COND: Cleaned by Kennedy North, Nov. 1939. Removed from Bulwer cabinet, March 1976. Double Mounted Royal.—*Verso*, paper from old mount at l. & r. corners.

PROV: See No. 1.

The richly coloured watercolour study on the *recto* shows the vibrancy of Thirtle's unfaded blues and greens. Stylistically close to No. 36 it can probably be dated to c. 1814.

Wroxham village is situated seven miles north-east of Norwich on the way to the nearby Hoveton House where Thirtle was drawing master to the Blofeld family, see No. 7. He may have also sketched the regatta at Wroxham, see the entry for No. 96.

The brown wash drawing on the *verso* is of the old church of St. Andrew's at Thorpe[1] of which only the south porch, tower and parts of the walls remain. Other Thorpe subjects are discussed in the entry for No. 38, see also No. 79.

1. In Thomas Lound sale 1861 was lot 101 Thirtle *Thorpe Church with Cattle* bt. Davey £1.3.0.

38 A view of Thorpe, with Steam Barge working up— Evening Pl. 24

Pencil, watercolour and some white bodycolour with slight scraping out on cream wove paper; 46·9 × 76·8 (18⁷⁄₁₆ × 30³⁄₁₆).

COND: Cleaned by Kennedy North, April 1940. Removed from Bulwer cabinet, March 1954. Framed 1976.— Worm holes l.r.—Colour faded.

PROV: Miss Weston sale, Mundesley, Spelman Fri. 11th Jan. 1889 lot 147 as *View of Thorpe (very fine) Watercolour* bt. J. J. Colman £24; his bequest to R. J. Colman 1898; R. J. Colman Bequest 1946, registered 1951.

EXH: Norwich Society 1815 (149); R. A. Winter Exhibition 1892; London 1897 (26); Norwich, St. Andrew's Hall 1902 (238); Norwich 1903 (87); Norwich, Thirtle Centenary 1939 (47); Norwich, Yare Valley 1968 (1)— with the exception of the first, in all as *Whitlingham Reach*.

REF: Dickes p. 227; Cundall *The Studio* 1922 p. 29 repro. pl. LXX; Norwich, Thirtle Centenary Catalogue 1939 repro.; Frank Leney, *EDP* 24th July 1939 'The Thirtle Exhibition/An Appreciation'; Othinal to the editor *EDP* 25th July 1939 'First Steam Vessel on the Yare'; *Illustrated London News* 29th July 1939 repro.; Paul Oppé, *Country Life* 5th Aug. 1939 'The Thirtle Centenary Exhibition at Norwich' p. 115 repro. p. 114; Barnard repro. pl. 54; Hervey Penham, *Once upon a tide* repro. between pp. 208 & 209; P. A. Darvill and W. R. Stirling, *Britain and the World, Book 4* repro.

This drawing is undoubtedly that exhibited with the Norwich Society in 1815. There is a fluid watercolour study of the same view in the collection, No. 39. The two drawings are one of five pairs recorded of studies and larger, finished, more elaborated watercolours which have similar measurements and form a group dating from period c. 1814–1817. Of the four other pairs, two studies are in the collection, No. 42, *Cottage by the River at Thorpe, Norwich* and No. 35, *Scene at Costessey, the Seat of Sir G. Jerningham*. The finished watercolours related to these two studies may have been exhibited with the Norwich Society in 1814 and with the Secession in 1816 respectively and are now in the collection of Rowntree Mackintosh Ltd. The fourth pair is in the collection: the finished watercolour, No. 47 and the study, No. 48. The former may also have been shown with the Norwich Society in 1816. The fifth pair recorded is *View from Thorpe, Looking towards Bracondale—Evening* possibly that exhibited with the Norwich Society in 1817 and now in the Mackintosh collection[1] and its related study in the collection of Leeds City Art Gallery[2].

Like other exhibition drawings in this group this is an exceptionally serene and monumental drawing 'In it Thirtle sets off his Girtin-like breadth and simplicity of composition by a touch of movement which is rare in his work'[3]. An apt but not fully accurate comment as Thirtle was fond of boats slicing through the water creating reflections and colour, for example in the V & A and BM drawings discussed in the entry for No. 76.

It has been held traditionally that the steam barge shown is the *Experiment*; the first to be launched on the Yare:

> "Monday (the 9th) the first experiment was tried with the steam packet boat, on which occasion Sir Edmund and Lady Lacon and family with a party of ladies, went in the boat to Breydon, and expressed themselves highly pleased with their excursion. The packet afterwards went through the bridge, amidst the acclamations of thousands of spectators. She has since gone regularly to and from Norwich . . ." *The Ipswich Journal* 14th August 1813.

However as the picture was not exhibited until 1815 it may represent the *Telegraph* or the *Courier*, launched during 1814–1815[4]. The stretch of the Yare shown in the drawing lies between Thorpe Old Hall, whose chimneys are visible on the extreme left, and Thorpe Gardens. With several fine buildings of the eighteenth century and earlier, this part of the river earned renown in the nineteenth century as the Richmond of Norfolk. While some of the buildings remain, the future of others, in particular Thorpe Old Hall, is uncertain.

There are ten other Thirtle drawings of Thorpe in the collections, see the entries for Nos. 37, 39, 42, 76, 79, 80, 84, 103, 112, 113[5].

1. Pencil, watercolour, some white bodycolour and slight scraping out, $19\frac{3}{8} \times 28\frac{1}{2}$ ins. (sight measurement).

2. Pencil and watercolour, $10\frac{3}{4} \times 16\frac{3}{4}$ ins., 13.196/53.

3. Paul Oppé 1939 *op. cit.*

4. I am grateful to my colleague, Charles Lewis, for this information.

5. Other Thorpe subjects known to have been drawn by Thirtle on the evidence of his exhibits and of existing works, originals and copies are: *Thorpe Hall*, exh. Norwich Society 1806 (2), possibly the drawing called *Old Manor House*, watercolour, 13 × 17 ins., signed and dated l.r. *Thirtle 1806*, in the collection of the Huntington Library, San Marino, California, 59.55.1255; *Tan Yard, Thorpe near Norwich*, exh. Norwich Society 1808 (248), of which No. 1352.B35.235.951 in the collection is perhaps a record; *View near Thorpe—Evening*, exh. Norwich Society 1809 (202); *Cottage at*

Thorpe, exh. Norwich Society 1814 (138), possibly the drawing in the collection of Rowntree Mackintosh Ltd, see the entry for No. 42; *View from Thorpe looking towards Bracondale—Evening*, exh. Norwich Society Secession 1817 (73), possibly the drawing in the collection of Rowntree Mackintosh Ltd., mentioned this entry; *View looking from Thorpe to Whitlingham—Evening* and *Scene on the River at Thorpe—Evening*, both exh. Norwich Society 1829 (142), (180), see the entries for Nos. 112, 113.

39 Thorpe, Norwich Pl. 24

Pencil and watercolour on cream wove paper; 26·3 × 41·4 ($10\frac{3}{8} \times 16\frac{5}{16}$).

COND: Cleaned by Kennedy North, April 1940. Removed from Bulwer cabinet, March 1976. Mounted Royal.— *Verso*, gum along lower edge.

PROV: Thomas Lound sale, Norwich, Spelman Wed. 6th March 1861[1] bt. for J. J. Colman[2]; his bequest to R. J. Colman 1898; R. J. Colman Bequest 1946, registered 1951.

CAT: CC MS vol. 1 p. 119 No. 458 as *Landscape. River in foreground. Thorpe Old Hall by riverside on left, houses on right.*

One of the group of fresh watercolour studies in the collection that relates to more finished works. This one was done in preparation for the larger drawing, No. 38, and is discussed in that entry.

1. Most of the lots have no titles in the Catalogue. The only named Thorpe subjects were lot 101 *Thorpe Church with Cattle* bought Davey £1.3.0. and lot 103 which was bought by Titlow for £2 and was probably later sold at his sale, Spelman Wed. 13th June 1871 as lot 184 *Thorpe Village*.

2. CC records.

40 Riverside scene, near Norwich Pl. 3b

Pencil and watercolour on buff laid paper; 20·5 × 29·3 ($8\frac{1}{16} \times 11\frac{1}{2}$).

INSCR: V*erso*, inscribed in pencil c.l. *J. Thirtle/one*.

COND: Mounted Royal. Paper stained u. & r. edge.

PROV: See No. 25.

EXH: Norwich, Thirtle Centenary 1939 (45) lent by R. J. Colman, repro.

REF: *EEN* 28th July 1939 repro; Clifford pp. 61, 71, repro. pl. 19b; Day III repro. p. 95.

The silvery still light of this watercolour study is expressed by the sparing application of horizontal washes. The main tones of grey and green are enriched by dots of rich yellow by the sluice gate. Although some of the blue has gone the drawing remains one of the freshest in the collection. In this respect it belongs to the group of watercolour studies discussed in No. 38.

The site has not been identified. Although the bridge in the middle distance resembles Foundry Bridge, Norwich, its environs are too rural to represent that stretch of the river which even in Thirtle's day was built up on the city side.

41 Buxton Lamas, Norfolk Pl. 4a

Pencil and watercolour on cream laid paper; 28·1 × 39·8 ($11\frac{1}{16} \times 15\frac{5}{8}$).

COND: Cleaned by Kennedy North, March 1940. Removed from Bulwer cabinet, Dec. 1969. Mounted Royal.—Inlaid, pinholes u.l. & r. edges, slight foxing.

PROV: Thomas Lound sale, Norwich, Spelman Wed. 6th March 1861 bt. James Reeve[1]; bt. from him by H. S. Theobald; bt. from him by R. J. Colman Feb. 1910; R. J. Colman Bequest 1946, registered 1951.

EXH: Norwich 1903 (89) lent by James Reeve; Norwich, Thirtle Centenary 1939 (53) lent by R. J. Colman; Colnaghi 1970 (113); Harlow 1976 (20).

REF: *EEN* 28th July 1939 'Thirtle Paintings'.

As one of the drawings in which the original colour remains, this study shows clearly Thirtle's lavish use of greys, preferred above all colours to express light in water and skies.

Buxton Lamas is situated in North Norfolk four miles south-east of Aylsham. The identification of the site is that given in the Colman catalogue[2].

1. Reeve Coll. MS. p. 37 No. 10. Most of the lots have no titles in the Catalogue.

2. CC MS vol. 1 p. 37 No. 133.

42 Cottage by the River at Thorpe, Norwich   Pl. 4b

Sketch in pencil of a boat and figures upper right.
Pencil and watercolour on cream wove paper; 30·7 × 39·3 ($12\frac{1}{16} \times 15\frac{1}{2}$).

INSCR: Inscribed in pencil with colour notes u.r.

COND: Cleaned and ? cut down by Kennedy North, March 1940[1]. Removed from Bulwer cabinet, Dec. 1969. Mounted Royal.

PROV: See No. 39.

EXH: Norwich, Thirtle Centenary 1939 (50) as *Riverside Inn* (*Thorpe, near Norwich*), lent by R. J. Colman; Colnaghi 1970 (115) as *River-side Inn*; The Hague 1977 (56).

This drawing, one of the best preserved and most expressive of Thirtle's watercolours, can be dated to c. 1814–1817. It is related to a larger, finished drawing formerly in the collection of Sir Robert Bignold and now with Rowntree Mackintosh Ltd[2]. The two drawings belong to a group which are discussed in the entry for No. 38. Thirtle exhibited with the Norwich Society in 1814 (138) *Cottage at Thorpe* which may have been the Mackintosh version. However there is a related pencil drawing in the collection inscribed, signed and dated *Thorpe 1817*, No. 76. Still, as it differs in several details from the two watercolours: the keel of a boat breaks into the composition on the left, two figures are introduced on the bank and there is much less foliage to the right, this can be an independent work of the same subject post dating the watercolour versions. The relationship between the watercolour study and the finished version is close, although, as in other drawings in this group, Nos. 35, 39 and 48, the composition of the sketch is elaborated in the finished piece, in this case by the addition of a wherry and figures to the right. Thus the loose open character of the study is changed in the worked up watercolour to a much stronger, towering, triangular composition.

The riverside view seen in this study is continued in an exceptionally beautiful drawing in the Whitworth Art Gallery, *Old Waterside Cottages*, which was exhibited at the Thirtle Centenary in 1939 and was considered by Mr. Bernard Boswell to be a Crome[3]. The Whitworth drawing repeats the two trees and the summer house with adjoining shed then extends towards the right to include a double gabled cottage which is shown again in a finished watercolour of c. 1817 in the BM[4]. This cottage is also the subject of several compositions by and after Crome[5].

Both the sketch discussed here and the Whitworth drawing show a masterly use of reserved spaces, especially in the rendering of the summer house and the reflections.

1. The colour notes u.r. are cut.

2. Watercolour with slight scraping out; $19\frac{1}{4} \times 26$ ins. (sight measurement), exh. Norwich, Thirtle Centenary 1939 (3) as *Riverside Thorpe*, lent by Sir Robert Bignold.

3. Pencil and watercolour, $7\frac{5}{8} \times 11\frac{1}{4}$ ins., D4.1915; cit. *EDP* 24th July 1939.

4. $13\frac{1}{4} \times 19\frac{1}{2}$ ins., 1902–5–14–475. Repro. Dickes p. 231.

5. According to James Reeve the cottages in the drawing were still standing in 1866 (Reeve Coll. MS p. 73 Print Room, BM).

43 The Abbot's Bridge, Bury St. Edmunds, Suffolk   Pl. 25

Undefined sketch upper right.
Pencil and watercolour on cream laid paper; 24 × 30·9 ($9\frac{7}{16} \times 12\frac{3}{16}$).

INSCR: Inscribed in pencil u.r. *Light through/Bridge*.

COND: Cleaned by Kennedy North between 1939–1940. Mounted Royal.—Paper creased u.c. from l. to r.

PROV: See No. 1.

EXH: The Hague 1977 (58).

CAT: As *Riverside sketch* in the CC MS vol. 1 p. 115 no. 428.

The inscription on this exceptionally free drawing indicates the major function of the watercolour study in Thirtle's oeuvre, to summarise the main source of light. The subject of this study, not identified until 1939–40[1], represents the Abbot's Bridge, carrying part of the Abbey walls, which spans the River Lark, north-east of the Abbey site at Bury St. Edmunds.

1. CC records. It is identified on the typescript conservation lists of that date.

44 Bridge over the Bure, Coltishall, Norfolk   Pl. 26

Pencil and watercolour and some white bodycolour on cream wove paper; 27·3 × 42·3 ($10\frac{3}{4} \times 16\frac{5}{8}$).

COND: Cleaned and laid by Kennedy North, March 1940. Removed from Bulwer cabinet, March 1976. Mounted Royal.—Repair u.c.r. and l.c.l.

PROV: Thomas Lound sale, Norwich, Spelman Wed. 6th March 1861 bt. James Reeve[1]; bt. from him by H. S. Theobald; bt. from him by R. J. Colman Feb. 1910; R. J. Colman Bequest 1946, registered 1951.

EXH: Norwich, Thirtle Centenary 1939 (14) lent by R. J. Colman.

Thirtle applies a more extensive palette in this drawing than is usual with his watercolour studies. The plummy rich shadow under the bridge and the russet browns of the foreground are strongly reminiscent of de Wint.

Coltishall bridge spans the River Bure eight miles north-east of Norwich. In 1814 Thirtle exhibited with the Norwich Society (124) *Horstead Mills, near Coltishall,* see the entry for No. 104.

1. Reeve Coll. MS. p. 35 no. 42. Most of the lots have no titles in the Catalogue.

45 Bridge over the Bure, Coltishall, Norfolk   Pl. 26

Pencil and brown wash on buff wove paper; 18·2 × 29·5 ($7\frac{3}{16}$ × $11\frac{5}{8}$).

COND: Cleaned by Kennedy North, March 1940. Removed from Bulwer cabinet, March 1976. Mounted Royal.—Tear u.l.

PROV: See No. 1.

This drawing, which has some sensitive pencil work, seems to show the same view of the bridge, but it is probably not a sketch for No. 44 as the details differ.

46 River Scene   Pl. 25

Pencil and watercolour on cream wove paper; 28·2 × 42·3 ($11\frac{1}{8}$ × $16\frac{5}{8}$).

COND: Removed from Bulwer cabinet, Aug. 1976. Cleaned and laid by D. Lewisohn, Sept. 1976. Mounted Royal.

PROV: Thomas Lound sale, Norwich, Spelman Wed. 6th March 1861[1] bt. for J. J. Colman[2]; his bequest to R. J. Colman 1898; R. J. Colman Bequest 1946, registered 1951.

This is a rather unusual watercolour study for this period as even washes of colour are applied all over with few reserved spaces. Also the palette is exceptionally bright, the brilliant red detail of the boats contrasts vividly with the glassy slate blue of the water. On the other hand the feathery handling of foliage is entirely in character.

1. Most of the lots have no titles in the Catalogue.

2. CC records.

47 Evening River Scene with Bridge, Cows, Fisherman and Dog   Pl. 29

Pencil, watercolour, some white bodycolour and slight scraping out on cream wove paper with watermark upper right (inverted) *J WHATMAN/1811*; 50·4 × 68·7 ($19\frac{7}{8}$ × $27\frac{1}{16}$).

COND: Cleaned and laid by D. Lewisohn, Feb. 1977. Mounted Atlas.—Paper surface grazed along edges.

PROV: J. R. Nutman; Sir Henry Holmes by June 1931[1]; Sir Henry Holmes Bequest with thirteen Norwich School paintings, 1932.

EXH: ? Norwich Society Secession 1816 (11) as *Drawing—Evening*; NCM 1932[2]; Norwich, Thirtle Centenary 1939 (55) as *The Pool,* lent by Sir Henry Holmes.

REF: *Holmes Catalogue* 1932 p. 42 no. 42 as *The Pool*; *EDP* 24th May 1932 'Mr. H. N. Holme's Collection'; *EDP* 16th March 1940 'The Late Sir Henry Holmes'; *EEN* 9th Sept. 1940 'Sir Henry Holmes' Bequest'.

The wooden bridge in this drawing is similar to that at Flordon, a village seven and a half miles south-west of

Norwich and to that at Tasburgh eight miles south of Norwich[3].

A date of c. 1816 can be ascribed to this drawing for which there is a brilliantly fresh watercolour sketch in the collection, No. 48. The two drawings are one of five pairs recorded of sketches and larger finished, more elaborated watercolours, which are discussed in the entry for No. 38. The drawing under comment here is certainly an exhibition piece and may be that shown with the Norwich Society Secession in 1816 (11) *Drawing—Evening.* Thirtle's exhibits of that year drew a warm response from *Candidus* who wrote to the Editor of the *Norwich Mercury* 10th August 1816 'I know not which most to admire, the clear and silvery tones of LADBROOKE, the golden hues of THIRTLE, or the inviting and natural appearance of SILLETT's fruits, fish, and flowers.' Thirtle's 'golden hues', introduced for an evening effect, have become wretchedly hot in the museum's drawing through the loss of much of the blues. This is confirmed by the colour notes of the sketch where the middle centre sky is marked as *Grey,* a colour since reduced to a pinkish haze on the finished drawing. The lush richness of Thirtle's original unfaded colour can not be better emphasised than by the comparison between this drawing and its watercolour sketch. Thirtle's approach to an exhibition drawing is also clearly defined, the addition of the fisherman and dog and in particular the cows, give the composition a rounded picturesque character which is foreign to the direct spontaneity of the sketch.

1. A note from the donor in the museum accession book 'The before mentioned pictures are part of the collection formed by me in June 1931. . .'

2. As one of Sir Henry Holmes' collection which was shown at the museum that year.

3 Both bridges were etched by the Rev. E. T. Daniell (1804–1842) T8, T48; the plates are reproduced in Thistlethwaite 1974 pls. VIII, XLVIII.

48 River Scene with Bridge   Pl. 5b

Pencil and watercolour on cream wove paper with watermark lower centre right *J WHATMAN/1811*; 31·3 × 44·2 ($12\frac{5}{16}$ × $17\frac{3}{8}$).

INSCR: Inscribed in pencil with colour notes, with indication that the paper was cut down u. edge; *verso,* inscribed in pencil lower c. *J Thirtle.*

COND: Mounted Royal.—*Verso,* staining.

PROV: See No. 25.

EXH: Norwich, Thirtle Centenary 1939 (54) lent by R. J. Colman; Bedford and Cambridge 1966 (59); Rouen 1967 (52).

One of the small group of Thirtle sketches in the collection which is in almost pristine condition. It is a study for the composition of No. 47 and is discussed in that entry.

1. CC records.

49 Cattle on the River bank, Norwich Castle in the distance   Pl. 29

Pencil, watercolour, some white body colour and gum with slight scraping out on buff wove paper; 43·2 × 65·1 (17 × $25\frac{5}{8}$).

COND: Cleaned and laid by D. Lewisohn, Feb. 1977. Mounted Atlas.—Colour faded.

PROV: Horatio Bolingbroke by 1860[1]; his sale Norwich, Spelman 12th, 13th March 1879 first day lot 243 as *Meadows and Cattle at Whitlingham* bt. for J. J. Colman 4 gns.[2]; his bequest to R. J. Colman 1898; R. J. Colman Bequest 1946, registered 1951.

EXH: Norwich, Fine Arts Association 1860 (278) as *Norwich from the River*, lent by H. Bolingbroke; ?Norwich, St. Andrews Hall 1902 (237) as *Norwich from Back River*, lent by R. J. Colman[3].

CAT: As *On the Back River Norwich* in all catalogues.

The view of Norwich in this drawing is from the north-west; the column-like silhouette on the centre right horizon can be identified as the old spire of St. Gregory's church. This drawing dates from c. 1816 as it compares well with *Evening River Scene* No. 47. Another more finished version of similar size was lent by the Misses Levine to the Thirtle Centenary 1939 (89) as *Norwich from Back of New Mills*[4]. It differs from the museum's drawing in that it has a heavy bunch of foliage in the left foreground. With its Cuyp-like cows, reminiscent of the later paintings of George Vincent, this composition is rather uncharacteristic of Thirtle. As in many of the larger drawings in particular, the colour has faded badly.

1. See EXH.

2. CC records.

3. No lender is given in the Catalogue, but R. J. Colman lent No. 238, another drawing by Thirtle and the title is close to that given in the Colman catalogues.

4. 16½ × 24 ins., photo in NCM annotated Catalogue. It was considered incorrectly by Frank Leney, the curator, to be a late work (*EDP* 24th July 1939 'The Thirtle Exhibition An Appreciation'), John Berney Ladbrooke (1803–1879) the Norwich School landscape painter, had a large Thirtle drawing which was sold at his sale, Norwich, Ray Tues. 21st Oct. 1879 lot 105 *A fine Drawing, Cattle in Landscape with distant view of Norwich 30 × 20 ins.*

50 Crossing the Brook—after Thomson   Pl. 27

Pencil, watercolour, some gum and scraping out on white wove paper; 61·3 × 41·9 (24⅛ × 16½) subject, 63 × 43·4 (24¹³⁄₁₆ × 17¹⁄₁₆) paper.

INSCR: Inscribed in pencil lower margin *But one Step More: be not in haste; This Stone's as slippery as the last: Step Cautiously the danger's past Now we'll trudge homeward cheerily/you'l tell yr Brother wh[at you've done and what you've seen;] how gay the fair was on the Green & how the day past merrily* (part of the text cut at lower edge).

COND: Treated with Chloramine T, Sept. 1948. Deframed May 1964. Cleaned and laid by D. Lewisohn, Feb. 1977. Mounted Atlas.

PROV: Presented with No. 52 by W. M. Palmer 1937.

EXH: Norwich, Thirtle Centenary 1939 (108); Lowestoft 1948 (70); Leewarden 1948 (48); Harrogate 1953 (52) in all as *Crossing the Stream*.

REF: *EDP* 30th November 1937 'Additions to the Art Gallery' as *Crossing the Stream*.

This subject, of cloying sentiment, is copied from the colour mezzotint by William Say (1768–1834) the Nor-

wich born engraver, after Henry Thomson R.A. (1773–1843), published by Macklin January 1804. Thirtle's version is slightly smaller than the plate size of the print[1]. A study for the child is in the collection, No. 51. Thomson, a pupil of Opie, exhibited the oil, a large canvas 72 × 54 ins. at the R.A. in 1803 (166); it was in the collection of Leicester of Tabley House in 1827[2]. Henry Thomson had dealings with Norwich and might have visited the city in 1814 when he painted William Smith MP for the civic collection in St. Andrews Hall.

1. There is a copy in the BM, 10.11.31.1941.

2. Reproduced *Country Life* 18th June 1959 p. 1384 and *Apollo* November 1973 p. 107 (in colour) from Sally Mitchell coll., Newark. An oil sketch by Thomson, 25½ × 18 ins., is repro. *The Connoisseur* November 1925, p. LV. It was in Mrs. Louise C. Hoyle's coll. then.

51 Head and Shoulders of a Child   Pl. 27

Pencil and greyish-brown wash on white wove paper; 14 × 12 (5½ × 4¹¹⁄₁₆).

COND: Cleaned by D. Lewisohn, Sept. 1976. Unmounted.—*Verso,* paper surface grazed l.r. edge.

PROV: Squire Gallery; bt. from them £5 with three other Thirtle drawings, by Percy Moore Turner 11th May 1939[1]; presented by him 1940.

EXH: Norwich, Boswell Centenary 1939 (7)[2]; Norwich, Thirtle Centenary 1939 (92) lent by Messrs. W. Boswell & Son ?on behalf of Percy Moore Turner[3]; Lowestoft 1948 (69); Arts Council 1948 (30); Kettering 1952 (25); Harrogate 1953 (53); Kidderminster 1954 (35).

This drawing is a study for the child in No. 50 *Crossing the Brook*—after Thomson.

1. Entry No. 2546 Percy Moore Turner Stock Book in Art Dept. archives.

2. No lender is given in the Art dept. copy of the catalogue.

3. See PROV.

52 Dorothea after Clarke   Pl. 28

Pencil and watercolour on white wove paper; 62·6 × 42·2 (24⅝ × 16⅝).

COND: ? Treated with Chloramine T, Sept. 1948. Deframed May 1964. Removed from old backing paper, cleaned and inlaid by D. Lewisohn, Feb. 1977. Mounted Atlas.—Colour faded.

PROV: Presented with No. 50 by W. M. Palmer, 1937.

EXH: Norwich, Thirtle Centenary 1939 (109); Harrogate 1953 (51), in both as *Susannah and the Elders*.

REF: *EDP* 30th Nov. 1937 'Additions to the Art Gallery'; Iolo Williams, *Early English Watercolours*, 1952 p. 156 as *Susannah and the Elders*.

This is one of the few figure subjects by Thirtle after other artists. The composition was long accepted as representing Susannah and the Elders until doubt was expressed in the catalogue of the exhibition shown in Harrogate in 1953. A girl disguised as a boy, the subject was later thought to be Imogen from Shakespeare's Cymbeline, but the recent find of its source proves it to be Dorothea from Cervantes' *Don Quixote*[1]. Thirtle's composition is a copy of the engraving by William Say (1768–1834) after a painting by Theophilus

Clarke (1766–fl. 1832)[2] which was exhibited at the R A in 1802 (44) *Dorothea: Don Quixote, b. iv, ch. 1* . . .

The particular incident illustrated is from the First Part, Book IV, Chapter 1, when Dorothea is discovered on the Brown Mountain by the Curate, Cardenio and the Barber:

'they beheld a young youth behind a rock, sitting under an ash-tree, and attired like a country swain . . . as he sat washing of his feet in the clear stream that glided that way . . . the curate, who went before the rest, seeing they were not yet espied, made signs to the other two that they should divert a little out of the way, or hide themselves behind some broken cliffs that were near the place. . . The youth took off his cap at last, and, shaking his head . . . did dishevel and discover such beautiful hairs as those of Phoebus might justly emulate them; and thereby they knew the supposed swain to be a delicate woman. . .'[3]

Dorothea, the daugher of Cleonardo the rich, a farmer of Andalusia, is wooed, raped and deserted by one Don Fernando, younger son of a grandee of Spain. To avoid disgrace she runs away to the forest and, having rid herself of a servant and a forester for their immodest advances, is finally befriended by Cardenio and company.

Cervantes enjoyed a remarkable vogue in England in the first half of the eighteenth century[4]. The interest continued—for example Francis Hayman (?1708–76) exhibited two compositions from *Don Quixote* at the Royal Academy in 1769 (50, 51), but the range of popular subjects widened and taste encompassed not only wild tales of travel but more domestic themes and above all Shakespeare and the Bible, promoted by the publishing enterprises of Boydell and Macklin. Nevertheless, the 'Knight of the Doleful Countenance' still held some sway: Thomas Stothard (1755–1834) exhibited two scenes at the Royal Academy, in 1820 (26) and 1821 (109), and others were shown with the Norwich Society of Artists by Henry Liverseege (1803–1832) in 1828 (249) and George Cattermole (1800–1868) in 1833 (28).

1. I am grateful to my colleague, Sheenah Smith, for the initial suggestion, prompted by the resemblance to a parian figure of Dorothea by John Bell (1812–1895) an example of which is in the museum's collection. This led to the identification of the print.

2. Pub. in 1802 and 1804, copies in the BM, 1863–11–14–505 and 1864–3–9–289. Both Say and Clarke have Norwich connections: Say was born at Lakenham, Norwich, and Clarke was a pupil of John Opie, just like Thomson, the painter of *Crossing the Brook*. See No. 50. My thanks are due to Elizabeth Einberg and to Timothy Clifford for making researches on my behalf in the engraved oeuvres of other artists.

3. *The History of the Valorious and Witty Knight Errant Don Quixote of La Mancha* translated by Thomas Shelton, 3 vols. 1900.

4. See Hans Hammermann and T. S. R. Boase *Book Illustrators in Eighteenth-Century England* 1975.

53 The Reaper's Child asleep, Harvest Scene, after Westall   Pl. 28

Pencil and watercolour with slight scraping out on greyish blue laid paper; 41·6 × 32·8 (16$\frac{3}{8}$ × 12$\frac{7}{8}$).

COND: Mounted Royal.

PROV: See No. 25.

REF: Clifford repro. pl. 17b.

One of Thirtle's few figure subjects after other artists, this drawing is a copy after Richard Westall (1765–1836). Westall produced a series of watercolours of which *The Reaper Child Asleep*, dated 1793[1] was engraved by C. Knight in 1799[2]. Thirtle's watercolour is undoubtedly copied from the published engraving. It is a close copy although some detail, the grass in the foreground and the background landscape, is unfinished. While the handling of the figures, especially the heads, is typical of Thirtle's hand, that of the surrounding landscape is rather uncharacteristic. The harvester and corn stooks in the right distance are, in their loose handling and pencil work, close to Cristall, in drawings such as *The Fisher Boy*[3] of which Thirtle made a rather poor copy[4]. See also Nos. 50 and 52 in the collection for Thirtle's copies after Henry Thomson and Theophilus Clarke.

1. Watercolour, 17 × 14 ins., signed and dated l.r. 1793, coll. Agnew's, n.d., photo Witt.

2. 18$\frac{11}{16}$ × 14$\frac{3}{4}$ ins., copy in the BM, 12.13.204. 1873.

3. Pencil and watercolour, 14$\frac{7}{16}$ × 13$\frac{7}{16}$ ins., V&A, 444.

4. Watercolour, 13$\frac{11}{16}$ × 11$\frac{1}{2}$ ins., inscribed *verso, Fisher Boy—From Cr[istall] Jan. 1815*, V&A, Sidney D. Kitson Bequest 1939, E 199–1939. The inscription has not been checked by the compiler as the drawing is stuck down.

54 View of Norwich from the North-East   Pl. 31

Pencil and watercolour with some white bodycolour on cream wove paper with watermark upper left (inverted) *BE&S/1815*; 23·1 × 72·1 (9$\frac{1}{16}$ × 23$\frac{3}{8}$).

INSCR: Inscribed in pencil with colour notes.

COND: Cleaned by Kennedy North, March 1940. Removed from Bulwer cabinet, Dec. 1969. Cleaned and laid by D. Lewisohn, Feb. 1977. Mounted Royal.— Repairs along edges. According to the CC MS vol. 2 p. 322 no. 133 'The slightly tinted foreground in this drawing was added by L. S. Boden, Artist London, from whom it was purchased'.

PROV: L. S. Boden; bt. from him by J. J. Colman by 1886[1].

EXH: Norwich Art Circle 1886 (63) lent by J. J. Colman.

A panoramic view of Norwich from the north-east. The Cow Tower is just visible above the roof tops of Pockthorpe to the left; St. John Sepulchre, the Cathedral, Castle and St. Peter Mancroft stand on the horizon.

Thirtle exhibited four subjects which were probably panoramic views of Norwich: with the Norwich Society in 1810 (2) *Norwich, evening*, with the Secession in 1816 (56) *Norwich, from Hellesdon—Morning* and (78) *View of Norwich from Mousehold Heath—Evening* and with the Society again in 1830 (48*) *An East View of Norwich*. There is a very fine grey wash drawing[2], which may be a study for the 1810 exhibit, where the rays of the setting sun create a powerful essay in monochrome light and shade. No drawing has been traced of the view from Hellesdon exhibited in 1816[3], but the other exhibit of that year is probably the watercolour signed and dated 1816 in a private collection[4]. The versions of the composition shown in 1830 are discussed in the entry for No. 119. The museum's drawing seems to be part of a panoramic study of Norwich from beyond Pockthorpe. It is the more north-easterly view of two drawings: the other, of similar size, is in a private collection[5]. A third, smaller panoramic study,

51

from an even more easterly view point, is in the collection, No. 55. These three studies have retained most of their soft buff, green and purplish-blue palette and their handling and their liquid washes are close to a large watercolour study discussed in note 5(c) in the entry for No. 119[6].

Thirtle's panoramic watercolours of Norwich are connected with a well established popular art form said to have been invented by Robert Barker, a Scottish artist who came to London around 1789 and set up the first panoramic entertainment 'these wondrous cylindric views, in the centre whereof the spectator stood, as one transported, by a genius of Araby, into some distant land. . .'[7] Barker was assisted by his son Henry Aston Barker, a contemporary of Girtin and Robert Ker Porter (who became a friend of John Sell Cotman), both of whom took up panorama painting. Girtin's colossal panorama of London, which covered almost two thousand square feet of canvas, was exhibited in Spring Gardens, London, in August 1802 as 'Eidometropolis; a great Panorama Picture of London, Westminster and environs, now exhibiting at the Great Room, Spring Gardens. Admission 1s.'[8] The panorama is lost but six fine watercolour studies survive in the British Museum. Thirtle's palette and handling of washes in his Norwich studies may be compared with some of Girtin's studies such as *Albion Mills* of c. 1797–8[9]. Thirtle, must of course, have known well the engraving after the younger Barker's panorama of Norwich published in 1809[10], he may have even met the artist working on Castle Hill. There is no indication, not even a suggestion, that Thirtle ever took up painting large panoramas, but he is alone among Norwich School watercolourists in attempting panoramic landscape studies.

1. See EXH.

2. Brownish-grey wash, with some scraping out l.l. corner, $12\frac{1}{4} \times 16$ ins., exh. Mandells Gallery 1976 (121).

3. A *View from Hellesdon* watercolour, $5\frac{13}{16} \times 16$ ins., in the museum's collection, 4.116.935, exh. Norwich, Thirtle Centenary 1939 (2) is of doubtful attribution—the handling is very weak and mechanical.

4. Watercolour, $16\frac{11}{16} \times 24\frac{15}{16}$ ins. (sight measurement), signed and dated l.r. *I Thirtle 1816*, ex coll. Walkers Galleries, Fine Art Society. Photo Witt.

5. Watercolour, $8\frac{1}{2} \times 26\frac{1}{2}$ ins.

6. Other panoramic views of Norwich by Thirtle recorded in posthumous sales and exhibitions are: *View of Norwich* lent by Mr. Ladbrooke (? John Berney Ladbrooke 1803–1879) to the Norwich Fine Art Association exhibition 1860 (271); *Norwich from the River* lent by Mr. H. Bolingbroke to the same exhibition (278); *View of Norwich from Mousehold* lent by Mrs. Thirtle to the same exhibition (307); *Norwich from Mousehold, Evening* lent by William Dixon to the Norwich 1867 exhibition (764); *Distant View of Norwich* (*a most masterly drawing*) lot 635 bt. Nichol 13 gns., in the sale of T. H. Gladwell Tues.–Fri. 5th–8th April 1881 and lot 85 bt. Palser £5, in his second sale Wed. 29th June 1881; *View of Norwich*, $7\frac{1}{2} \times 16\frac{5}{8}$ ins., lent by James Reeve to the Norwich 1903 exhibition (94); *Norwich from Mousehold* lent by Leonard G. Bolingbroke to the Norwich Art Circle exhibition 1927 (11).

7. Roget i, p. 104.

8. *Times* 25th Aug. 1802, cit. William T. Whitley 'Girtin's Panorama', *The Connoisseur* May 1924, vol. LXIX No. 273.

9. Watercolour, $12\frac{1}{2} \times 20$ ins., BM, 1855–2–14–24.

10. Copy in NCM, 82.30.

55 View of Norwich from Mousehold Heath Pl. 31

Pencil and watercolour with slight scraping out on buff wove paper; $18 \cdot 8 \times 41 \cdot 9$ ($7\frac{3}{8} \times 16\frac{1}{2}$).
Verso, Landscape with Mill, River and Cattle (inverted). Pencil and watercolour.

INSCR: Numbered in pencil l.l. ?67; *verso*, inscribed in pencil with colour notes.

COND: Cleaned by Kennedy North, March 1940. Removed from Bulwer cabinet, March 1976. Double mounted Royal.—Slight foxing. *Verso*, gum along lower edge.—Colour faded.

PROV: See No. 25.

This drawing is one of several panoramic views of Norwich, which are discussed in the entry for No. 54. The view is from the north-east above Pockthorpe, looking towards the Hospital Meadows with the Cow Tower centre left.

The colours of this drawing and its *verso* have remained unusually fresh and clear.

56 Haymarket, Norwich Pl. 30

Pencil, watercolour and some white bodycolour on buff wove paper with watermark parallel with lower right edge *C/1815* (only the upper half of the digits visible); $26 \times 33 \cdot 5$ ($10\frac{3}{16} \times 13\frac{3}{16}$).

COND: Cleaned by Kennedy North, March 1940. Removed from Bulwer cabinet, Dec. 1969.—Inlaid. Mounted Royal. *Verso*, paper surface grazed and gum u. edge.

PROV: Col. Philip Back by 1885[1]; bt. from him by R. J. Colman July 1909; R. J. Colman Bequest 1946, registered 1951.

EXH: Norwich 1885 (498) lent by P. Back; Norwich, Thirtle Centenary 1939 (11) lent by R. J. Colman; Colnaghi 1970 (109) repro. Pl. xxv.

REF: *EEN* 28th July 1939 'Thirtle Paintings, Norwich Scenes'; Cotman and Hawcroft p. 93, repro. pl. 5 pp. 92–93.

This is one of the few townscape subjects in Thirtle's oeuvre. Another, probably of c. 1816, St. Magnus Church, London, is in the V&A[2]. The two watercolours are probably slightly faded but the ghostly insubstantial pink and grey buildings of the middle distance and touches of white bodycolour are common to both. This view of the Haymarket, Weavers Lane and Gentleman's Walk, Norwich, still exists with the east turrets and clerestory windows of St. Peter Mancroft still towering above this picturesque corner of Norwich. However the gabled White Horse Inn in the left foreground is today replaced by an open square and the Georgian doorway of the fine house to the right is now a shop front. There is a later drawing, of the 1840s, of the same view by Henry Ninham, in the collection, showing some changes that have already taken place in the intervening period[3].

1. See EXH.

2. Pencil, watercolour and some white bodycolour, $13\frac{5}{16} \times 19\frac{1}{16}$ ins., inscribed *verso* u.r. *Thirtle*, V. & A., 1272–1871. Thirtle exhibited two London subjects with the Norwich Society Secession in 1816 (61) *View on the Thames* and (62) *Ditto*.

3. Pencil, $10\frac{3}{8} \times 14\frac{3}{4}$ ins., 1051.76.94.

57 New Mills, Norwich   **Pl. 32**

Pencil and watercolour on cream wove paper 26·8 × 42·3 (10$\frac{9}{16}$ × 16$\frac{5}{8}$).

COND: Cleaned by Kennedy North, April 1940. Removed from Bulwer cabinet, Dec. 1969. Mounted *Royal.*—Paper stained along edges. *Verso,* paper surface grazed, remains of old backing mount, tear u.c. edge.—Colour faded.

PROV: Thomas Lound sale, Norwich, Spelman Wed. 6th March 1861 *Water-colour Drawings* lot 228 *'Scene near the New Mills' rich and effective in colour* bt. D. Dalyrymple ?for J. J. Colman £3.6.0[1]; J. J. Colman bequest to R. J. Colman 1898; R. J. Colman Bequest 1946, registered 1951.

EXH: Norwich, Art Circle 1886 (33) lent by J. J. Colman; Colnaghi 1970 (116).

REF: Dickes pp. 225, 233.

Virtually all the blue has gone from this watercolour. A band made up of the original brilliant greens of the foliage, of the grey and mauve of the brickwork and the deep blue of the water, remains under the mount.

The subject is the millpond on the city side of New Mills, Norwich, situated on the River Wensum to the north-west of the city. The first New Mills, which replaced four old water mills destroyed by a riot in 1440, were later rebuilt in 1709[2]. From the late sixteenth century the mills supplied water to the city. Thirtle appears to have made at least two other drawings of the New Mills, which were sold at P. E. Hansell's sale 1921[3]. The theme was also painted by Crome, he exhibited four New Mills subjects, the first in 1806, the last in 1821 and must have painted more as six appeared in his memorial exhibition in 1821. The two genuine works known of this theme by Crome are in the museum's collection[4]. He also etched the subject in 1813.

1. CC records.
2. P. Browne, *History of Norwich* 1814, p. 55.
3. P. E. Hansell sale, Wroxham, Tues. 12th July 1921 lot 286 *Pair watercolour drawings, Back of New Mills, Norwich,* £2.2.0.
4. *Back of the New Mills,* 2.4.99 and *New Mills: Men Wading,* 531.970.

58 Fye Bridge, Norwich   **Pl. 32**

Pencil and watercolour on buff laid paper; 19·8 × 29 (7$\frac{13}{16}$ × 11$\frac{3}{8}$).

COND: Cleaned by Kennedy North, April 1940. Removed Bulwer cabinet, Dec. 1969. Laid. Mounted Royal.—Colour faded.

PROV: Charles Thompson; bt. from him by J. J. Colman by 1886[1]; his bequest to R. J. Colman 1898; R. J. Colman Bequest 1946, registered 1951.

EXH: Norwich, Art Circle 1886 (34) lent by J. J. Colman; Norwich 1903 (88) lent by R. J. Colman; RA 1934 (918) repro. pl. CLXXV; Colnaghi 1970 (118) repro. pl. XXIX.

REF: Norwich Art Circle, *Third Exhibition Catalogue, John Thirtle* 1886 illus. in litho by Minna Bolingbroke (1857–1939) p. 5[2]; Dickes pp. 221, 233; H. E. Conrad *England* 1976, repro. pl. 18.

The present buff and pinkish brown tones of this drawing

are misleading. A narrow band of the original unfaded colour remains along the edge showing that the sky was a very bright blue and the rest, tones of grey and blue with brown.

Thirtle showed the subject twice with the Norwich Society: in 1807 (50) *Fye-bridge* and in 1809 (201) *North-west View of Fyebridge, Norwich.* The museum's drawing is a view down river from above the bridge, another drawing of the same view but closer to the bridge is in the V. & A.[3] A third drawing looking up river from below the bridge is in a private collection[4]. All three drawings seem to be too late to be considered as possible candidates for the 1807 or 1809 exhibits. Although a shadow of its former self the museum's drawing is still impressive. The underlying pencil work is also very fine.

Fye Bridge spans the River Wensum at Quayside, Magdalen Street, Norwich (see No. 169). The first stone bridge was carried away by floods in 1570 and the bridge was rebuilt by 1573. 'This bridge is the most frequented of any in the city, being the principal passage from the northern parts of the County.'[5] It was replaced by a new bridge in 1829.

1. CC records. See EXH.
2. Compiler's pagination.
3. Watercolour, 11$\frac{1}{4}$ × 9$\frac{1}{4}$ ins., V & A, P 12–1948, exh. Norwich, Thirtle Centenary 1939 (81) lent by F. J. Nettlefold.
4. Pencil and watercolour, 7$\frac{3}{4}$ × 10$\frac{15}{16}$ ins., an old label on the backing board is inscribed *The Bishop's Bridge Norwich/By Girtin./Very Fine Specimen . . .*
5. P. Browne *History of Norwich* 1814, p. 247.

59 St. Edmund's Church, Costessey, Norfolk   **Pl. 30**

Pencil, watercolour and some white bodycolour on cream wove paper; 32·3 × 40·6 (12$\frac{11}{16}$ × 15$\frac{15}{16}$).

INSCR: Signed and dated l.l. in brown watercolour. *Thirtle. 1816.*

COND: Cleaned by Kennedy North, April 1940. Removed from Bulwer cabinet, April 1975. Laid. Mounted Royal.—Tear l.c.l.; *verso,* gum and remains of old backing paper.—Colour faded.

PROV: Thomas Brightwell; ? by descent to Barron Brightwell by 1886[1]; ? by descent to Henry Brightwell; his sale, Norwich, Spelman Wed. 26th Nov. 1890 lot 111 *Cossey Church* bt. J. J. Colman[2]; his bequest to R. J. Colman 1898; R. J. Colman Bequest 1946, registered 1951.

EXH: Norwich, Art Circle 1886 (1) lent by Barron Brightwell.

The autumnal tints of this drawing are misleading; a thin line of the original colours shows the foreground grass to have been a bright spring green and the sky a soft deep blue. Apart from this drawing there are three others dated 1816 recorded: Thirtle's *Self portrait* and that of his wife, Nos. 130 and 131 in this catalogue and *Norwich from Mousehold Heath* mentioned in note 4 in the entry for No. 54. *The Haymarket, Norwich,* No. 56, is also probably of the same date as the washes of the building and touches of bright blue and of white bodycolour compare well with *St. Edmund's Church, Costessey.*

53

Costessey village is situated four miles north-west of Norwich. Thirtle exhibited other drawings of Costessey scenes in 1814 and 1816, see No. 35.

1. See EXH.

2. CC records.

60 Hoveton Little Broad, Norfolk   Pl. 33

Pencil and watercolour on cream wove paper with watermark parallel with upper centre left edge (inverted) *J WHATMAN/1809*; 20·2 × 31·2 (8 × 12¼) subject, 22·5 × 32·8 (8⅞ × 12⅞) paper.

COND: Mounted Royal.—Staining around edges. Pin holes along lower & r. edges.

PROV: See No. 1.

EXH: Norwich, Art Circle 1886 (68) as *Hoveton little Broad with indication of boat and figure in left foreground*, lent by J. J. Colman; Norwich, Thirtle Centenary 1939 (24) as *Thatched Cottage*, lent by R. J. Colman.

REF: Dickes p. 240.

CAT: As *Thatched Cottage* in all catalogues.

The title of this drawing is that given when it was exhibited in 1886. It is probably accurate for the cottages are reminiscent of those at Hoveton Broad. Thirtle also painted Hoveton House, see No. 75, and what is probably another view of the broad in the companion drawing, No. 61. Both these drawings have retained their blues and greens and their handling is close to the watercolour *Under Bishop Bridge* in the BM of c. 1814–1817[1].

1. Watercolour, 11 × 15½ ins., 1902–5–14–478. Discussed in the entry for No. 30 note 10.

61 Cottages, Cattle and Figure by a Broad   Pl. 33

An undefined sketch in pencil upper left corner. Pencil and watercolour on cream wove paper; 19·2 × 30·8 (7 9/16 × 12⅛) subject, 22·5 × 33·1 (8 13/16 × 13) paper.

INSCR: Inscribed in pencil with colour notes; *verso*, numbered in pencil u.c.l. *?No 1* (indistinct, paper cut).

COND: Mounted Royal.—Staining around edges; *verso*, staining and remains of old backing paper. Pin holes along lower and r. edges.

PROV: See No. 1.

CAT: As *Riverside Cottages* in all catalogues.

This drawing is probably a study of Hoveton Broad: it is a companion drawing to No. 60 and is discussed in that entry.

62 A Norfolk Church   Pl. 39

Pencil on cream wove paper; 24·2 × 38·3 (9 9/16 × 15 1/16).

INSCR: Inscribed in pencil with colour notes.

COND: ?Cleaned by Kennedy North[1]. Removed from Bulwer cabinet. Mounted Royal.—*Verso*, paper surface grazed l.r., slight foxing l.l.

PROV: Thomas Lound sale, Norwich, Spelman Wed. 6th March 1861 bt. by J. J. Colman[2]; his bequest to R. J. Colman 1898; R. J. Colman Bequest 1946, registered 1951.

EXH: Norwich 1940; The Hague 1977 (59).

The church with its octagonal tower has not been identified[3]. This drawing, one of the best preserved in the collection, belongs to the group of studies of Norfolk houses and compares closely with Nos. 70, 75. These three drawings represent Thirtle at his peak as a watercolourist. The stringently economic use of pencil, of washes and of the paper for lights is nowhere better expressed in the artist's oeuvre.

1. The title is not included in Kennedy North's restoration lists, but the drawing bears mounter's numbers etc. similar to drawings treated by him.

2. CC records. Very few of the titles in this sale are specific.

3. It does not seem to be included among the plates of *Ladbrooke's Churches*.

63 Italianate Building   Pl. 34

Pencil and watercolour on buff wove paper; 21·6 × 33 (8½ × 12 15/16). *Verso*, slight sketch in pencil ?of foliage (indistinct) lower left.

INSCR: Inscribed in pencil with colour notes u.r. *low Distance/Buildg Rich Yellow/Bright Blue/& warm Murky sky.*

COND: Cleaned by Kennedy North, April 1940. Removed from Bulwer cabinet, April 1976. Mounted Royal.— Paper stained along l.u. & r. edges; *verso*, staining.— Colour faded.

CAT: As *White House, Whitlingham* in all catalogues.

PROV: Mrs. Thirtle sale, Norwich, Spelman Tues. 9th May 1882 ?lot 41 *Whitlingham White House* bt. Thompson[1] £3.5.0; J. J. Colman by 1886[2]; his bequest to R. J. Colman 1898; R. J. Colman Bequest 1946, registered 1951.

EXH: Norwich, Art Circle 1886 (59) as *White House, Whitlingham*, lent by J. J. Colman.

REF: Dickes p. 233 as *White House, Whitlingham*.

Fortunately some of the unfaded colour survives to substantiate Thirtle's aims as stated in the colour notes.

In the Colman catalogues the drawing is called *Whitlingham White House* and it comes from Mrs. Thirtle's sale which included a drawing of this subject. However the known representations[3] of this house, a thatched Victorian gothic building still standing, contradict this identification.

1. CC records. Probably Charles Thompson, see Nos. 11, 58.

2. See EXH.

3. *Whitlingham White House, with church in distance looking East, Kell Bro^s· Lith. London* [perhaps c. 1850–1860's] NCLN2 ref. 1697; *Whitlingham White House, looking towards Thorpe,* NCLN2 ref. 1696a.

64 Figures, standing beside Barrels, in a Square   Pl. 35

Studies in pencil, lower left, of the head of the seated girl on the left. Pencil and watercolour on white wove paper; 25·1 × 38·6 (9⅞ × 15 3/16).

INSCR: *Verso*, inscribed in pencil l.c.r. *John Thirtle.*

COND: Cleaned by D. Lewisohn, Sept. 1976. Mounted Royal.

PROV: See No. 1.

EXH: Norwich, Thirtle Centenary 1939 (104) as *Costume Figure Study,* lent by R. J. Colman.

CAT: As *Costume Figure Study* in all catalogues.

An unusual subject for Thirtle. Similar groups of figures, leaning on barrels, are familiar in the foreground of port scenes by Vernet, but there seems to be no direct relation between Thirtle's study and any known Vernet composition[1]. It is possible, of course, that one should rather look for a source in another direction such as the oeuvres of English artists, like Samuel Scott.

1. See, for example, *Seaport* no. 22, repro. in the exhibition catalogue *Claude Joseph Vernet 1714–1789,* Kenwood 4th June–19th Sept. 1976.

    I am grateful to Lindsay Stainton and to Philip Conisbee, author of the catalogue, for their comments.

65 Three Fishing Luggers and Two Figures on a Beach
Pl. 35

Pencil and watercolour on cream wove paper; 23·6 × 31·5 ($9\frac{1}{4}$ × $12\frac{3}{8}$).

COND: Deframed, old backing removed and treated with Thymol vapour, ?July 1960. Mounted Royal.—*Verso,* remains of old backing paper; staining.

PROV: Dr. Ernest Egbert Blyth Bequest with No. 104, 1934[1].

This is a rather weak drawing, almost certainly copied after Prout: the composition is similar to several of the plates in Prout's *Studies of Boats and Coast Scenery* published by Ackerman in 1816[2].

    Thirtle exhibited with the Norwich Society Secession in 1816 (96) *Fishing Boats—Storm coming on* and (123) *Fishing Boats—Calm,* probably the Proutesque drawings now in the collection of Rowntree Mackintosh Ltd.[3] The closely followed Prout original of the first of the two drawings is in a private collection[4]. Another copy dated 1822 and probably derived from one of the four lithographs of Dover published as an instalment of Prout's *Marine Sketches* 1820, is in the collection of the Laing Art Gallery, Newcastle[5]. Thirtle's copies after Prout are strong, rugged drawings but nonetheless they are rather dull. He evidently continued with his Prout imitations for years as there is a more successful watercolour of this kind, dating from as late as 1827, in a private collection[6].

1. Both drawings entered the collection wrongly attributed to John Joseph Cotman (1814–1878).

2. For example *At Worthing* and *At Brighton.* There is another Thirtle drawing of this type in a private collection, watercolour, 9 × $9\frac{1}{4}$ ins., exh. Boswell Centenary 1939 (27) lent by Boswell.

3. (96) pencil, watercolour, some white bodycolour with slight scraping out, $18\frac{3}{8}$ × $22\frac{3}{4}$ ins. (sight measurement), exh. Norwich, Thirtle Centenary 1939 (65) lent by Sir Robert Bignold; (123) pencil, watercolour and some white bodycolour, $19\frac{3}{8}$ × $24\frac{5}{8}$ ins. (sight measurement), exh. Norwich, Thirtle Centenary 1939 (59) lent by Sir Robert Bignold. A study for the latter, pencil, brown wash and some white bodycolour, 13 × $17\frac{1}{4}$ ins., was exhibited at the Norwich Thirtle Centenary 1939 (126) lent by the Rev. Canon Parr and at Mandells Gallery 1976 (120).

4. Pen and brown ink, brown wash, some yellow watercolour and white bodycolour,, $12\frac{3}{4}$ × $17\frac{1}{8}$ ins.

    I am most grateful to the owner for bringing this drawing to my notice.

5. Pencil and watercolour, $8\frac{3}{4}$ × $11\frac{1}{2}$ ins., signed and dated l.l. *I. Thirtle 1822.*

6. Pencil and watercolour, $8\frac{5}{8}$ × $12\frac{13}{16}$ ins. (sight measurement), signed and dated l.l. in brown ink *I. Thirtle 1827.*

66 Petch's Boat House opposite Cow Tower, Norwich
Pl. 36

Pencil and watercolour on cream wove paper; 11·6 × 22·7 ($4\frac{9}{16}$ × 9) subject, 17·4 × 28·5 ($6\frac{7}{8}$ × $11\frac{3}{16}$) paper.

COND: Cleaned by D. Lewisohn, Feb. 1977. Mounted Royal.—Colour faded.

PROV: Miss E. Woolmer by 1939[1]; her Bequest 1959.

EXH: Norwich, Thirtle Centenary 1939 (73) lent by Miss E. Woolmer.

REF: *EEN* 28th July 1939 'Thirtle Paintings. "Modern" Watercolours'.

The immediacy of Thirtle's watercolour studies is nowhere better seen than in this little drawing. The dramatic effect of fading is visible on the margins which indicate the clarity of the original colours.

    The title is that given in the 1939 Thirtle exhibition. Petch's boatyard does not appear in local directories. Berry's *Norwich Directory* 1811 gives a James Petch, but he was a publican of the Angel, Trowse Millgate.

1. See EXH.

67 The Riverside, King Street, Norwich
Pl. 36

Pencil and watercolour on cream laid paper; 20·1 × 25·1 ($7\frac{7}{8}$ × $9\frac{7}{8}$).

COND: Cleaned by D. Lewisohn, Feb. 1977. Mounted Royal.

PROV: ?Spelman coll.[1]; Rev. C. T. Rae by 1939[2]; presented by him 1956.

EXH: Norwich, Thirtle Centenary 1939 (34) as *St. Martin's Wharf,* lent by the Rev. C. T. Rae.

Stylistically this drawing is close to No. 66 but it has suffered more badly from fading.

    The drawing was first registered with the title given at the 1939 exhibition, however the group of buildings shown in the drawing: the timber framed house and triple gabled warehouses behind, are to be found in a coloured aquatint of *KING STREET, NORWICH, from the River/London Published Dec.[r] 1822*[3]. The site is a short way up river from the Devil's Tower, on the opposite bank.

1. Note on old card, Art Dept. archives.

2. See EXH.

3. NCM, Todd coll. vol. 2, box 7, Great Ward of Conisford, p. 15.

68 Cluster of Houses by Water
Pl. 39

Pencil and watercolour on cream wove paper; 16·2 × 28·1 ($6\frac{3}{8}$ × $11\frac{1}{16}$).

INSCR: *Verso,* numbered in pencil u.c. (inverted) *No. 1.*

COND: Cleaned by Kennedy North, Nov. 1939. Removed from Bulwer cabinet, March 1976. Mounted Royal.

PROV: See No. 1.

CAT: As *Thorpe Tea Gardens* in the CC MS vol. 1 p. 117 no. 436.

One of several drawings in the collection which are close to de Wint, especially in the wine red roofs and the washes of inky blue applied with a dry brush in the background trees.

In the Colman catalogues the site is given as Thorpe but this seems unlikely as such a cluster of buildings, set in open countryside, is not characteristic of the fairly continuous development along the river at Thorpe even in the first half of the nineteenth century.

69 Lenwade Mill, Norfolk — Pl. 40

Pencil and watercolour with some white bodycolour on cream wove paper; 20·3 × 32·7 (8 × $12\frac{7}{8}$).

COND: Cleaned by Kennedy North, Nov. 1939. Removed from Bulwer cabinet, March 1976. Mounted Royal.

PROV: Mrs. Clowes; bt. from her[1] by James Reeve by 1902[2]; bt. from him by H. S. Theobald after 1903[2]; bt. from him by R. J. Colman Feb. 1910; R. J. Colman Bequest 1946, registered 1951.

EXH: Norwich 1902 (223) lent by James Reeve; Norwich 1903 (90) lent by James Reeve.

Lenwade is situated ten and a half miles north-west of Norwich: 'a picturesque group by the bridge, with Sayer's Mill . . .'[3] A photograph of the mill, dating from c. 1880–90[4], gives no help in identifying Thirtle's subject as the mill, but as it may have been altered or rebuilt in the intervening period the title is retained. Lenwade Mill is of some art historical interest because of its connections with the Le Neve family from the mid 1700's until 1853. Peter le Neve-Foster (1809–1879), who inherited the mill in Thirtle's lifetime, had not only legal and mathematical interests but was a member of an artistic circle which included the Norwich artists Horace Beevor Love, J. B. Crome and Elizabeth Rigby and her distinguished husband Sir Charles Eastlake. In 1837 he was elected a member of the Society of Arts of which he became Secretary in 1853. He was also at the centre of the early developments in photography.

There is no documentary evidence that Thirtle was acquainted with Le Neve Foster but is seems more than likely, especially as the family was related by marriage to the Prestons of Stanfield Hall whose portraits were drawn by Thirtle[5].

1. Reeve Coll. MS p. 33 no. 40.
2. See EXH.
3. Pevsner p. 244.
4. Peter Le Neve Foster *The Le Neves of Norfolk* 1969 repro. p. 47.
5. See the entry for No. 71.

70 Canal House, Ashwellthorpe, Norfolk — Pl. 38

Pencil and watercolour on cream wove paper; 20 × 30·2 ($7\frac{7}{8}$ × $11\frac{7}{8}$).

COND: Cleaned by Kennedy North between 1939–1940. Removed from Bulwer cabinet, Aug. 1976. Mounted Royal.—Tear c.l.

PROV: See No. 74.

EXH: Norwich 1940.

This drawing is one of a group of five watercolour studies of Norfolk country houses; the others are Nos. 71, 72, 74, 75. They are discussed in the entry for No. 75. The identity of the house was established when the five studies were exhibited in 1940. Ashwellthorpe is a village three miles south-east of Wymondham, Norfolk.

This is perhaps the finest of all five studies; the colours are exceptionally brilliant and the handling confident and economical.

71 Stanfield Hall, Norfolk — Pl. 38

Pencil and watercolour on cream wove paper; 20·4 × 37·4 (8 × $14\frac{3}{4}$).

INSCR: Inscribed in pencil with colour notes lower edge.

COND: Cleaned and ?cut down[1] by Kennedy North between 1939–1940. Removed from Bulwer cabinet, Sept. 1976. Cleaned and laid by D. Lewisohn, Feb. 1977. Mounted Royal.—*Verso*, paper surface grazed u.l. and u.r.

PROV: See No. 1.

EXH: Norwich 1940.

REF: *EEN* 17th May 1940 'Where are they?'.

This drawing is one of five studies of Norfolk country houses in the collection; the others are Nos. 70, 72, 74, 75. Its identity was established when these studies were exhibited in 1940. They are discussed in the entry for No. 75.

Stanfield Hall is situated two and a half miles east of Wymondham, a market town nine miles east of Norwich. The Hall was built by William Wilkins, the Norwich born architect, in 1792 and was the seat of the Rev. George Preston. Thirtle painted watercolour portraits of his two sons, Jermy William Preston in 1819 and the Rev. George Preston in 1820[2]. The Hall was engraved by Hobson after John Preston Neale (?1780–1847), who published the print in 1819. Thirtle's watercolour study is very close to the engraving which he may have copied, although the house appears to have been always drawn from the same viewpoint. It was externally Tudorized c. 1830–1835[3]. In 1848 Stanfield Hall was the scene of the Rush murders and became infamous through the endless press reports which ensued.

1. The colour notes are cut along the lower edge.
2. Duleep Singh *Portraits in Norfolk Houses* vol. II p. 326, 327; the portraits are now untraced.
3. Pevsner, *North-West and South Norfolk* p. 398. An engraving by William Freeman, showing this alteration, was published Yarmouth 1848.

72 Burlingham House, Norfolk — Pl. 37

Pencil and watercolour on buff wove paper; 14·5 × 27·4 ($5\frac{11}{16}$ × $10\frac{13}{16}$).

COND: ?Cleaned by Kennedy North[1]; removed from Bulwer cabinet, March 1976. Mounted Royal.

PROV: See No. 1.

EXH: Norwich 1940.

This drawing is one of a group of five watercolour studies

of Norfolk country houses; the others are Nos. 70, 71, 74, 75. They are discussed in the entry for No. 75. The House, in North Burlingham, was built in 1790 by William Heath Jary who owned the estate with the Burroughes of Burlingham Hall, see No. 141.

73 Caister Castle, Norfolk   Pl. 34

Pencil and watercolour on buff wove paper; $20 \cdot 7 \times 26 \cdot 8$ ($8\frac{1}{8} \times 10\frac{9}{16}$).

COND: Cleaned by Kennedy North, March 1940. Removed from Bulwer cabinet, March 1976. Mounted Royal.—*Verso*, paper stained l.

PROV: See No. 1.

EXH: Norwich, Thirtle Centenary 1939 (72) lent by R. J. Colman.

The pencil work of this drawing is characteristic of Thirtle but the rather flat unsubstantial washes lend some doubt to the attribution. Another drawing of Caister Castle attributed to Thirtle, in the Ulster Museum, Belfast, is unlikely to be by him[1].

Caister Castle is situated three miles north of Great Yarmouth, Norfolk; it was built for Sir John Fastolf in 1432–5 and is one of the most impressive of the fifteenth century castles in England. It was painted, drawn and etched by other Norwich School artists, notably John Crome and John Sell Cotman, and also by Sir George Beaumont whose grey wash drawing of c. 1784 is in the collection.

1. Pencil and brown wash, $12\frac{1}{4} \times 19\frac{7}{8}$ ins., 1137. Another Caister Castle subject attributed to Thirtle was in the C. C. R. Spelman sale Tues.–Thurs. 17th–19th March 1914 second day *Water Colour Drawings In Folios* lot 447 *Two—Caister Castle, An Old Rectory* bt. Walker 17s.

74 Old Hall, Lakenham, Norwich   Pl. 37

Pencil and watercolour on cream wove paper; $22 \cdot 3 \times 32 \cdot 5$ ($8\frac{13}{16} \times 12\frac{13}{16}$).

COND: Cleaned by Kennedy North between 1939–1940. Removed from Bulwer cabinet, Aug. 1976. Mounted Royal.

PROV: See No. 1.

EXH: Norwich 1940.

CAT: As *Private House and Carriage Drive* in CC MS vol. I p. 117 no. 437.

This drawing is one of a group of five watercolour studies of Norfolk country houses; the others are Nos. 70, 71, 72, 75. Its identity was established when the five studies were exhibited in 1940. They are discussed in the entry for No. 75.

75 Hoveton House, Norfolk   Pl. 5a

Pencil and watercolour on buff wove paper with watermark lower right $S \& C$[1]; $23 \times 39 \cdot 3$ ($9\frac{1}{16} \times 15\frac{7}{16}$). *Verso*, sketch in pencil of a rider on a donkey with figures and a dog parallel with left edge; sketch of a ground plan of a house on the right.

COND: Cleaned by Kennedy North, March 1940. Removed from Bulwer cabinet, Dec. 1969. Inlaid. Mounted Royal.—*Verso*, glue at u. edge.

PROV: See No. 1.[2]

EXH: Norwich, Thirtle Centenary 1939 (38) as *Study of Mansion* lent by R. J. Colman; Norwich 1940; Colnaghi 1970 (112) repro. pl. XXVIII.

REF: Ian Bennett, *The Connoisseur* Jan. 1971 repro. p. 63.

Hoveton House is situated north of Norwich near Wroxham, 'Built towards the end of the C17 and one of the most attractive, if not most perfect, houses of its time in Norfolk. It is a naive but most lovable design[3].' The house was built, and is still lived in, by the Blofeld family.

By 1824 Thirtle was a drawing master to Mary Catherine Blofeld[4] (1803–1851). She was the daughter of Thomas Calthorpe Blofeld and his wife Mary Caroline, daughter of the antiquary Francis Grose. Thirtle's exuberant study shows a girl, probably Mary Blofeld, sketching under the tree. A watercolour by her of the same view is still in the family's possession[5], as is the Thirtle watercolour of *Horstead Mill*, probably the one exhibited with the Norwich Society in 1814 (124), see No. 104, and presumably acquired by her father, Thomas Blofield.

Hoveton House is one of a group of five watercolour studies of country houses; the others are 70, 71, 72, 74. Its identity was established when the five studies were exhibited in 1940. Stylistically the group belongs with the outstanding watercolour studies of c. 1814–1817 discussed the entry for No. 38. However these studies of houses may be later—from after 1819[6]—in view of Thirtle's recorded portraits of 1819 and 1820 of the Preston family of Stanfield Hall and of his documented connection with the Blofelds of Hoveton House in 1824[4].

Hoveton House and *Canal House, Ashwellthorpe*, No. 70, are the finest of the group but all five are remarkably fresh and retain their original colour[7].

1. Churchill records (p. 69, fig. 94) a watermark of Marten Schouten & Co. (1783) where the name is shown as *MS & Cº*.

2. Two lots may have included this drawing: lot 5 *Four sketches architecture* bt. Thompson £13 or lot 7 *Twelve Sketches houses, etc.* bt. Fox £4.

3. Pevsner p. 175.

4. Payment in the family diaries for April 1824 'Paid Thirtle DM [Drawing Master] £9 16s. 9d.'

5. Watercolour, $14\frac{1}{4} \times 25\frac{1}{4}$ ins., the frame bears Thirtle's trade label (I am grateful to Mr. T. R. C. Blofeld for drawing my attention to this). The family has a sketchbook and another watercolour after Thirtle by Mary Blofeld, see the entry for No. 96.

6. Although he was definitely engaged in this type of work before 1818 as is shown by his two other known views of country seats; *Westwick House, Norfolk* and *Bracondale* which were engraved by J. Ransom and W. Wallis respectively for *Excursions through Norfolk* 1818, opp. pp. 131,155.

7. There are two other drawings said to be of Hoveton in the collection, Nos. 60 and 61.

76 Thorpe 1817   Pl. 42

Pencil on white wove paper with watermark lower right corner, parallel with right edge *J WHA*[TMAN] *18* (paper cut); $32 \cdot 9 \times 47 \cdot 2$ ($12\frac{15}{16} \times 18\frac{9}{16}$).

INSCR: Inscribed, signed and dated in pencil l.c.r. *I. Thirtle 1817 Thorpe.*

COND: Cleaned and laid by D. Lewisohn, Sept. 1876. Mounted Imperial.

PROV: W. Henry Parr; bt. from him out of the Walker Bequest Fund, £5, 1932.

EXH: Norwich, Thirtle Centenary 1939 (129).

According to the donor[1] the house shown is Thorpe Old Hall which it clearly is not, as the Hall is an early seventeenth century building with tudor windows, those on the ground floor, pedimented. This drawing is related to two watercolours of similar composition, including a study in the collection, No. 42, and is discussed in that entry. The strong motif of the keel gliding in from the left of the picture is found in a watercolour in the V & A, *The River at King Street, Norwich*[2], an exceptionally Cotman-esque drawing. The use of a boat to break the edge of a composition is also seen in a paintbox fresh watercolour in the BM, *Under Bishop Bridge, Norwich*[3]. Both these watercolours are probably of the period c. 1814–1817.

1. Letter to the curator, Frank Leney, 29th March 1932 in the Art Dept. archives.

2. Pencil and watercolour, 15 × 17¼ ins., P. 26—1926.

3. 11 × 15½, 1902–5–14–478.

77 Rainbow Effect, on the River, King Street, Norwich 1817   Pl. 41

Pencil, watercolour, some white bodycolour and slight scraping out on cream wove paper; 42·5 × 64·9 (16¹¹⁄₁₆ × 25⁹⁄₁₆).

INSCR: Signed and dated l.r. *I.Thirtle.1817.*

COND: Mounted Atlas.—Gum, and paper surface grazed, at edges; *Verso,* gum at corners and edges; foxing.— Colour faded.

PROV: Charles Turner by 1860[1]; Rev. Charles Turner by 1878 and still in 1905[2]; by descent to his wife Gertude Mary Turner; her bequest with a painting by Vincent through the Rev. A. E. Alston 1919.

EXH: Norwich Society Secession 1817 (51); Norwich, Fine Arts Association 1860 (252) as *Norwich River, with Rainbow,* lent by Mr. C. Turner; Norwich 1878 (420) as *On the Wensum, Norwich,* lent by Rev. Charles Turner[4]; Norwich, Art Circle 1886 (44), lent by Rev. Charles Turner; Norwich, Thirtle Centenary 1939 (20); Nottingham, Portsmouth and Bolton 1953–54 (33).

REF: *Norfolk Chronicle* 2nd Aug. 1817; *Norwich Mercury* Sept. 1860; *EDP* 13th Dec. 1878 'St. Peter Mancroft Art Loan exhibition IV. The Water-Colour Drawings'[5]; Norwich Art Circle *Third Exhibition Catalogue, John Thirtle* 1886 illus. in litho. by C. M. Nichols (1847–1923) p. 6[6]; *Norwich Mercury* 7th July 1886; Frank Leney, *EDP* 24th July 1939 'The Thirtle Exhibition an appreciation'; Dickes p. 230; Barnard repro. pl. 55; Barnard 1951 repro. pl. 8B; Day III repro. p. 101; Mallalieu repro. pl. 32, p. 44; Norwich Union Calendar 1975 repro. in colour March and April; RHM Flour Mills Ltd. Calendar 1977 repro. in colour April, May, June.

A view of the River Wensum looking down river just beyond the sharp, almost right angle bend after Foundry Bridge. The ruins of St. Anne's Church are on the right and beyond them St. Anne's Staithe[7]. The Black Tower is on the middle horizon. A sketch of this composition, but without the ruined arch on the right, is in the collection, No. 78[8]. A similar view called *Harrison's Wharf* was

engraved by J. H. Kernot after Stark and published in 1829 for *Scenery of the Rivers of Norfolk*, 1834, pl. 31.

Thirtle was secretary to the breakaway group of the Norwich Society in 1817 when his exhibited drawings won warm praise from the *Norwich Mercury* 9th August 1817: 'Mr. Thirtle's drawings in watercolours are certainly without rivals in either place. They have a warmth, a richness and a brilliancy that is very captivating'. *Rainbow Effect* was singled out by the *Norfolk Chronicle* 2nd August 1817: 'The 'Scene on the King Street River' is a singular and beautiful Drawing the gleam of light over the meadow beyond the Rainbow, is well executed, and has a very pleasing effect.'

The rainbow is the exclusive subject of a small sketch, No. 20, and appears in two further drawings of Dilham Staithe, Nos. 115 and 116. The seven colours of the spectrum are clearest in *Rainbow Effect*, in spite of the overall fiery red colour of the drawing which is the 'lurid' and sad result of indigo fading that had already occurred by 1878[5].

1. See Exh.

2. Dickes p. 230.

3. *View in Glen Sherrah* (sic), *near Inverary*, 39.19.

4. See REF.

5. 'The lurid glare of the cloud is still further heightened by a rainbow, which crosses it with a perfect arch, and is reflected in the river.'

6. Compiler's pagination.

7. Campbell, *Norwich*, Map. 3. No trace of the church remains today.

8. Other River Wensum/King Street subjects (excluding the Devil's Tower) known to have been drawn by Thirtle on the evidence of exhibited works, of sales and of existing works, originals and copies are: Norwich Society of Artists 1808 (25) *View on the river Wensum near King-Street Gates*; Mrs. Thirtle sale, Norwich, Spelman Tues. 9th May 1882 lot 33 *River, King Street, Norwich* bt. Hansell 2 gns; same sale lot 49 *Boats, near King Street* bt. Hansell £6.16.6; *River at King Street, Norwich.* exh. Norwich, Thirtle Centenary 1939 (82) lent by E. M. Hansell, presumably the drawing in the collection of E. P. Hansell 1971, 8× 10¹³⁄₁₆ ins. (sight); *River at King Street, Norwich,* watercolour, 10⅜ × 15⅜ ins., Cooper Art Gallery, Barnsley, Cat. 15; *Old Houses on the Wensum, Norwich,* watercolour, 8¼ × 5⅞ ins., BM, 1902–5–14–480; *The River at King Street, Norwich,* watercolour, 15 × 17¼ ins. V & A, P26–1926.

    The River at King Street, Norwich, 10 × 15 ins. (photo Witt), lent by Sir Michael Sadler to the Norwich Thirtle Centenary 1939 (125) is not King Street but the River Wensum north of the city, looking towards St. Giles church.

78 View on the river Wensum, King Street, Norwich   Pl. 41

A thumbnail sketch in pencil of a composition with two figures upper right. Pencil and watercolour on cream wove paper; 25·8 × 35·2 (10³⁄₁₆ × 13⅞).

COND: ?Treated with Chloramine T, Sept. 1948. Cleaned by J. MacColum 1967. Mounted Royal.—Paper surface grazed u. & lower edges. Paper damaged u.c.

PROV: ?Thomas Lound sale, Norwich, Spelman Wed. 6th March 1861[1] or ?Mrs. Thirtle sale, Norwich, Spelman Tues. 9th May 1882 ?lot 33 *River, King Street, Norwich* bt. Hansell 2 gns;[2] P. E. Hansell by ?1867[3]; presented by him to the EAAS between 27th June 1894 and 27th Feb. 1895[4]; presented by the Society in 1895 as an addition to the rest of its collection presented the previous year.

EXH: ?Norwich 1867 (770) *Four Water Colour Drawings* lent by P. E. Hansell; Norwich, Thirtle Centenary 1939 (83).

The composition is similar to No. 77. A rather weak drawing, further weakened by the loss of blue leaving a dull indian red in the shadows.

1. Very few of the titles in this sale are specific. Hansell bought ten drawings by Thirtle in two lots: 101 and 112, also a portfolio, lot 116, which may have included Thirtle drawings.

2. Hansell also bt. lot 49 *Boats, near King Street* for £6.16.0. but this would be a high price for an unfinished watercolour.

3. See EXH.

4. This drawing is not listed in the last report of donations and purchases (*Norwich Mercury* 27th June 1894) but is included in the Deed of Settlement dated 27th Feb. 1895.

79 Thorpe Watering   Pl. 42

Pencil, watercolour and some white bodycolour with slight scraping out on cream wove paper; 32·6 × 47·9 (12$\frac{7}{8}$ × 18$\frac{13}{16}$). *Verso* Trees by a River, with Watermill, Windmill and Two Figures. Pencil and watercolour.

COND: Cleaned by Kennedy North, April 1940. Removed from Bulwer cabinet, March 1976. Double Mounted Imperial.—Staining along l.u. & r. edges. *Verso,* paper surface badly grazed u.l., remains of old backing paper u.r. corner, repair l.r. corner.—Colour faded.

PROV: Miss Davey sale, Lowestoft 1897[1] bt. J. J. Colman; his bequest to R. J. Colman 1898; R. J. Colman Bequest 1946, registered 1951.

EXH: Norwich 1903 (85).

The view in this drawing is Thorpe Watering seen from the west with the church of St. Andrews, Thorpe, the subject of No. 61, on the left. A similar composition but without the wherries, also in watercolour, was lent by Sir Henry Holmes to the Thirtle Centenary 1939 (5)[2]. The inn in the centre left distance figures more prominently in another drawing in the collection, No. 80, taken further down river. The peculiar mottled appearance of the water in the drawing is the result of uneven fading; only a thin band of the original blue remains along the edges. Stylistically, especially in the 'blotting' treatment of foliage and in the thin hazy distance, this drawing is close to *Putney Bridge,* dated 1819, No. 81. The abandoned composition of the *verso,* uncharacteristic with its heavy forms, may be a copy, perhaps after Vincent[3]. Thorpe was a favourite sketching ground for Thirtle: other recorded drawings are discussed in the entry for No. 38.

1. CC Records. The catalogue, if there was one, of this sale is untraced.

2. 10$\frac{1}{4}$ × 16$\frac{3}{4}$ ins., photo in NCM annotated catalogue.

3. One is reminded of the kind of composition as *Old Mill on the Yare* printed after Vincent by Walker & Cockerell (photo Witt).

80 Thorpe St. Andrew, Norwich   Pl. 40

Pencil and watercolour on cream wove paper; 24·3 × 35·3 (9$\frac{9}{16}$ × 13$\frac{7}{8}$).

INSCR: *Verso,* ? signed in pencil c. *J Thirtle.*

COND: Cleaned by Kennedy North, Nov. 1939. Removed from Bulwer cabinet, March 1976. Mounted Royal.—*Verso,* paper stained.

PROV: See No. 25.

A view of Thorpe Watering from the west[1], a similar view taken from further up river is the subject of a large watercolour in the collection, No. 79. The handling and palette of this drawing are close to *Putney Bridge* dated 1819, No. 81.

1. What may have been the same view or perhaps this very drawing was in the Thomas Turner sale, Norwich, Maddison Miles & Maddison, Mon. 5th April 1897 lot 203 *Thirtle. Watercolour The Old Buck Inn, Thorpe.* 9$\frac{1}{4}$ × 12 ins.

81 Putney Bridge, London   Pl. 43

Pencil, watercolour and some white bodycolour on cream wove paper; 21·5 × 30·1 (8$\frac{7}{16}$ × 11$\frac{7}{8}$).

INSCR: Signed and dated in brown watercolour l.r. *J Thirtle/1819* (paper cut).

COND: Deframed and treated with Thymol vapour, Sept. 1960. Cleaned and laid by D. Lewisohn, Feb. 1977. Mounted Royal.

PROV: W. A. Brooke Bequest received through his sisters, Mrs. Chamberlain and Mrs. Clarke, with four other Norwich School pictures, 1944.

EXH: Lowestoft 1948 (68).

This is the only drawing known which bears the date of 1819. It is rather weak but has suffered badly through fading. The old backing paper is inscribed in pencil in an unknown hand *Putney Bridge* and the drawing may well represent the bridge which was a wooden structure built in 1729, not replaced until 1886[1]. Thirtle had drawn London subjects by 1816 as he exhibited two views on the Thames with the Norwich Society Secession in 1816 (61, 62)[2].

1. Eric de Mary *Bridges of Britain* 1975 p. 124.

2. Thirtle may have drawn Putney Bridge more than once as a watercolour attributed to him *River Scene near Putney* was in the William Willins sale, Norwich, Dennis Barnard Tues. 8th 1855 lot 6 bt. King 12s. and a *Putney Bridge* was in the Rev. John Bailey sale, Stoke Holy Cross, Spelman Tues. Wed. 4th, 5th March 1884 first day lot 32. Either of these may of course be the museum's drawing.

82 Cottages and Trees beside the East End of Trowse Newton Church, Norfolk   Pl. 44

Pencil, watercolour and some white bodycolour on greyish wove paper; 19·2 × 27·5 (7$\frac{9}{16}$ × 10$\frac{13}{16}$).

COND: Cleaned by Kennedy North, April 1940. Removed from Bulwer cabinet, March 1976. Cleaned and laid by D. Lewisohn, Feb. 1977. Mounted Royal.—*Verso,* paper surface grazed; repairs at u.c.l. and lower edges and l.l. and l.r. corners.—Colour faded.

PROV: James Reeve[1]; bt. from him by H. S. Theobald[1]; bt. from him by R. J. Colman Feb. 1910[2]; R. J. Colman Bequest 1946, registered 1951.

The overall greyish tone is probably the result of fading and cleaning.

Trowse with Newton is situated on the south-east outskirts of Norwich. Thirtle exhibited with the Norwich

Society in 1815 (135) *Trowse Bridge, near Norwich* and later made a copy of a painting of Trowse by Vincent, see the entry for No. 110.

1. Reeve Coll. MS. p. 81 no no. as *Trowse—nr. Norwich Church on left, cottage on right—trees in centre.*

2. The CC MS vol. 2 p. 326 no. 137b gives 'Bought at the Agricultural Hall, Norwich; but the Reeve description is so accurate that the Theobald provenance is more probable.

83 Landscape with a Road to a Thatched Farmhouse
Pl. 43

Pencil and watercolour on white wove paper; 17 × 26·3 (6$\frac{11}{16}$ × 10$\frac{3}{8}$).

COND: Cleaned and laid by D. Lewisohn Feb. 1977. Mounted Royal.—*Verso*, paper surface grazed; repair u.l. edge, centre; l.l., u.r., l.r. corners torn.—Colour faded.

PROV: R. J. Colman Bequest 1946, registered 1951[1].

One might be prompted to doubt the attribution of this rather weak drawing, but it is probably only a ghost of its former self, having suffered badly from fading. The handling and pencil work is close to No. 81.

1. The CC MS vol. 2 p. 322 no. 134a gives no provenance.

84 Thorpe looking towards Whitlingham
Pl. 44

Pencil and watercolour on buff wove paper with watermark upper right (inverted) *1818*; 22·2 × 29 (8$\frac{5}{8}$ × 11$\frac{1}{2}$) subject; 26·7 × 32·6 (10$\frac{9}{16}$ × 12$\frac{7}{8}$) paper.

INSCR: Inscribed in pencil, in the artist's hand, on the lower edge with lines of colour notes (indistinct, paper torn away); inscribed in pencil, in an unknown hand, l.l. *Thorpe looking towards Whitlingham J Thirtle . . .*

COND: Deframed, old backing and mount removed, treated with Thymol vapour 1960. Mounted Royal.—Tear u.l.; *recto* and *verso*, gum along edges;—colour faded.

PROV: Mrs. Thirtle sale, Norwich, Spelman Tues. 9th May 1882 ?lot 42 *At Thorpe* bt. Thompson £1.7.6; J. J. Colman by 1886[1]; his bequest to R. J. Colman 1898; R. J. Colman Bequest 1946, registered 1951.

EXH: Norwich, Art Circle 1886 (73) lent by J. J. Colman.

A wide band of the original clear blues and greens of this drawing exists under the mount. Apart from its sadly faded condition, important colour notes have been lost because of careless mounting in the past.

Thirtle's exhibits of Thorpe subjects and other known works of this, one of Thirtle's favourite sketching grounds, are discussed in the entry for No. 38.

1. See EXH.

85 Lady sewing
Pl. 45

Pencil and grey wash on cream wove paper with watermark centre right parallel with right edge *E&P/1801*[1]; 11·9 × 14·8 (4$\frac{11}{16}$ × 5$\frac{13}{16}$). *Verso*, (?) random pencil marks and a blue stain, with indication that it was cut down from a larger sheet.

COND: Mounted Royal with No. 86.—*Verso*, gum at corners.

PROV: See No. 7.

1. Churchill records (p. 50) *1801 Edmonds & Pine.*

86 Study of a half length Figure, Two Heads and a Boat
Pl. 45

Pencil and watercolour on white wove paper; 10·5 × 16·1 (4$\frac{1}{8}$ × 6$\frac{5}{16}$).

INSCR: Inscribed in pencil with colour notes.

COND: Mounted Royal with No. 85.—Staining. *Verso*, gum at corners.

PROV: See No. 7.

87 Woman standing by a Font
Pl. 45

Pencil and watercolour on white wove paper; 10 × 8·8 (3$\frac{15}{16}$ × 3$\frac{7}{16}$).
Verso, sketch in pencil of ?a river scene with two figures.

INSCR: Inscribed in pencil with colour notes.

COND: Unmounted.—*Verso*, gum at corners.

PROV: See No. 25.

A figure study of bright clear colours similar to that in the BM, *Girl seated with a child*[1].

1. Watercolour, 4$\frac{1}{2}$ × 6 ins., 1902–5–14–487.

88 Study of a Farm Cart
Pl. 60

Pencil and grey-brown wash on white laid paper; 5·4 × 12·4 (2$\frac{1}{8}$ × 4$\frac{7}{8}$).

COND: Cleaned and inlaid by D. Lewisohn, Feb. 1977. Unmounted.—Foxing stain left edge.

PROV: See No. 7.

89 Two Horses between Shafts and Three Figures on the left
Pl. 60

Pencil and brown wash on greyish brown wove paper tinted with brown wash; 17·5 × 22·6 (6$\frac{7}{8}$ × 8$\frac{15}{16}$).
Verso, undefined sketches in pencil of foliage and ?figures in two boats.

COND: Cleaned by J. MacColum 1967. Mounted Royal.—Paper joined $\frac{1}{2}$ in. from lower edge.

PROV: See No. 12.

EXH: Norwich, Thirtle Centenary 1939 (112) as *Study of Horses;* Kettering 1952 (23); Harrogate 1953 (54); Kidderminster 1954 (36); Wisbech 1960.

This drawing is difficult to date. The use of grey and brown wash predominates in Thirtle's early work of c. 1803–1811 while tinted papers are usually found in or after 1811. The subject is unusual because of its scale; most of Thirtle's known sketches are smaller such as those in the Fitch collection[1]. However the attribution is confirmed by the handling of the washes and the characteristic pencil sketches on the *verso*.

1. Nos. 7, 16–20, 85, 86, 88, 90–102, 134–169.

90 *Recto* **Riverside Scene with Wherry**   **Pl. 48**

Slight sketch in pencil of chimney stack upper left.
Pencil and brown wash on white wove paper; 9·5 × 16·1
($3\frac{3}{4}$ × $6\frac{3}{8}$).
Verso, Foundry Bridge from the Bank opposite Pulls
Ferry. Pencil, grey and brown wash.
COND: Mounted Royal with Nos. 18, 91.—Paper stained
u.l.; *verso,* gum at corners.

This drawing is closely related to its *verso* and to No. 91.
The subject is probably Pulls Ferry. The pencil sketch of a
gable end and a chimney stack is that of the house in No.
91. The view on the *verso,* with the tower of St. John
Sepulchre in the distance is taken from the opposite side of
the river looking downstream towards Foundry bridge.
This was the first bridge on the site; of wood on stone
piers, it was built to the plans of a Mr. Mendham of Holt,
in 1810 and replaced in 1844 by a cast iron bridge.
Another drawing by Thirtle of Old Foundry Bridge is in
the B.M., it shows the bridge looking up river[1].

1. Pencil, watercolour and white body colour, $5\frac{5}{8}$ × $8\frac{3}{4}$ ins., ex coll.
   James Reeve, who lent it to the Art Circle exhibition 1886 (17),
   1902–5–14–482.

91 Old House with Foundry Bridge in the Distance
                                                     Pl. 48

Pencil, grey and brown wash on white wove paper; 9 ×
15·8 ($3\frac{9}{16}$ × $6\frac{1}{4}$).
Verso, slight sketch in pencil of ? clouds.
COND: Mounted Royal with Nos. 18 and 90. *Verso,* gum
at corners.
PROV: See No. 7.

It is practically the same view as the verso of No. 90 but
taken from a spot further upstream so as to include the
house on the left. A similar view of the river, with the
gabled houses on the left bank, is shown in an unattributed
coloured aquatint *The Ferry near Bishops Bridge Norwich
London Published Decr 1822*[1].

1. NCM Todd coll. vol. II Box 8 p. 264.

92 Duke's Palace Bridge, Norwich   **Pl. 49**

Pencil and watercolour on cream wove paper; 11·3 ×
18·1 ($4\frac{7}{16}$ × $7\frac{1}{8}$).
COND: Mounted Royal with Nos. 17 and 93. *Verso,* gum
at corners.
PROV: See No. 7.
EXH: Rouen 1967 (54c).

This drawing can be dated between 1822 when the bridge
was completed and 1830, when Thirtle showed a drawing
with the Norwich Society (25 *) *Duke's Palace Bridge*[1],
for which it is probably a study. According to Bolingbroke's MS notes[2], the exhibited drawing was, at the time
of his writing, in the collection of Miss Parr[3]; it is now
untraced. On the evidence of the lithograph after Stark's
Dye Works/Duke's Palace Bridge, frontispiece to the
Norwich Art Circle Exhibition catalogue of his works
June 1887, the museum's drawing is a view of the other
bank, looking down river from above the bridge. With its
clear tones of the complementaries: blue and orange,

yellow and purple, this is one of the freshest drawings in
this group. A full view of the bridge looking up river, in
chalk and white bodycolour on blue paper, attributed to
Thirtle, is in a private collection[4]. What may be a view of
the site of the bridge is shown in No. 11.

Duke's Palace Bridge was built to connect Pitt Street
with the market place; until then there was no bridge on
the stretch of the river between Coslany bridge to the west
and Blackfriars to the east. The foundation stone was laid
on 28th August 1821 and the bridge completed by
December 1822. It was designed by Henry Lock, engineer, and cast by John Brown of Norwich[5]. The bridge took
its name from the Duke's Palace, built by Henry Howard,
6th Duke of Norfolk, which stood between St. Andrews
Street and the river, and was partly demolished by 1711.
Duke's Palace Bridge with its sixty-foot wide elliptical
arch and pierced ballustrading was a fine example of early
nineteenth century cast iron work. Despite a Ministry
preservation order, the bridge was demolished in 1972 to
allow for road widening.

1. Pictures asterisked in the catalogue were for sale.
2. Bolingbroke MS (Thirtle) in Art Dept. archives.
3. A drawing of this subject was sold at James Mill's sale, Norwich,
   Spelman Wed. 14th June 1865, *Water colour drawings in gilt frames
   & glazed* lot 187 *VIEW on the NORWICH RIVER—the Duke's
   Palace Bridge & Craft Painted for the late Michael Stark. Very fine,*
   bt. Dalrymple £14.14.0.
4. $9\frac{7}{8}$ × $14\frac{13}{16}$ ins. (sight measurement).
5. A. Paget Baggs 'Some notes on the history of cast iron in Norwich
   architecture', the *Handbook of the Norfolk and Norwich Association
   of Architects* 1960–61 p. 40.

93 Wherry on River   **Pl. 47**

Pencil and watercolour on cream wove paper; 11 × 9·1
($4\frac{3}{8}$ × $3\frac{9}{16}$).
COND: Mounted Royal with Nos. 17 and 92.—*Verso,*
gum at corners.
PROV: See No. 7.
EXH: Rouen 1967 (54b).

94 A Wherry   **Pl. 47**

Pencil and brown wash on cream wove paper with watermark upper edge [RUSE & TU]*RNERS*[1]; 18·7 × 12·9
($7\frac{3}{8}$ × $5\frac{1}{16}$).
Verso, sketch in pencil and brown wash of top of boat
masts at lower edge, indicating that it was cut down from a
larger sheet.
INSCR: Inscribed in pencil with colour notes.
COND: Mounted Royal with No. 95.—Horizontal crease
mark. u.c. *Verso,* gum at corners.
PROV: See No. 7.

1. Churchill records (p. 53) papers dated between 1805–45 with the
   watermark of *Ruse and Turner,* with no *s;* however a drawing in the
   collection, previously attributed to Thirtle, 1335.235.951, bears the
   watermark *RUSE & TURNERS/1823* which is not recorded by
   Churchill.

61

95 River Scene with Wherries, with Sketch of Boat in Sky
Pl. 46

Pencil and brown wash on white wove paper; $11 \cdot 5 \times 23 \cdot 7$ ($4\frac{1}{2} \times 9\frac{5}{16}$).

INSCR: Inscribed in pencil with colour notes.

COND: Mounted Royal with No. 94.— Vertical crease stain c.r. *Verso*, gum at corners.

PROV: See No. 7.

96 Wherries and Figures
Pl. 46

Pencil and brown wash on cream wove paper with watermark lower right *JWH*[ATMAN]; $10 \cdot 1 \times 16 \cdot 2$ ($4 \times 6\frac{3}{8}$). *Verso*, slight sketch in pencil of the gable end of two houses, overlapped by an undefined sketch with colour note.

COND: Mounted Royal with Nos. 97 and 98.—Vertical crease c.l. *Verso*, gum at corners.

Probably a study of a water frolic, a subject which Thirtle did not exhibit, but which is treated in two watercolour sketches attributed to him called *Carrow Water Frolic* and *Wroxham Regatta*[1].

A watercolour copy of the latter composition, with slight variation, by Thirtle's pupil Mary Catherine Blofeld (1803–1851), is in the collection of Mr. and Mrs. T. R. C. Blofeld[2]. See also Nos. 158–164.

1. $4\frac{3}{8} \times 8$ ins. and $6\frac{3}{16} \times 10\frac{1}{4}$ ins., both in the collection of H. Bolingbroke 1972.

2. $15\frac{1}{4} \times 30$ ins.

97 Wherry with Sail lowered
Pl. 46

Pencil and brown wash on cream wove paper tinted with light brown wash; $10 \cdot 6 \times 12 \cdot 2$ ($4\frac{3}{16} \times 4\frac{13}{16}$).

COND: Mounted Royal with Nos. 96 and 98.—Vertical stain line l. *Verso*, gum at corners.

PROV: See No. 7.

98. Riverside, Boats with Figures
Pl. 46

Pencil and brown wash on cream wove paper; $11 \cdot 7 \times 18 \cdot 8$ ($4\frac{9}{16} \times 7\frac{3}{8}$).

COND: Mounted Royal with Nos. 96 and 97.—*Verso*, gum at corners.

PROV: See No. 7.

99 A Sail, Sailing Boat with Figure, and a Figure Pl. 48

Pencil and brown wash on white wove paper with watermark lower left *J WH*[ATMAN]/ *18* . . ; $9 \cdot 2 \times 17 \cdot 4$ ($3\frac{5}{8} \times 6\frac{13}{16}$). *Verso*, sketches in pencil and brown wash of two sailing boats and a group of a cow and a donkey.

COND: Mounted Royal with Nos. 100, 101, 102.—*Verso*, gum at corners.

PROV: See No. 7.

100 Stranded Sailing Vessel
Pl. 45

Pencil and grey-blue wash on white wove paper; $10 \cdot 8 \times 13 \cdot 1$ ($4\frac{1}{4} \times 5\frac{1}{8}$).

COND: Mounted Royal with Nos. 99, 101, 102.—Staining and slight foxing. *Verso*, gum at corners.

PROV: See No. 7.

101 Wherry and Sailing Boat
Pl. 47

Pencil and brown wash on cream wove paper with watermark lower centre right edge [WHA]*TMAN/* . . .8; $9 \cdot 2 \times 10 \cdot 8$ ($3\frac{5}{8} \times 4\frac{1}{4}$). *Verso*, ? cloud study in pencil and watercolour with colour notes, with indication that it was cut from the same sheet as No. 102.

COND: Mounted Royal with Nos. 99, 100, 102.—*Verso*, gum at corners.

PROV: See No. 7.

102 Wherry
Pl. 47

Pencil and brown wash on cream wove paper; $9 \times 6 \cdot 2$ ($3\frac{9}{16} \times 2\frac{7}{16}$). *Verso*, ? cloud study in pencil and watercolour with colour notes with indication that it was cut from the same sheet as No. 101.

COND: Mounted Royal with Nos. 99, 100, 101.—*Verso*, gum at corners.

PROV: See No. 7.

103 River Scene with a Billy Boy at Thorpe, Norwich
Pl. 48

Studies of sailing boats upper left.

Black chalk, pencil, some white bodycolour and brown wash on greyish-green wove paper with watermark lower centre *S & A/1828*[1]; $24 \cdot 1 \times 30 \cdot 2$ ($9\frac{1}{2} \times 11\frac{7}{8}$).

INSCR: Inscribed in pencil with colour notes; *verso*, numbered in pencil u.c.r. *No 2*.

COND: Mounted Royal.—*Recto & verso*, gum along edges.

PROV: See No. 1[2].

EXH: Norwich, Thirtle Centenary 1939 (128) *River at Thorpe* lent by R. J. Colman.

Possibly a study for No. 112 which has the same composition. This is an unusual drawing, as the use of dark tinted paper and black chalk is not common in Thirtle's oeuvre, although it is found in Nos. 116 and 118. The same watermark occurs yet again in No. 120 but this time with watercolour. The colour notes also support the attribution.

The subject is too summary to identify the site but the general impression suggests Thorpe looking up river towards the city. The 'Billy Boy' was a coastal merchant trading vessel.

1. Churchill records (p. 53) *1816–54 Smith & Alnutt*. The watermark of No. 103 is found also in No. 120 and the watermark *SMITH & ALNUTT* in No. 121.

2. The only Thorpe subject specified in Mrs. Thirtle's sale 1882 was lot 42 *At Thorpe* bt. Thompson £1.7.6 but this would have been a high price for a chalk drawing.

104 Beach Scene, Cromer with Sailing Ship and Figures
Pl. 51

Pencil, watercolour, white bodycolour and some scraping out on cream wove paper with watermark parallel with left edge *J WHATMAN/1811*; 23·2 × 35·1 ($9\frac{1}{8}$ × $13\frac{13}{16}$).
Verso, Horstead Mill with two Cows.
Pencil and watercolour.

COND: Deframed and treated with Thymol vapour, Sept. 1960. Cleaned by J. MacColum 1967. Double Mounted Royal.—Remains of old backing paper along edges; *verso*, staining along edges. Pin holes l. edge.

PROV: Dr. Ernest Egbert Blyth Bequest with No. 65, 1934[1].

The dishevelled look of the handling and crude palette of this drawing make it one of the most unsuccessful in the collection. Nevertheless the attribution to Thirtle is confirmed by the treatment of the pier in the middle distance, by the ghost-like pencil figures in the lower centre, and by the green and silvery study of *Horstead Mill* on the *verso*. Horstead is situated on the River Bure six miles north-east of Norwich. Thirtle showed with the Norwich Society in 1814 (124) *Horstead Mills, near Coltishall* for which the museum's drawing may be a study[2].

1. Both drawings entered the collection wrongly attributed to John Joseph Cotman (1814–1878).
2. Watercolour, $16\frac{1}{2}$ × $24\frac{13}{16}$ ins., in the collection of Mr. & Mrs. T. R. C. Blofeld. There is another drawing of the mill, pencil, watercolour and some white bodycolour, $9\frac{1}{16}$ × $12\frac{1}{4}$ ins., in the collection of H. Bolingbroke 1972.

105 Buckenham Ferry, Norfolk 1827
Pl. 52

Pencil, watercolour and some white bodycolour on buff wove paper; 17 × 37·1 ($6\frac{11}{16}$ × $14\frac{5}{8}$).

INSCR: Inscribed and dated in pencil l.c.r. *Buckenham Ferry Oct 1827*.

COND: Mounted Royal.—Slight foxing. *Verso*, paper stained l.—Colour faded.

PROV: W. Miles Parr by 1886[1]; by descent to W. Henry Parr by Feb. 1915; bt. from him out of the Walker Bequest Fund, £5, 1915.

EXH: Norwich, Art Circle 1886 (58) lent by W. M. Parr; Norwich, Thirtle Centenary 1939 (21).

REF: *EDP* 10th March 1916 'Some recent picture acquisitions'; Dickes p. 236; *EDP* 25th April 1921 'New light on Crome—some Ladbrooke Memories'.

Buckenham is a small village on the River Yare, seven and a half miles south-east of Norwich. According to Henry Ladbrooke, he and Thirtle sketched there on 17th October [?1827].

The pallid yellow and brown tones of this drawing are misleading, a thin band of the original blue colour remains along the lower edge.

There is an amateur, naive drawing of Buckenham Ferry[2], wrongly attributed to Thirtle, in the collection which is inscribed in pencil along the top *Buckingham (sic) Ferry pray. . . . of all* (paper cut) *these objects particularly the/Carriage & Horses/you are to make a good finished Drawing of the view in/your best manner*

according to the size I have marked as/the paper it is for Sir Thomas Beauchamp[3] may be of/Infinite service to you take care of this sketch & let/me have it again and lower right *Ferry Boat here/* . . .

There is no evidence, apart from his name twice inscribed by later hands, to assume that these instructions were addressed to Thirtle. The composition of his watercolour, the only version of this subject recorded, shows a more oblique view of the ferry house and differs from the amateur sketch in several other details: it has no horse and carriage and its main motif is the wherry to the left. The Beauchamp collection did include by 1829 'a very sparkling little picture, a View of Buckenham Ferry—Mr. J. Stannard'[4]. However, this oil by Stannard similarly does not follow the composition of the amateur drawing the instructions on which moreover specify that the work commissioned is a drawing not a painting. Taking all this into consideration it is not proven that Thirtle painted a view of this scene for Beauchamp, but the possibility cannot be ruled out.

1. See EXH.
2. Pencil and grey wash, $8\frac{3}{16}$ × $12\frac{1}{4}$ ins. (cut down), inscribed in pencil with instructions, colour notes and l.r. *Thirtle*, in the same hand as the inscription of No. 84; *verso*, sketches in pencil of boats u.l. and inscribed in pencil in another hand u.r. *Thirtle*, l.r. one, 1352.B57.235.951.
3. Sir Thomas Beauchamp Proctor Bt. (1756–1827), connoisseur and collector, of Langley Hall, Norfolk.
4. Chambers' *Norfolk Tour* vol. II 1829 p. 847. Presumably the painting, with E. D. Levine some years back (photo in Art dept. archives), oil on panel, $15\frac{3}{4}$ × 24 ins., and now in the collection of the Yale Center for British Art and British Studies, New Haven, U.S.A. having acquired a 'signature' and the 'date' 1826 in the meantime. A watercolour of a similar composition by Stannard, $5\frac{3}{16}$ × $13\frac{5}{8}$ ins., is in the NCM collection, 69.942.

106 The Devil's Tower, Norwich
Pl. 50

Black chalk, brown wash with some white bodycolour on grey wove paper; 22·6 × 32·7 ($8\frac{7}{8}$ × $12\frac{7}{8}$).
Verso, sketch in black chalk with some white bodycolour of river scene with wherry (inverted).

INSCR: Inscribed in pencil with colour notes u.l. *Bright Blue*; u.r. *yellowish/Grey/* . . . (indistinct).

COND: Cleaned by Kennedy North, April 1940. Cleaned by D. Lewisohn, Feb. 1977. Mounted Royal.—Repair u.l. corner, l.l. corner torn, paper surface grazed. Foxing stains.

PROV: Mrs. Thirtle sale Norwich, Spelman Tues. 9th May 1882 bt. for ?J. J. Colman[1]; his Bequest to R. J. Colman 1898; R. J. Colman Bequest 1946, registered 1951.

EXH: Norwich, Art Circle 1886 (30) as *King Street, Norwich*.

REF: *Norwich Mercury*, 7th July 1886 'The John Thirtle Exhibition'[2]; Dickes p. 236 as *King Street, Norwich*.

CAT: As *River at Carrow* in all catalogues.

Although this is a rather weak drawing and the use of chalk is not common in Thirtle's oeuvre, the colour notes are in his hand and this lends weight to the attribution. In the 1886 exhibition catalogue the drawing is stated to be a *Sepia Sketch for No. 27, but without fishing boat to the left*. The drawing, No. 27, referred to was lent by H. D.

Geldart: *Fishing Boat, Carrow . . . signed and dated 1827*, $9\frac{3}{8} \times 13\frac{1}{4}$ ins., and was illustrated in lithograph by Miller Smith (1854–1937) p. 6. Its present whereabouts is untraced[3].

A similar view of the Devil's Tower was etched by Thomas Lound[4].

1. CC records. Many of the lots have no titles. However lot 17 specifies *Four watercolour sketches in sepia* bt. Jackson, £4, and there are two King Street subjects: (a) lot 33, *River King Street, Norwich*, bt. Hansell £2.2.0 and (b) lot 49, *Boats, near King Street* bt. Hansell £6.10.6.

2. The press report mentions 'two drawings of the river at King Street, the Devil's tower in each showing just what part of the Waveney [Wensum] is the scene' but there were three exhibited: No. 27 *Fishing Boat, Carrow* mentioned above, this drawing and *Devil's Tower near King Street Gates Evening*, see No. 13.

3. A poor copy of this composition, with slight variations, is in the collection: watercolour, $7\frac{11}{16} \times 11\frac{1}{2}$ ins., 1352.B55.235.951. According to the CC records it came from Benjamin Russell, brother-in-law of the artist, but it cannot be accepted as by Thirtle.

4. Plate size $4\frac{5}{8} \times 6\frac{1}{16}$ ins. Bol. 3.

107 The Devil's Tower and Carrow Bridge   Pl. 50

Pencil, watercolour and some white bodycolour on cream wove paper with watermark lower centre right *B.E. & S/18.3* (probably 1803—3rd digit indistinct); $23 \cdot 7 \times 34 \cdot 1$ ($9\frac{5}{16} \times 13\frac{7}{16}$).

COND: Cleaned by Kennedy North, March 1940. Removed from Bulwer cabinet, April 1975. Mounted Royal.—Corner split l.l. *Verso*, foxing stains lower edge.

PROV: Benjamin Russell by 1886[1] and still in 1905[2]; H. S. Theobald by 1910; bt. from him R. J. Colman Feb. 1910[3]; R. J. Colman Bequest 1946, registered 1951.

EXH: Norwich, Art Circle 1886 (7) as *Carrow Bridge from King Street*, lent by B. Russell; Norwich, Thirtle Centenary 1939 (22) as *Carrow Bridge, Norwich*.

REF: Norwich Art Circle, *Third Exhibition catalogue, John Thirtle* 1886 illus. in litho. by J. Miller Marshall (1830–1900) p. 1[4]; *Norwich Mercury* 7th July 1886 'The John Thirtle Exhibition'; Dickes p. 236 as in the collection of Benjamin Russell.

A view down river with the 1810 Carrow Bridge in the middle distance. The malthouses on the left were in existence by at least 1825[5]. The 1886 exhibition catalogue suggests a date of 1827 and Percy Moore Turner gives 1828[3], assumptions presumably based on the drawing in the Geldart collection dated 1827, see the entry for No. 106.

The touches of what appears to be a cobalt or ultramarine blue in the figures and the predominant use of a turquoise (probably prussian blue and a yellow) are characteristic of Thirtle's later work and support the above dating. A smaller, close version of this composition, watercolour, $7\frac{1}{4} \times 10$ ins., attributed to Thirtle, was exhibited by Manning Galleries June 1968 (51) and Nov. 1971 (66)[6]. The composition was also used as the subject for an etching by Thomas Lound[7].

1. See EXH.
2. See REF.
3. CC Records.
4. Compiler's pagination.

5. cf. a dated drawing by B. S. Norgate, on deposit from the Norfolk and Norwich Record Office, NCM L1974.7.3.

6. Also *The Devils Tower and Carrow Bridge* attributed to Thirtle was lent by William Runacres to the Norwich 1878 exhibition (425).

7. Plate size $4\frac{5}{8} \times 6$ ins., Bol. 2.

108 The Devil's Tower and Carrow Bridge   Pl. 49

Sketch of a boat upper left.
Pencil and watercolour on grey green wove paper; $21 \cdot 7 \times 31 \cdot 2$ ($8\frac{9}{16} \times 12\frac{1}{4}$).

INSCR: Inscribed in pencil with colour notes.

COND: Cleaned by Kennedy North, March 1940. Removed from Bulwer cabinet, Aug. 1976. Mounted Royal.

PROV: Mrs. Thirtle sale, Norwich, Spelman Tues. 9th May 1882 bt. ?for J. J. Colman[1]; his bequest to R. J. Colman 1898; R. J. Colman Bequest 1946, registered 1951.

CAT: CC MS vol. I, p. 119 no. 439 as *The River at Carrow. Devils Tower on left, wherries on right*.

One of the finest of Thirtle's unfinished drawings, the silvery tonal values and broad washes demonstrate the remarkable economy of the medium in able hands. The composition is loosely related to the more finished watercolour, No. 107.

1. See No. 106 note 1.

109 Hilly landscape with a House and two Cows   Pl. 54

Pencil and watercolour on cream wove paper; $14 \cdot 2 \times 20$ ($5\frac{9}{16} \times 7\frac{7}{8}$).
Verso, Sunset Landscape with Windmill, two Figures and a Horse.
Pencil and watercolour.

COND: Cleaned by D. Lewisohn, Sept. 1976. Double Mounted Royal.

PROV: Miss Alice Geldart sale, Norwich, Hanbury Williams Tues. 14th July 1942 lot 275 *Watercolour Frettenham Common* bt. ?Hansell £5.10.0; purchased out of the Southwell Bequest Fund, £5.5.0, 1942.

While some features of this drawing are characteristic of the late Thirtle: the Vincent-like treatment of the sky and the treatment of foliage, the use of a dark ultramarine blue for the distant horizon and the weak handling overall on both the *recto* and *verso* call for caution in accepting the attribution.

110 Trowse near Norwich—after Vincent   Pl. 55

Pencil, watercolour and some white bodycolour with slight scraping out on cream wove paper; $31 \cdot 2 \times 47 \cdot 4$ ($12\frac{1}{4} \times 18\frac{5}{8}$).

COND: Cleaned by Kennedy North, April 1940. Removed from Bulwer cabinet, March 1954. Mounted Imperial.—Tear u.c.r. and a notch u.r. edge. Paper surface slightly grazed along edges.—Colour faded.

PROV: Mrs. Thirtle; given by her, shortly after the artist's death in 1839, to Mr. Root, the artist's gilder[1]; James Reeve by 1873 and still in 1886[2]; J. J. Colman by 1894[2]; his bequest to R. J. Colman 1898; R. J. Colman Bequest 1946, registered 1951.

EXH: Norwich 1873 (9) as *Crown Point from Trowse Bridge—a very choice and characteristic work, lent by James Reeve*; Norwich 1874 (113) as *The Harvest Waggon—Trowse, looking towards Crown Point* lent by James Reeve; Norwich, Art Circle 1886 (57) as *Trowse looking from Second Bridge towards Crown Point* lent by James Reeve; Norwich 1894 (67) as *Trowse Hythe* lent by J. J. Colman; Norwich, Thirtle Centenary 1939 (12) lent by R. J. Colman.

REF: *Norwich Mercury* 15th Aug. 1874; Norwich Art Circle, *Third Exhibition Catalogue, John Thirtle* 1886 illus. in litho. by J. Miller Marshall (1830–1900) p. 10[3]; Dickes pp. 226–227, incorrectly dated to 1815.

This drawing is a faithful copy of an oil by George Vincent (1796–1832) in the collection[4] which may have been exhibited with the Norwich Society in 1828 as (107*) *Norfolk Scenery*[5] or (142) *Scene at Trowse near Norwich*. The frame of the Vincent painting bears Thirtle's trade label indicating that he had the picture to frame, possibly for the Norwich Society exhibition. His copy has all the stylistic qualities of the late drawings of c. 1827–1830, discussed in the entry for No. 111. In this period Thirtle seems to have imitated, in the lighter medium, the feathery rendering of clouds in the oil paintings by Vincent and this treatment of skies occurs in other watercolours as well. This suggests that by the twenties his aim in a finished watercolour was to approach the colour and power of an oil, which resulted in an overtaxing of the medium.

1. CC records.

2. See EXH.

3. Compiler's pagination.

4. *Trowse Meadows, Norwich*, oil on canvas, $28\frac{1}{4} \times 43\frac{1}{8}$ ins., J. J. Colman Bequest 1898, registered 1899, 13.4.99.

5. *Norfolk Scenery* was reviewed 16th Aug. 1828 '. . . in which we recognise the fine verdant range of Thorpe meadows, and the sweetly picturesque heights near Crown Point and Trowse. The figures of horses, cows and men which animate, without disturbing the repose of, this agreeable composition are judiciously introduced and ably executed.' (*Norfolk Chronicle* vol. LIX No. 3037).

111 Carrow Bridge, Norwich   Pl. 55

Pencil, watercolour and some white bodycolour on cream wove paper with watermark left, parallel with left edge. *J WHATMAN/1828*; $33 \times 51\cdot7$ ($13 \times 20\frac{3}{8}$).

COND: Cleaned by Kennedy North, April 1940. Removed from Bulwer cabinet, March 1975. Mounted Imperial.— Bleached foxing stains. Tear l.c.l. edge.

PROV: W. Miles Parr by 1886[1]; by descent to W. Henry Parr; bt. from him R. J. Colman, £20, April 1915[2]; R. J. Colman Bequest 1946, registered 1951.

EXH: Norwich, Art Circle 1886 (32) lent by W. M. Parr; Norwich, Thirtle Centenary 1939 (9).

REF: *Norwich Mercury* 7th July 1886 'John Thirtle Exhibition'; Norwich Art Circle, *Third Exhibition Catalogue, John Thirtle* 1886 illus. in litho. by C. J. Watson (1846–1927) p. 3[3].

A view of Carrow Bridge, built in 1810, demolished and replaced by another one in 1833, showing part of the medieval fortifications of Norwich: the Black Tower on Butter Hills to the left. The tower of St. John Sepulchre stands on the right horizon.

With its strong localised light, curious block-like forms and sharp touches of blue, this is a late drawing of c. 1830. It compares well with a watercolour of *Cromer Beach*, $9\frac{1}{8} \times 12\frac{1}{8}$ ins. (sight measurement), dated 1830, in a private collection. Thirtle exhibited *Boat Builders, Carrow* with the Norwich Society in 1829 (127) which may have been the museum's drawing as it shows a boatyard on the left.

A similar composition, in the catalogue stated to be an early drawing, was lent by J. J. Colman to the Norwich Art Circle exhibition 1889 (17)[4]. What was probably the same work was lent to the Norwich Art Circle exhibition 1913, loan collection (75). A closer view of the bridge and Black Tower is shown in a sketch in black and white chalk, which bears colour notes *The Sky & Water the Principle Light. . .*[5]

An earlier watercolour of the same but narrower view by Henry Ninham is in the museum's collection[6] and a wider aspect was engraved after Stark by William Miller and published in Stark's *Scenery of the Rivers of Norfolk* 1834 pl. 18.

1. See EXH.

2. Correspondence in Art Dept. archives.

3. Compiler's pagination.

4. It was still in the Colman collection in 1905, see Dickes p. 226.

5. $9 \times 12\frac{5}{16}$ ins., in the collection of H. Bolingbroke 1972. A *Carrow Bridge* was also lent by Mrs. Thirtle to the Norwich Fine Arts Association exhibition 1860 (284) and was reviewed by the *Norwich Mercury* Sept. 1860.

6. $13 \times 19\frac{1}{4}$ ins., 1190.B35.235.951.

112 Thorpe Staithe   Pl. 53

Pencil, watercolour and some white bodycolour with slight scraping out on cream wove paper; $25\cdot3 \times 34\cdot2$ ($9\frac{15}{16} \times 13\frac{1}{2}$).

COND: Cleaned by Kennedy North, April 1940. Removed from Bulwer cabinet, March 1954. Mounted Royal.— *Verso*, gum a t u.l. & r. corners; remains of old backing paper.

PROV: J. B. Aldis by 1886[1]; his sale 1909 bt. for R. J. Colman[2]; R. J. Colman Bequest 1946, registered 1951.

EXH: ?Norwich Society 1829 (180) *Scene on the* [Yare] *River at Thorpe—Evening*; Norwich, Art Circle 1886 (65) lent by J. B. Aldis; Norwich 1903 (83) lent by J. B. Aldis.

REF: Norwich Art Circle, *Third Exhibition Catalogue, John Thirtle* 1886 illus. in litho. by W. J. Churchyard (fl. 1886–1925) p. 8[3]; Dickes p. 231.

With its angular forms, illuminated by an all enveloping light, this is a typical late work. It may well have been that exhibited with the Norwich Society in 1829 when the local press gave the artist his usual acclaim 'Mr. Thirtle has given a rich harmonious tone to his watercolour painting'[4]. A chalk study of the same composition is in the collection, No. 103, which Thirtle may have used for the the worked up watercolour, as it bears colour notes such as 'whole of the distance/light [?] Purplish Gray'. For other Thorpe subjects see No. 38.

1. See EXH.

2. CC records: CC MS vol. 2 p. 320 no. 128a. The catalogue of this sale is untraced.

3. Compiler's pagination.

4. *Norwich Mercury* 25th July 1829.

113 River Scene with laden Wherries and Figures Pl. 53

Pencil and watercolour with slight scraping out on cream wove paper; 24·7 × 33·5 ($9\frac{11}{16}$ × $13\frac{3}{16}$).

COND: Cleaned and laid by D. Lewisohn, Feb. 1977. Mounted Royal.—Colour faded.

PROV: The Misses Thirkettle by 1927[1]; Miss F. C. Thirkettle by 1939[1]; her Bequest 1957.

EXH: Norwich 1927 (283) lent by the Misses Thirkettle; Norwich 1939 (15) lent by Miss Thirkettle; Derby and Nottingham 1959 (62).

Much of the pinkish glow of this drawing was not the artist's intention. A band of the original greyish blue of the sky and water still survives around the edges. The strong diagonal of the composition is unusual for Thirtle and the drawing is more than likely a copy after Joseph Stannard (1797–1830). The hay laden wherry on the left bank, with fishermen and the wherry in the middle distance are all to be found in Stannard's *River at Thorpe* in the museum's collection[2]. Indeed in 1939 Messrs. William Boswell of Norwich had in their possession[3] an oil, attributed to Stannard, of the same composition as the Thirtle drawing. However it was suggested at the time[4] that it might be an oil by Thirtle, in which case it would be the only one recorded. Its quality is certainly too poor for it to be by Stannard but whether it might be a watercolourist's unsuccessful attempt at oil painting must remain unresolved.

1. See EXH.

2. Oil on canvas, $37\frac{1}{2}$ × 43 ins., 1263.235.951.

3. In a Norfolk private collection 1974, photo in NCM.

4. A typescript comment against the Thirkettle loan (15) in the annotated copy of the Thirtle Centenary Catalogue 1939, Art dept. library.

114 Whitlingham Reach Pl. 52

Pencil, watercolour, white bodycolour and slight scraping out on cream wove paper; 32·1 × 63·7 ($12\frac{5}{8}$ × $25\frac{1}{16}$).

COND: ? Treated with Chloramine T, 1949. Removed from old backing board, cleaned and laid by D. Lewisohn, Feb. 1977. Mounted Atlas.—Foxing stains in sky; *verso*, paper surface grazed.—Colour faded.

PROV: W. Miles Parr by 1886[1]; by descent to Mrs. Elizabeth Parr; bt. from her, with two others, by the EAAS, £80, 14th July 1894[2]; presented by the EAAS 1895 as an addition to the rest of its collection presented the previous year.

EXH: ? Norwich Society of Artists 1829 (143 *)[3] *View Looking from Thorpe to Whitlingham Evening*; Norwich, Art Circle 1886 (40) lent by W. M. Parr; Tate 1922 (248); Norwich, Thirtle Centeenary 1939 (46).

REF: ? *Norfolk Chronicle* 1st Aug. 1829; *Norwich Mercury* 7th July 1886 'The John Thirtle Exhibition'; Nor-

wich Art Circle, *Third exhibition catalogue, John Thirtle 1886* illus. in litho. by C. J. Watson (1846–1927) p. 3[4]; Dickes p. 237.

There is another, larger version of this composition: watercolour, $15\frac{3}{8}$ × $25\frac{15}{16}$ ins., in the Walker Art Gallery, Liverpool[5]. The Liverpool drawing is called *Bramerton Woods End Reach on the Yare*, a correct alternative title as Whitlingham and Bramerton are close to each other on the right bank of the river. The names have been used indiscriminately to describe a three mile picturesque stretch south-east of Norwich. There are slight variations between the two drawings: the Liverpool version has less foliage in the left foreground and there is an unfinished sketch of a boat in the middle right distance. The sky seems stronger in this version although the Norwich drawing has suffered through foxing and the complete loss of indigo which gives an overall hot tonality. As it is more finished, the Norwich drawing is likely to be the one that was shown with the Norwich Society in 1829 and reviewed in the *Norfolk Chronicle* 1st Aug. 'Mr. Thirtle's Views of Thorpe and Whitlingham Meadows are fraught with rich effects of sunset.'

There is a watercolour of this scene in Mr. Eric Hinde's collection, with a profusely annotated fresh study of the same view on its *verso*[6].

1. See EXH.

2. EAAS records: Minutes Book (Minutes for 11th July 1894 p. 165) and cheque to Mrs. Bessie Parr dated 14th July 1894.

3. Pictures marked by asterisks in the catalogue were for sale.

4. Compiler's pagination.

5. Presented by Lord Wavertree in 1914. Very probably the drawing lent by Samuel Harvard to the Norwich 1878 exhibition (470) and reviewed in the *EDP* 23rd Nov. 1878 'No. 470 is "Whitlingham Reach", taken from the meadows close to the station. The same ruddy glow is introduced, but not to the same extent. A storm is rising to the right [left] . . . The left of the picture is a little wanting in finish . . .' It was still with Harvard in 1885 when he lent it to the Norwich exhibition of that year (322) and was probably sold at his sale, Norwich, Spelman Thurs., Fri. 30th, 31st Oct. 1890 second day lot 691 *Whitlingham*, £11.0.6.

6. Other Whitlingham subjects attributed to Thirtle known on the evidence of posthumous sales and exhibitions are: *View at Whitlingham*, lot 99 in Thomas Lound sale, Norwich, Spelman Wed. 6th March 1861 bt. Gilman £1.13.0; *Meadows and Cattle at Whitlingham*, lot 243 in Horatio Bolingbroke's sale, Norwich, Spelman Wed.–Thurs. 12th, 13th March 1879 first day, 4 gns.; *The Whitlingham Lime Pits* (in monochrome) lot 480 in C. C. R. Spelman sale, Norwich Tues.–Thurs. 17th–19th March 1914, bt. Walker, 48s., possibly the drawing in the Sir Hickman Bacon Collection, grey wash, $10\frac{3}{4}$ × $15\frac{1}{4}$ ins., 513. See also the entry for No. 38.

115 Dilham Staithe Pl. 57

Pencil and watercolour with slight scraping out on cream wove paper; 36·5 × 49·9 ($14\frac{3}{8}$ × $19\frac{5}{8}$).

INSCR: Backing board of gilt frame inscribed and signed in black ink *Dilham Staithe*/. *Thirtle*.

COND: ? Treated with Chloramine T, 1949; cleaned and laid by D. Lewisohn, Feb. 1977. Mounted Imperial.—Repair u.r. (above rainbow).

PROV: Miss Parr by 1886[1]; W. Miles Parr by 1889[1]; by descent to Mrs. Elizabeth Parr; bt. from her with two others by the EAAS, £80, 14th July 1894[2]; presented by the EAAS 1895 as an addition to the rest of its collection presented the previous year.

EXH: ? Norwich Society of Artists 1830 (18*) *Dilham Staithe*[3]; Norwich, Art Circle 1886 (48) lent by Miss Parr; Great Yarmouth 1889 (81) lent by W. Miles Parr; Norwich, Thirtle Centenary 1939 (6).

REF: ? *Norwich Mercury* 7th Aug. 1830; Norwich Art Circle, *Third Exhibition Catalogue, John Thirtle*, 1886 illus. in litho. by J. Miller Smith (1854–1937) p. 4[4]; *Norwich Mercury* 7th July 1886 'The John Thirtle Exhibition'; Dickes p. 238; *EDP* 25th April 1921 'New light on Crome—some Ladbrooke memories'; Barnard, *The Studio*, Aug. 1947 p. 31.

According to Henry Ladbrooke, Thirtle sketched at Dilham when staying with Ladbrooke at Swafield (see REF). Dilham is a small village on the River Ant in northeast Norfolk four miles south-east of North Walsham. The river was only navigable as far as Dilham until a canal to North Walsham was opened in 1826. Thirtle's drawing shows a limekiln, granary and watermill on the canal, probably at Dilham lock[5]. Unfortunately the rainbow and sunset effect has suffered with the loss of blue, see No. 77. This drawing is probably that exhibited with the Norwich Society in 1830, a date which is acceptable on stylistic grounds. It is also the largest and most finished of the recorded versions of this composition. A brown wash sketch in the collection, No. 116, also has a rainbow, although in this case a double one, but is closer in other respects to a watercolour, $7\frac{3}{8} \times 12\frac{1}{2}$ ins., in Newport Museum and Art Gallery[6]. In both these drawings the composition ends on the right with the buildings, there is a horse on the far left and no figure in the left foreground. There are two other drawings of Dilham Staithe, but viewed from the canal, in the collection (Nos. 117 and 118)[7].

1. See EXH.

2. See No. 114, note 2.

3. Pictures marked with an asterisk in the catalogue were for sale.

4. Compiler's pagination.

5. See Martin H. Press 'The North Walsham and Dilham Canal', *The Edgar Allen News* vol. 32 No. 368, Feb. 1953, sketch map 2.

6. $7\frac{1}{2} \times 12\frac{1}{2}$ ins., exh. Norwich 1927 (268) lent by Miss E. M. and E. C. Colman; bequeathed in 1949 by them to the NACF, who presented it to Newport. This drawing is possibly that lent by Mrs. Thirtle to the Norwich Fine Art Association exhibition 1860 (301); ? her sale, Norwich, Spelman Tues. 9th May 1882 lot 54 bt. C. C. R. Spelman £ 5.15.6d.; ? exh. Norwich, Art Circle 1886 (14) $7\frac{3}{8} \times 12\frac{1}{2}$ ins., lent by C. C. R. Spelman.

7. There is one other Dilham Staithe drawing by Thirtle recorded. It was lent by Mrs. Kye to the British Medical Association Norwich, St. Andrew's Hall, *Loan Collection of the works of Norfolk and Suffolk Artists* 1874 (108).

116 Dilham Staithe   Pl. 57

Black chalk, brown and blue wash and some white body colour on greenish-grey wove paper $20 \cdot 2 \times 29 \cdot 5$ ($7\frac{15}{16} \times 11\frac{5}{8}$).

COND: Cleaned by Kennedy North, March 1940. Removed from Bulwer cabinet, March 1976. Mounted Royal.—Paper stained along edges.

PROV: Mrs. Thirtle sale, Norwich, Spelman Tues. 9th May

1882[1]; bt. for J. J. Colman[2]; his bequest to R. J. Colman 1898; R. J. Colman Bequest 1946, registered 1951.

EXH: Norwich, Art Circle 1886 (42), lent by J. J. Colman; Norwich Thirtle Centenary 1939 (4) lent by R. J. Colman.

REF: *Norwich Mercury* 7th July 1886 'The John Thirtle Exhibition'; Dickes p. 238.

This drawing was dated to 1830 by Percy Moore Turner[3], presumably because of its relationship with the finished drawing No. 115. It is perhaps wiser to suggest a wider date range of c. 1827–30. The use of black chalk, which marries well with the monochrome washes in this drawing, is only occasionally found in Thirtle's work, although he prefers it to pencil in Nos. 103, 106, 118, also in a small drawing in the Witt collection[4] and in another of *Duke's Palace Bridge* in a private collection[5]. The handling of the museum's drawing is close to that of a sketch, also on tinted paper, by De Wint, in the Fitzwilliam Museum, Cambridge[6].

1. The only *Dilham Staithe* title specified was lot 54 which is discussed in the previous entry, note 6. Lot 17 *Four watercolour sketches in sepia* bt. Jackson 4s. may have included the wash drawing discussed here.

2. CC records.

3. CC records; typescript of works in the Colman collection with dates ascribed to them by Percy Moore Turner.

4. *Two sailing barges*, black chalk and watercolour on grey paper, $5\frac{5}{16} \times 6\frac{15}{16}$ ins., Witt collection 4195. See No. 92 note 4.

5. See No. 92 note 4.

6. *The Sawpit*, black chalk and brown wash with some white body colour on blue paper, $8\frac{5}{16} \times 12\frac{3}{8}$ ins., 1468. This is a sketch for the watercolour, 15×23 ins., V&A, 1934–1900.

117 Dilham Staithe from the River   Pl. 58

Pencil, watercolour and some white bodycolour on cream wove paper; $18 \cdot 1 \times 29$ ($7\frac{1}{8} \times 11\frac{7}{16}$).

INSCR: Inscribed in pencil c.l. edge *Green*.

COND: Cleaned by Kennedy North, April 1940. Removed from Bulwer cabinet, March 1976. Mounted Royal.— Paper creased l. Foxing. *Verso*, gum along edges.— Colour faded.

PROV: See No. 116.

EXH: Norwich, Art Circle 1886 (37) lent by J. J. Colman; Tate 1922 (240) lent by R. J. Colman.

REF: *Norwich Mercury* 7th July 1886 'The John Thirtle Exhibition'; Dickes p. 238.

A view of the watermill, granary and limekiln from the water. The loose fluid handling is close to that of the drawing in Newport Museum and Art Gallery, discussed in the entry for No. 115. The colour in the museum's drawing has faded, especially in the sky, as it is clearly shown by the band of original colour on the right.

118 Dilham Staithe, from the River   Pl. 58

Black chalk, watercolour and some white bodycolour on blue paper; $23 \cdot 8 \times 30 \cdot 5$ ($9\frac{1}{2} \times 12$).

INSCR: Inscribed in pencil l.c.r. *Reeds*.

COND: Laid. Mounted Royal.—Colour faded.

PROV: See No. 116[1].

EXH: Norwich, Art Circle 1886 (45) lent by J. J. Colman.

REF: *Norwich Mercury* 7th July 1886 'The John Thirtle Exhibition'; Dickes p. 239.

This drawing is stylistically close to No. 116 and seems to be of the same period c. 1827–1830.

1. There are three Dilham Staithe subjects listed in the Colman collection records: Nos. 116, 117 and another, similar in size to this one, *Dilham Staithe/Sketch on tinted paper;* $8\frac{5}{8} \times 11\frac{1}{2}$ *ins.* (CC MS vol. 2 p. 320 no. 127). This last drawing has been recorded as missing, or according to a note in the catalogue *op. cit.* as possibly sent to Christie's during the 1914–1918 War; however it seems more likely that it is identical with *Watermill,* watercolour, $8\frac{1}{2} \times 11\frac{1}{2}$ ins. (sight measurement when covered by the mount, CC MS vol. 2 p. 320 no. 130), renamed and recatalogued as such by a compiler who did not recognise it as a view of Dilham Staithe.

119 An East View of Norwich   Pl. 59

Pencil, pen and brown ink and watercolour on cream wove paper squared; $20 \cdot 6 \times 37$ ($8\frac{1}{8} \times 14\frac{9}{16}$) subject, $21 \cdot 3 \times 38 \cdot 3$ ($8\frac{3}{8} \times 15\frac{1}{16}$) paper.

COND: ? Treated with Chloramine T, 1948. Cleaned and laid by D. Lewisohn, Feb. 1977. Mounted Royal.

PROV: W. Miles Parr by 1886[1]; by descent to Mrs. Elizabeth Parr; bt. from her with two others, by the EAAS, £80, 14th July 1894[2]; presented by the EAAS 1895 as an addition to the rest of its collection presented the previous year.

EXH: Norwich, Art Circle 1886 (38) lent by W. M. Parr; Norwich, University of East Anglia 1964 (5).

REF: Dickes p. 239.

This is a preliminary drawing for a larger watercolour, $15\frac{1}{2} \times 28\frac{1}{2}$ ins., signed and dated 1830[3], which is probably that exhibited by Thirtle at the Norwich Society Exhibition in 1830 (48*)[4] *An East View of Norwich* and reviewed by the *Norwich Mercury* 7th August 1830 'Mr. J. Thirtle's watercolour drawings of Cromer, Dilham Staithe, and East View of Norwich display that regard to the beauties of nature, combined with the elegance which has ever been his characteristic.'

This watercolour is of particular interest as the only known example by Thirtle of a drawing squared-up for a larger composition. The sketch is fluid and summary, it has all the main elements of the larger work, but the curious block like forms are less pronounced and the colour less richly and densely worked than in the finished drawing[5].

See the entry for No. 54 for details of other recorded panoramic views of Norwich by Thirtle.

1. See EXH.

2. See No. 114 note 2.

3. Norwich, Thirtle Centenary 1939 (48) lent by Sir Henry Holmes; by descent to the present owner, Mrs. G. E. Bracecamp.

4. Pictures marked with an asterisk in the catalogue were for sale.

5. There are four other drawings of the same composition recorded: (a) watercolour, $19\frac{1}{4} \times 38\frac{1}{4}$ ins., lent by Mr. John Cator to the Norwich School exhibition 1927 (266), photo in NCM annotated catalogue; (b) watercolour, 16×29 ins., signed and dated 1829, in the collection of Mrs. Clarke of Wymondham in 1886, mentioned in the entry for No. 39. in the Norwich Art Circle exhibition catalogue of that year;

(c) watercolour on tinted paper joined at the centre, 12×32 ins. an earlier study for (b) above—lent by C. J. Watson to the Norwich Art Circle exhibition 1886 (39), now in the National Gallery of Canada, Ottawa, 6566; (d) watercolour, $8\frac{1}{4} \times 12\frac{7}{8}$ ins., lent by H. G. Barwell to the Norwich Art Circle exhibition 1886 (15), now untraced.

120 Sunset Landscape with Thorpe Hospital, Norwich Pl. 56

Pencil, watercolour and white bodycolour on greyish green wove paper with watermark parallel with l. left edge $S \& A/1828$[1]; $26 \cdot 8 \times 41 \cdot 8$ ($10\frac{9}{16} \times 16\frac{7}{16}$).

COND: Cleaned by Kennedy North, Nov. 1939. Removed from Bulwer cabinet, Dec. 1969.—Inlaid. Mounted Royal. Tear l. corner.

PROV: See No. 39.

EXH: Colnaghi 1970 (111) repro. pl. XXVII; Harlow 1976 (19).

REF: Clifford repro. pl. 23a wrongly captioned as Major-General James Pattison Cockburn (1779–1847) and incorrectly called *Cavalry Barracks, Norwich.*

The intensity of colour and assured handling of this drawing make it one of the most impressive of Thirtle's late drawings. The use of a dark coloured paper and the unusually heavy application of white bodycolour in the sky, contribute to the rich luminosity of the sunset effect.

The 'County Lunatic Asylum, Thorpe'[2] shown in the middle distance was begun in 1811 and completed in 1814 to the designs of the Norwich architect Francis Stone (1775–1835). Stone exhibited an *Elevation* of the Asylum with the Norwich Society in 1811 (143) and a *Perspective View* in 1812 (152). The building is still in use as St. Andrew's Hospital, Thorpe.

1. See No. 103 note 1.

2. Engraved by T. Barber after J. B. Ladbrooke, published 1825, copy in Bol. coll. NCM.

121 Near Norwich, Trees and Figures on the right Pl. 56

Pencil and watercolour on cream wove paper with watermark lower edge *SMITH & ALNUTT*[1]; $21 \cdot 2 \times 31 \cdot 5$ ($8\frac{5}{16} \times 12\frac{3}{8}$).

Verso, Three Cows in a Hilly Landscape.
Pencil and watercolour.

COND: Cleaned by D. Lewisohn, Sept. 1966. Double Mounted Royal.—*Verso,* staining, paper surface grazed, especially along edges.

PROV: Mrs. Thirtle sale, Norwich, Spelman, Tues. 9th May 1882 ?lot 18 *Three water colour sketches–Norwich* bt. Thompson £1.10.0 ?for J. J. Colman[2]; his bequest to R. J. Colman 1898; R. J. Colman Bequest 1946, registered 1951.

A pleasing late watercolour study, close in the handling of the sky and foliage to *Sunset Landscape,* No. 120. The large forms on the verso are similar in treatment to another abandoned drawing on the *verso* of No. 79.

1. See No. 103 note 1.

2. CC records.

122 Tombland, Norwich **Pl. 59**

Pencil and watercolour with some white bodycolour on cream wove paper with watermark l.c.r. *J WHATMAN/1830*; 35·8 × 55 (1 4$\frac{1}{8}$ × 21$\frac{5}{8}$).

COND: Laid. Mounted Imperial.—Colour faded.

PROV: ? Thomas Lound[1]; the Misses Thirkettle by 1927[1]; presented by Miss F. C. Thirkettle 1945.

EXH: Norwich, Norwich School 1927 (282) lent by the Misses Thirkettle; Norwich, Thirtle Centenary 1939 (35) lent by Miss F. C. Thirkettle; Kidderminster 1954 (39); Worthing 1957 (32); Derby and Nottingham 1959 (61); Manchester, Whitworth 1961 (42); USA 1967 (23); Kenwood 1969 (69); The Hague 1977 (55) repro. pl. 24.

REF: *EEN* 28th July 1939 'Thirtle Paintings'; Barnard *The Studio* Aug. 1947 p. 31; Clifford 1965 repro. pl. 19a; Clifford *OWCS* 1966, repro. pl. xx; Day III repro. p. 101; Mallalieu repro. p. 47 pl. 35.

A narrow band of the original blue tones of this drawing remains around the edge. The colour laid over fine pencil work has changed considerably.

Thirtle did not exhibit the subject but he painted it at least twice as another version was lent by Dean Cranage to the Thirtle Centenary 1939 (16)[2]. This smaller version is a narrower view of Tombland, it does not include the porch on the extreme left nor the tower of St. George's Tombland on the right. The museum's drawing, or more likely[3], the Cranage version may have been that included in Mrs. Thirtle's sale in 1882[4].

The watermark of 1830 in the paper of the museum's drawing suggests a slightly later date for the drawing itself. As there are no works dated later than 1830 recorded, the two Tombland drawings seem to be the latest watercolours with a verifiable date in the artist's oeuvre yet traced.

The odd name *Tombland* 'has nothing to do with tombs'[5]; it is probably derived from the Danish word *Toom* meaning empty place. Tombland adjoins the Cathedral precinct and is reached from there through the Erpingham Gate which is shown on the left in the museum's drawing.

The square became an annual fair ground and remained as such well into Thirtle's lifetime. 'The fair now kept on the south part of Tombland is a mart for wicker and tunnery wares, toyes, hardware and gingerbread. The last two fairs are entirely discontinued.'[6] Although fairs are seldom held there today, Tombland is still one of the most charming thoroughfares in Norwich. The curious obelisk shown in the centre right of the drawing was erected in 1786 'containing the aqueduct and a hydraulic machine forcing the water through the pipes to the highest parts of the City.'[7] The obelisk became redundant in the 1850's and is commemorated today by an obelisk-shaped drinking fountain donated in 1860 by John Henry Gurney[7]. The Regency house and porch on the extreme left of the drawing was the home of Emanuel Cooper, surgeon; it was demolished in 1871[7]. Set back on the right is the sixteenth century half timbered house of Augustine Steward, Mayor of Norwich. One of the finest buildings surviving in Norwich, today it is occupied, appropriately by the East Anglian Tourist Board. Adjoining it is the gabled Jacobean Samson and Hercules house. The gigantic stuccoed wooden statues of Samson and Hercules stand today, as

they originally did, either side of the door but in the early nineteenth century they were moved inside, 'the house having been altered, the figures are removed to the sides of the door within the court[8].'

1. Ellen Margaret and Florence Catherine Thirkettle were the granddaughters of Thomas Lound and the drawing probably descended to them from his collection. See EXH.

2. 11$\frac{3}{4}$ × 18$\frac{1}{8}$ ins., photo in NCM annotated catalogue.

3. See PROV.

4. Lot 58 *Tombland—Norwich* bt. Hansell £17.16.6. Probably the version lent by Sir Samuel Hoare to the Norwich exhibition 1894 (55) and sold at his sale, Cromer, Mealing Mills, Wed.–Fri. 25th–27th Sept. 1935, first day, lot 10 *Tombland* 11$\frac{1}{4}$ × 17$\frac{1}{2}$ ins., 9$\frac{1}{2}$ gns.

5. Pevsner p. 280.

6. P. Browne, *History of Norwich* 1814 p. 245.

7. P. Browne, *op. cit.* p. 75. I am grateful to Mr. H. W. Earl for these references.

8. P. Browne, *op. cit.* p. 243. The statues are shown, in this inner court, by Henry Ninham in a drawing in the museum's collection, 27.89.929.

123 Portrait of a Gentleman **Pl. 70**

Oval miniature.
Watercolour, bodycolour and gum on ivory; 8·5 × 6·7 (3$\frac{3}{8}$ × 2$\frac{5}{8}$).

INSCR: Signed with initials l.r. *J.T.*

COND: Restored by J. Murrell 1976. Framed 1977.— Vertical crack u.c.l. to l.c.l. and transverse cracks u.l.

PROV: W. Henry Parr by 1927[1]; bt. from him out of the Walker Bequest Fund, £5, 1932.

EXH: Norwich, Norwich School 1927 (275) as one of *Two Miniature Portraits*[2] lent by H. W. (sic) Parr; Norwich, Thirtle Centenary 1939 (101).

REF: *EDP* 20th July 1939 'Thirtle Centenary Exhibition/Mr. Laurence Binyon on the Norwich School', repro.

This miniature entered the collection as a self portrait but the only basis for this assumption is a statement from the vendor W. Henry Parr in a letter[3] of 16th March 1932 to the curator, Frank Leney: 'I have also a miniature painted by himself (his only portrait I have ever seen of himself).' However, the miniature was not called a self-portrait in the catalogue of the 1927 Exhibition. Kitson was also doubtful in a letter[3] of 21st May 1932 to Leney. He dated it to c. 1806 which is reasonable as most of Thirtle's exhibited and recorded portraits are early and the one other recorded signed miniature is dated 1807[4].

1. See EXH.

2. Photograph in NCM annotated catalogue.

3. Art Dept. archives.

4. *Portrait of an unknown man*, watercolour on ivory, oval 2$\frac{5}{8}$ × 2$\frac{1}{4}$ ins., signed and dated l.r. *J. Thirtle 1807*, verso inscribed on card *Painted by / J. Thirtle Norwich / March 28 1807*, V & A, P28–1949.

124 William Cowper 1731–1800 **Pl. 70**

Pencil on cream wove paper; 28·3 × 24 (11$\frac{1}{8}$ × 9$\frac{7}{16}$).

INSCR: Inscribed in pencil l.l. by an unknown hand *Drawn by John Thirtle* and in pencil l.r. by another hand *Cowper*.

COND: Mounted Royal.—Paper discoloured. Corners cut. *Verso*, gum at corners.

PROV: Presented by Dawson Turner, with a collection of twenty-nine portraits, mostly engravings, of Norfolk interest, 1830.

The drawing is a copy of the stipple-engraved portrait by Blake after Lawrence published by J. Johnson in 1802 as a frontispiece to William Hayley's *Life of Cowper*, Vol. II 1803[1]. Cowper and Lawrence were close friends: a letter from Cowper dated 18th October 1793 is published in the *Life of Lawrence* by D. E. Williams, London 1831, Vol. I, pp. 162–163. Cowper spent his declining years in Norfolk from 1795 under the care of Mrs. Unwin; he died in East Dereham where his monument by Flaxman is in St. Edmund's Chapel of St. Nicholas Church. A drawing of this monument, by Francis Stone (c. 1769–1835) the Norwich architect, was exhibited with the Norwich Society of Artists in 1805 (208) and it was engraved by Blake.

The attribution to Thirtle must be regarded with caution because the firm, almost sharp lines of the drawing are uncharacteristic of Thirtle's portraits in watercolour. However, while no other purely pencil portraits by Thirtle are recorded, the handling can be compared to the pencil drawing of a landscape inscribed *Thorpe*, No. 76. Moreover even if the inscription is not autograph, it may have been added by Dawson Turner, or someone of his circle, in which case it is contemporary and therefore lends weight to the attribution to Thirtle. The hatching and accents are reminiscent of Cotman's pencil portraits.

1. There is an amateur drawing, probably after the engraving, in the collection, pencil $10\frac{1}{2} \times 7\frac{3}{16}$ ins., signed and dated l.l. *Maria Heath delin! 1804* and inscribed W*m Cowper Esq!*, Bol. coll. no no.

125 Portrait of a Gentleman   Pl. 71

Pencil and watercolour on cream wove paper; $10 \cdot 9 \times 10 \cdot 9$ ($4\frac{5}{16} \times 4\frac{5}{16}$).

COND: Cleaned by D. Lewisohn 1976. Framed.—Paper surface grazed at corners. Corners repaired u. & l.r.

PROV: Percy Moore Turner by 1927[1]; A. T. Chittock sale, Norwich J. R. E. Draper Wed. 3rd Feb. 1954 lot 381 as Portrait of John Crome (circular) bt. for the Museum out of the Beecheno and Fitch Bequest Funds £3.15.0.

EXH: Norwich, Norwich School 1927 (286) lent by Percy Moore Turner.

This drawing entered the collection as a portrait of John Crome but the resemblance to authentic portraits is too slight to justify this identification. When it was shown at the Norwich School 1927 exhibition the sitter was not identified. The drawing is not typical of Thirtle's miniatures or small finished portrait drawings, but the washes compare with the slight sketch for No. 126 indicating that the attribution should not be rejected too readily.

1. See EXH. Photo in NCM annotated catalogue.

126, 127, 128, 132 and 133

The following group of five portraits of members of the Miles family entered the collection from a grandson of Catherine Miles. It seems therefore reasonable to accept the traditionally stated identities of the sitters. On comparison with recorded portraits dated 1805 and judging from the age of the sitters, the four portraits seem later, post 1810 at least. The 1805 portraits that they should be compared with are: (a) *Portrait of a girl*, pencil and watercolour, $7\frac{5}{16} \times 6\frac{3}{16}$ ins. (sight measurement), signed and dated l.r. *Thirtle Pin^{xt} / 1805*, in the collection of E. D. Levine; (b) called *Portrait of Lady Willoughby of Middleton*, watercolour, $10\frac{3}{4} \times 7\frac{1}{2}$ ins., signed and dated l.l. *THIRTLE 1805*, in the collection of the Huntington Museum and Art Gallery, San Marino, California, U.S.A., exh. Norwich, Thirtle Centenary 1939 (95) as *Portrait of [?] Ann Miles, wife of John Sell Cotman* lent by Messrs. W. Boswell & Son. Photo in NCM annotated catalogue.

126 Portrait of Miss Miles   Pl. 71

Pencil and watercolour on cream wove paper with indistinct watermark right edge (paper cut); $12 \cdot 1 \times 10$ ($4\frac{3}{4} \times 3\frac{15}{16}$).

COND: Cleaned and laid by D. Lewisohn, Sept. 1976[1]. Framed.—Colour faded.

PROV: W. Henry Parr; bt. from him out of the Walker Bequest Fund, £3, 1932.

EXH: Norwich, Thirtle Centenary 1939 (98).

Edmund and Mary Miles had at least six daughters born between c. 1787 and 1801. As the sitter in this drawing, which is probably from the 1810–20 period, must be in her twenties, she is either Mary who married in 1808, or Ann, who married Cotman in 1809 or Elizabeth who married Thirtle in 1812. The large eyes, hairstyle and somewhat prominent nose are rather close to two portraits of Ann Miles by John Sell Cotman[2].

The sketch found during conservation, No. 127, sheds light on Thirtle's method of working up a portrait study. The pencil drawing is lightly touched in and the main planes of the face are laid on with pale washes.

1. A sketch in pencil and watercolour was found on a second layer of paper during conservation, No. 127.

2. (a) Leeds Art Gallery 9.694/49, (b) in the collection of A. M. Cotman repro. Kitson 1937 opp. p. 171.

127 Portrait of Miss Miles   Pl. 71

Pencil and watercolour on cream wove paper; $12 \cdot 3 \times 10 \cdot 2$ ($4\frac{13}{16} \times 4$).

COND: Cleaned and laid by D. Lewisohn, Sept. 1976. Unmounted.

PROV: See No. 126.

A sketch found during conservation, on a second layer of the paper of No. 126; it is discussed in that entry.

128 Portrait of the Artist's Mother-in-law, Mrs. Edmund Miles   Pl. 71

Pencil and brown wash on cream wove paper; $9 \cdot 3 \times 7 \cdot 4$ ($3\frac{11}{16} \times 2\frac{15}{16}$).

COND: Cleaned and laid by D. Lewisohn, Sept. 1976. Framed.

PROV: W. Henry Parr by 1927[1]; bt. from him out of the Walker Bequest Fund, £3, 1932.

EXH: Norwich, Norwich School 1927 (275) as one of

Two Miniature Portraits[2] lent by H. W. (sic) Parr; Norwich, Thirtle Centenary 1939 (99).

A portrait of Mary Hancock, wife of Edmund Miles one of whose daughters, Ann, married John Sell Cotman in 1809 and another, Elizabeth, married Thirtle in 1812. Assuming that Mary Miles was a young woman when she started having children in c. 1787 the portrait can hardly be earlier than 1810. The pencil work with its sharp dark accents is characteristic of Thirtle's hand (see Nos. 130 and 131) and the watercolour modelling of the face compares well with the sketch, No. 127, and with the portrait No. 125.

1. See EXH.

2. Photograph in NCM annotated catalogue.

129 Portrait of a small Boy   Pl. 73

Pencil, watercolour and some white bodycolour on cream wove paper tinted with brown wash; 12·4 × 9·5 (4$\frac{7}{8}$ × 3$\frac{3}{4}$).
Verso, part of a squared-up watercolour by an unknown hand, of a female figure with fruit in her lap.
Pencil, watercolour and bodycolour.

COND: Cleaned by Kennedy North, March 1940. Removed from Bulwer Cabinet, May 1972. Mounted Royal.

PROV: C. C. R. Spelman sale, Norwich, Tues.–Thurs. 17th–19th March 1914 lot 549 as *Portrait of Cotman when a boy* bt. Mase ?for R. J. Colman £5[1]; R. J. Colman Bequest 1946, registered 1951.

This charming portrait traditionally has been thought to be of John Sell Cotman (1782–1842) as a boy[2]. While the portrait is likely to be by Thirtle, the sensitive pencil work and facial treatment are similar to No. 133 in the collection, it seems most improbable that the sitter could be Cotman, only five years his junior: at the time when Cotman was five or six years old, the apparent age of the sitter, Thirtle was still a young boy of ten or eleven.

1. In the same sale was lot 548, also stated to be by Thirtle, *The three children of John Sell Cotman—Walter, Ann and Alfred,* bt. Mase ?for R. J. Colman (CC records) 17$\frac{1}{2}$ gns. and bequeathed by R. J. Colman to NCM 1946, registered 1951, 1352.235.951. The attribution to Thirtle is doubtful. The pencil work, the handling of the watercolour and treatment of the faces is uncharacteristic of portraits by him in the collection. The profuse use of pencil with fine diagonal hatching suggest a reattribution to the portrait artist Henry Edridge (1769–1821). However the CC records (CC MS vol. 2 p. 325 no. 137j) give a date of 1824 to the drawing: 'Ann was born July 13th 1812, she was 12 years of age, Francis Walter was born July 5th 1816, being 4 years younger, Alfred Henry born October 11th 1819 was 5 years old, when these portraits were taken.' The basis of the identification of the sitters and the definition of their age is not known.

2. The CC records (CC MS vol. 2 p. 325 no. 137i) suggest that Cotman must have been 'scarcely 8 or 9 years of age' and thus Thirtle '13 or 14 when he commenced it'. The portrait is surely of a younger child.

130 Self Portrait   Pl. 74

Pencil and watercolour on cream wove paper tinted with grey wash faded to pink; 24·6 × 19·8 (9$\frac{11}{16}$ × 7$\frac{3}{4}$).

INSCR: *Recto,* signed and dated in pencil with initials l.c.r. *IT 1816.*

COND: Cleaned by J. R. England Sept. 1932. Deframed and treated with Thymol vapour, Sept. 1960. Cleaned by J. Skillen, Dec. 1969. Mounted Royal with No. 131.—*Verso,* paper surface grazed l.l. edge. Repair lower c. and u.r. edge.

PROV: Miss Maria Woodrow by 1886[1]; her sale bt. L. O'Malley[2]; presented by him with No. 131 in memory of his mother 1932.

EXH: ?Norwich Society Secession 1816 (102); Norwich Art Circle 1886 (70) lent by Miss Woodrow; Norwich, Thirtle Centenary 1939 (96).

REF: Norwich Art Circle, *Third Exhibition Catalogue, John Thirtle,* 1886, illus. as frontispiece in litho. by C. J. Watson (1846–1927); Dickes p. 228.

The modelling of the face in this drawing and its pair, No. 131, is less defined than that of the Miles portraits, Nos. 126, 132, and is closer to No. 125, especially in the sharp accents of the eyes. If not the 1816 exhibit itself it is presumably a study for it. The Norwich, Boswell Centenary Exhibition 1939 also included a portrait which was stated to be Thirtle by himself[3]. A portrait of Thirtle attributed to Horace Beevor Love (1800–1838), similar in the dress and in the incline of the head to the museum's self portrait, was exhibited at the Norwich School Exhibition 1927 (219)[4].

1. See EXH.

2. The catalogue of this sale is untraced.

3. 'Portraits Principals of the Firm, 1800–1939, *John Thirtle 1777–1839, Water-Colour Drawing by Himself.*' Not numbered in the catalogue; repro. p. 2, now untraced.

4. Watercolour, 6$\frac{1}{4}$ × 5$\frac{1}{4}$ ins., lent by Charles R. Bignold, now untraced.

131 Portrait of the Artist's Wife, Elizabeth Miles Pl. 74

Pencil and watercolour on cream wove paper, tinted with grey wash faded to pink, with watermark parallel with left edge *J BUDGEN/1813*[1]; 24·9 × 20 (9$\frac{13}{16}$ × 7$\frac{7}{8}$).

INSCR: Signed and dated in pencil l.c.r. *Thirtle 1816.*

COND: Deframed and treated with Thymol vapour, Sept. 1960. Cleaned by J. Skillen, Dec. 1970. Mounted Royal with No. 130.—Repair l.c.r. edge; paper stained.

PROV: See No. 130.

EXH: ?Norwich Society Secession 1816[2]; Norwich Art Circle 1886 (71) lent by Miss Woodrow; Norwich, Thirtle Centenary 1939 (97).

REF: Dickes p. 229.

A pair to the *Self Portrait,* the subject of the previous entry. The portraits are obviously a pair, so it is reasonable to accept that the subject of this drawing is Thirtle's wife, Elizabeth Miles, who was born in 1787, and whom he married in 1812. Elizabeth was one of at least ten children, six daughters and four sons, born to Edmund and Mary Miles of Felbrigg, Norfolk. Her sister Ann, married Cotman in 1809 and another, Mary, married Samuel Kitton, a printer of Norwich, in 1808.

1. Churchill records (p. 48) *1818 Budgen, J.*

2. Apart from a self portrait Thirtle showed (110) *A Portrait* and (116) *Portrait.*

132 Portrait of Catherine Miles on Cromer Beach Pl. 72

Pencil, watercolour and white bodycolour with some scraping out on cream wove paper; 38·3 × 29·7 (15$\frac{1}{16}$ × 11$\frac{5}{8}$).

INSCR: Signed by wiping out l.l. *Thirtle P* [?inx^t].

COND: Cleaned by D. Lewisohn, Sept. 1976. Mounted Royal.—Laid on original backing mount with wash lines.—Colour faded.

PROV: W. Henry Parr by 1927 and still in 1932[1]; bt. from him by F. Base; bt. from him, with a half length version, out of the Southwell Bequest Fund, £25, 1937.

EXH: Norwich, Norwich School 1927 (276) as "*Portrait*", lent by H. W. (sic) Parr; Norwich, Thirtle Centenary 1939 (94).

REF: Kitson 1937 p. 129 (as dated 1813); *EDP* 30th Nov. 1937 'Additions to the Art Gallery'.

A portrait of Catherine Miles, born at Felbrigg in 1791 who later married into the Burrell Parr family. She was a witness at the wedding of her sister Elizabeth to Thirtle in 1812. A thin band of blue around the original tinted mount indicates that this drawing too has faded badly. The use of turquoise, of white body colour and the treatment of the distance compare with the sketch of *Putney Bridge* dated 1819 in the collection, No. 81. The age of the subject, who must be in her mid to late twenties, also supports this dating. Thirtle attempted at least four other full length portraits two of which were shown at the Norwich School exhibition in 1927[2].

1. See EXH. Parr offered it to the museum for £30 in 1932 (letters to the curator, Frank Leney, March and April 1932, in the Art Dept. archives).

2. Photos in NCM annotated catalogue: (a) (259) *Miniature Portrait of Charles Turner, Mayor of Norwich 1834, as a child, 12 × 9½ ins.*, lent by Mrs. Alston, untraced; (b) (260) *Portrait of Mr. Hay Gurney, 16¼ × 12 ins.*, lent by Mr. Charles Barnard, untraced; (c) see the introductory paragraph to this section, note 1 (2); (d) Isaac Jermy sale, Stanfield Hall, Tues.–Fri. 27th Feb.–2nd March 1849 3rd day lot 100 *A full length portrait of Nelson (a watercolour drawing by Thirtle)*, untraced.

133 Portrait of Catherine Miles Pl. 73

Pencil, watercolour, bodycolour with some gum on cream wove paper tinted with ?grey wash faded to pink; 12 × 9·9 (4$\frac{11}{16}$ × 3$\frac{15}{16}$).

COND: Cleaned and laid by D. Lewisohn, 1976.—Colour faded.

PROV: See No. 132.

A half length, slightly less finished version of No. 132. The sitter is discussed in that entry.

134 Church Porch with broken Cross in Foreground Pl. 61

Pencil on cream wove paper; 18·5 × 23·6 (7$\frac{5}{16}$ × 9$\frac{5}{16}$).

COND: Unmounted. Crease stain across corner u.l.

PROV: See No. 7.

A drawing possibly copied from Prout; there is for example a similar chapel also with a window of four lights, in Prout's *Easy Lessons in Landscape Drawing*, published by Ackermann c. 1819[1], pl. 33. The emptiness of this drawing is probably due to its being a copy; the handling of the pencil lines is not inconsistent with other drawings by Thirtle.

1. No date, but the plates are dated from Feb.–Nov. 1819.

135 A Barn with three Figures in front Pl. 61

Pencil on cream wove paper; 11·1 × 15·3 (4$\frac{3}{8}$ × 6). *Verso*, sketch in pencil of a woman on the left, with indication that it was cut down from a larger sheet.

COND: Mounted Royal with No. 136.—*Verso*, gum at corners.

PROV: See No. 7.

136 Building by Water with Boats and Figures Pl. 61

Pencil on cream wove paper; 20 × 27 (7$\frac{7}{8}$ × 10$\frac{5}{8}$) subject, 20·6 × 28 (8$\frac{1}{8}$ × 11) paper.

COND: Mounted Royal with No. 135.—Some foxing. *Verso*, gum at corners.

PROV: See No. 7.

A drawing possibly after Prout: there is for example a similar composition, *At Freshwater*, in Prout's *Studies of Boats and Coast Scenery*, published by Ackerman in 1816.

137 Gateway of St. Benet's Abbey, Norfolk Pl. 68

Pencil on white wove paper; 17·7 × 25·6 (6$\frac{15}{16}$ × 10$\frac{1}{16}$).

INSCR: Inscribed in pencil with ?colour note u.r.

COND: Cleaned and laid by D. Lewisohn, Feb. 1977. Mounted Royal with No. 138.—Crease stain across u.r. corner. Hole u.c.r. *Verso*, surface grazed u. and l.l. corners.

PROV: See No. 7.

This is an unusual view of the gateway and mill, because Thirtle, Cotman, Lound and others usually showed it from the south-east, which is its most picturesque aspect[1]. In rendering the gateway from the north-east, it relates to the only other Thirtle composition of this view recorded, a watercolour, lent by H. P. Gowen to the Norwich School Exhibition 1927 (269) and to the Thirtle Centenary 1939 (76) and now untraced[2].

1. See the entry for No. 23.

2. 7¼ × 12¼ ins., poor photographs in NCM annotated catalogues. Yet another drawing of the north-east view, once with the Walker Gallery, was wrongly attributed to Thirtle (photo Witt).

138 Manor House in a Park Pl. 68

Pencil on greyish white laid paper; 20 × 28·1 (7$\frac{7}{8}$ × 11$\frac{1}{16}$).

INSCR: *Recto*, inscribed in pencil with colour notes.

COND: Mounted Royal with No. 137.—*Verso*, gum at corners.

PROV: See No. 7.

This is one of the most sensitive sketches by the artist and can be grouped with others in the Fitch collection: Nos. 137, 139, 140. Unfortunately the house has not been identified.

139 St. Margaret's Church, Felthorpe Pl. 69

Pencil on buff laid paper; 20·4 × 25·9 ($8\frac{1}{16}$ × $10\frac{3}{16}$).

COND: Mounted Royal with No. 140.—*Verso*, gum at corners.

PROV: See No. 7.

Felthorpe is a small village seven miles north-west of Norwich. This drawing shows the north view of the church which had clerestory windows on the south side but it was almost rebuilt in 1846 and extensively restored again in 1878 when t he south aisle was added. The Rev. Henry Stebbing, submaster of Norwich Free Grammar School, was curate at Felthorpe in the 1820s, but whether there was any connection between him and Thirtle is not known.

140 Bishop Bridge, Norwich Pl. 69

Pencil on buff wove paper; 19·1 × 26·8 ($7\frac{9}{16}$ × $10\frac{9}{16}$).

INSCR: Inscribed in pencil with colour notes.

COND: Mounted Royal with No. 139.—*Verso*, gum at corners.

PROV: See No. 7.

A sketch of the south side of the bridge from the left bank of the River Wensum.

For notes on Bishop Bridge see the entry for No. 30. This drawing, with sure, almost Turnerish, pencil work, is one of the finest of Thirtle's sketches. It must be pre 1831 in date, for in the engraving of the subject after Stark of that year[1] the third house beyond the bridge has the addition of an upper floor with weather boarding, which is not apparent in Thirtle's sketch.

1. Stark's *Scenery of the Rivers of Norfolk* 1834 pl. 19.

141 Burlingham St. Peter's Church, Norfolk Pl. 67a

Pencil on white lined wove paper; 20·3 × 29·4 (8 × $11\frac{9}{16}$).

COND: Cleaned and laid by D. Lewisohn, Sept. 1976. Unmounted.—Crease stain across corner u.l.

PROV: See No. 7.

The subject was previously thought to be St. Benedict's church, Norwich, but comparison with a lithograph by J. B. Ladbrooke dated 1822[1] shows it to be a north-east view of Burlingham St. Peter. The fifteenth century church stood a quarter of a mile from the church of Burlingham St. Andrew in North Burlingham, a village situated nine and a half miles to the east of Norwich, near Blofield. Of flint with freestone dressings, the church had a chancel, nave, north and south porches. The tower fell in 1906 and today the whole church is in ruins. Burlingham Hall nearby was the seat of the Burroughes family. There is no record of Thirtle being connected with the Burroughes, but as a son of the family, M. S. Burkin Burroughes, died at Hoveton in 1823[2], Thirtle may have known them through his acquaintance with the Blofelds of Hoveton House[3].

1. Ladbrooke's *Norfolk Churches* 1843 vol. 1. Ladbrooke shows the church from the south-east.

2. T. Hugh Bryant, undated press cutting in Bol. coll. NCM library.

3. The Burroughes were connected with Hoveton House: 'James Burkin Burroughes married Christabelle, daughter and heiress of Henry Negus of Hoveton Hall. . . His second son Jeremiah was my Great Grandfather and died in 1803' (kindly communicated by Mr. T. R. C. Blofeld March 1977).

142 A Country House with a female Figure in front Pl. 67a

Pencil on white wove paper; 17·2 × 26·5 ($6\frac{3}{4}$ × $10\frac{7}{16}$).

COND: Cleaned and laid by D. Lewisohn, Feb. 1977. Unmounted.

PROV: See No. 7.

Although the buildings in this drawing have distinctive features they have not been identified.

143 Two Figures by a ? Pump Pl. 67b

Pencil on greyish wove paper; 16 × 18 ($6\frac{5}{16}$ × $7\frac{1}{16}$).

COND: Cleaned, laid and inlaid by D. Lewisohn, Feb. 1977. Unmounted.

PROV: See No. 7.

144 Two Figures and Trees with Pedimented Building Pl. 67b

Pencil on white wove paper; 17·4 × 17·5 ($6\frac{7}{8}$ × $6\frac{7}{8}$). *Verso*, horizontal rough pencil markings.

INSCR: *Verso*, inscribed in pencil with colour notes.

COND: Cleaned and inlaid by D. Lewisohn, Feb. 1977. Unmounted.—Hole u.r.

PROV: See No. 7.

This is an unusual drawing; the colour notes on the *verso* seem to be in Thirtle's hand but the lacy outline of the foliage is not characteristic of others of his drawings in the collection, neither is the paper found elsewhere among the Fitch drawings. The attribution to Thirtle should be regarded with caution.

145 Scene at Gillingham, Norfolk Pl. 62

Pencil on white wove paper; 10·7 × 16·2 ($4\frac{1}{4}$ × $6\frac{3}{8}$).

COND: Cleaned and laid by D. Lewisohn, Feb. 1977.

PROV: See No. 7.

The ruined tower of All Saints church on the left, St. Mary's on the right. The Hall, just outside the drawing on the left, was the seat of Francis Schutz's widow, the daughter of Sir Edmund Bacon, in Thirtle's time. She entertained John and Cornelius Varley in 1801 and probably knew John Sell Cotman who drew both St. Mary's church and the Hall for the *Excursions through Norfolk* 1818.

With its overall hatching this drawing is rather uncharacteristic of Thirtle's hand. However it does compare with the drawing of No. 142, and the soft hatching of the sky is typical of the summary sketches of skies and landscapes on the *verso* of drawings in the Fitch collection.

146 Studies of Figures **Pl. 63**

Pencil on white lined wove paper with watermark centre right, parallel with right edge [WH]*ATMAN*/[18]*10*; 12 × 18·4 ($4\frac{3}{4}$ × $7\frac{1}{4}$).

INSCR: Inscribed in pencil with colour notes.

COND: Cleaned and laid by D. Lewisohn, Feb. 1977. Unmounted.

PROV: See No. 7.

147 Woman with a Jug beside and a Seated Man **Pl. 64**

Pencil on white wove paper; 8·5 × 12·5 ($3\frac{3}{8}$ × $4\frac{15}{16}$). *Verso,* sketch in pencil of a woman, half length, wearing a bonnet, with indication that it was cut down from a larger sheet.

COND: Cleaned by D. Lewisohn, Feb. 1977. Unmounted.

PROV: See No. 7.

148 A Group of Five Sailors **Pl. 63**

Pencil on white wove paper; 6·5 × 10·5 ($2\frac{1}{2}$ × $4\frac{1}{8}$).

COND: Cleaned and laid by D. Lewisohn, Feb. 1977. Unmounted.

PROV: See No. 7.

The following sixteen sketches are all studies of figures and boats

Pencil on small pieces of white wove paper, hand cut in varying sizes from larger sheets.

COND: They were all cleaned and inlaid by D. Lewisohn, Feb. 1977. Surface is grazed on *verso* of Nos. 149, 152, 158, 160, 161, 164 and the paper creased in Nos. 162 and 163. They are placed in one Royal mount.

PROV: See No. 7.

149 Leaning Figure **149–157 Pl. 66**

3·2 × 5 ($1\frac{1}{4}$ × 2)

150 Half length Figure

3 × 4·4 ($1\frac{3}{16}$ × $1\frac{3}{4}$)
Verso, slight sketch in pencil and brown wash which seems to be part of the landscape sketch on the *verso* of No. 164.

151 Half length Figure

3 × 4·5 ($1\frac{3}{16}$ × $1\frac{3}{4}$)

152 Two Figures by a Mast

4·6 × 3·3 ($1\frac{13}{16}$ × $1\frac{5}{16}$)

153 Boat crowded with Musicians

4·3 × 8·4 ($1\frac{1}{16}$ × $3\frac{5}{16}$)

154 Seated Sailor

4 × 3·1 ($1\frac{9}{16}$ × $1\frac{1}{4}$)

155 Bonneted Ladies in a Boat

4·8 × 7·2 ($1\frac{7}{8}$ × $2\frac{13}{16}$)

156 Three Figures in a Boat, one punting

5·3 × 6·3 ($2\frac{1}{8}$ × $2\frac{1}{2}$)

157 Two Figures in a Boat, one seated the other standing

5·3 × 6 ($2\frac{1}{16}$ × $2\frac{3}{8}$)

158 Three Figures in a Boat, two seated one standing **158–164 Pl. 65**

4·3 × 5·7 ($1\frac{11}{16}$ × $2\frac{1}{4}$)

159 Two Sailors and a Child standing beside a winch

4·7 × 5·1 ($1\frac{13}{16}$ × 2)

160 Figure in a Rowing Boat on the beach, beside a winch

4·5 × 6 ($1\frac{13}{16}$ × $2\frac{3}{8}$)

161 Two Figures

4·8 × 5·4 ($1\frac{7}{8}$ × $2\frac{1}{8}$)

162 Two Fishermen hauling Nets

4·7 × 6·5 ($1\frac{7}{8}$ × $2\frac{9}{16}$)
Verso, slight sketch in pencil and brown wash which seems to be part of the landscape sketch on the *verso* of No. 164.

163 Three Figures in a Sailing Boat

6·4 × 9 ($2\frac{1}{2}$ × $3\frac{9}{16}$)

164 Three Fishermen hauling Nets

5·4 × 6·9 ($2\frac{1}{8}$ × $2\frac{11}{16}$)
Verso, sketch in pencil and brown wash, of clouds or a landscape, other parts of which appear on the *verso* of Nos. 150 & 162.

At least two of these small sketches seem to be studies of a water frolic (Nos. 153, 155), see the entry for No. 96. Some of them, especially Nos. 149, 150, 151, 158, 159, 160, 162, are remarkably Cotmanesque.

165 Studies of a Horse and four Figures **Pl. 61**

Pencil on white wove paper; 11·2 × 19·1 ($4\frac{7}{16}$ × $7\frac{1}{2}$). *Verso,* sketches in pencil of a horse and several of figures.

INSCR: *Recto*, inscribed in pencil with colour note u.c.r. *HorseCloth Red*.

COND: Cleaned by D. Lewisohn, Feb. 1977. Unmounted.

PROV: See No. 7.

166 Studies of Coaches   Pl. 64

Pencil on white wove paper; $7\cdot3 \times 13\cdot5$ ($2\frac{7}{8} \times 5\frac{5}{16}$). *Verso*, sketches in pencil of six male figures, with indication that it was cut down from a larger sheet.

COND: Cleaned and inlaid by D. Lewisohn, Feb. 1977. Unmounted.—Vertical crease stain c.r.

PROV: See No. 7.

167 Beach Scene with Pole and Figures   Pl. 62

Pencil on cream wove paper with watermark left, parallel with left edge *J WHA*[TMAN] / *18. .* ; $11\cdot8 \times 18\cdot2$ ($4\frac{11}{16} \times 7\frac{3}{16}$).

INSCR: Inscribed in pencil with colour notes along lower and r. edge.

COND: Mounted Royal with Nos. 168 and 169.—*Verso*, gum at corners.

PROV: See No. 7.

168 Boats and Figures on a Beach   Pl. 62

Pencil on cream wove paper with watermark centre right, parallel with right edge *WHA*[TMAN] / [18]*13*; $12 \times 16\cdot8$ ($4\frac{3}{4} \times 6\frac{5}{8}$). *Verso*, slight sketch in pencil of a beach scene.

INSCR: *Recto* and *verso*, inscribed in pencil with colour notes.

COND: Mounted Royal with Nos. 167, 169.—*Verso*, gum at corners.

PROV: See No. 7.

169 Quayside, Norwich   Pl. 62

Pencil on cream wove paper; $12\cdot5 \times 19\cdot2$ ($4\frac{15}{16} \times 7\frac{9}{16}$).

INSCR: Inscribed in pencil with colour notes.

COND: Mounted Royal with Nos. 167, 168.

PROV: See No. 7.

A view of Quayside, Norwich, from Fye Bridge, looking down river towards Whitefriars Bridge:

'There is a strong brick wall along the side of the river, extending the whole length of Fye-bridge quay, at the end of which is Fye-bridge staithe. This was formerly a great fish market and there were likewise several butchers' stalls as well as fish stalls, all of which were taken down in 1662.'[1]

Little or nothing remains today of the buildings standing in Thirtle's day. The range of early gabled buildings on the right were re-developed in the nineteenth century. The fifteenth century building on the extreme right, the New Star Inn, was demolished, amid heated controversy, in 1963.

Three watercolour versions of this subject attributed to Thirtle are on record: (a) pencil and watercolour, $12\frac{3}{4} \times 18\frac{7}{8}$ ins., V & A, 23–1874[2]. According to the V & A catalogue this drawing is said to have been finished by Henry Ninham. This may account for the uncharacteristic handling of the foreground and figures. In other respects the attribution to Thirtle is upheld by the fine pencil work and the handling of the washes. (b) pencil, brown wash and some white bodycolour, $6\frac{11}{16} \times 10\frac{7}{16}$ ins. (sight measurement), in the collection of H. Bolingbroke 1972[3]. (c) pencil, watercolour with some white bodycolour, $9\frac{3}{16} \times 12\frac{7}{8}$ ins., NCM[4]. According to the Colman catalogue, this last drawing has a good provenance: 'it was given to Mr. Root, the Artist's gilder shortly after his decease by Mrs. Thirtle, as a memento of his master. It was subsequently sold by Root and bought by Mr. Colman'. However the drawing is so lacking in clarity and in skill with the medium that it cannot be accepted as by Thirtle in spite of the underlying pencil work which is not uncharacteristic. The painting is probably the work of a Thirtle pupil.

All three versions differ from the sketch and from each other in details of composition, but the wall in both versions (a) and (b) follows the main line of the sketch by curving into the left corner, while in version (c) it breaks off in the centre. Similarly the sails of the wherries in the sketch and in versions (a) and (b) echo each other's shape whereas in version (c) the sail of the left wherry billows at the top. The figure groups differ in all four drawings, but, overall, versions (a) and (b) seem more closely related to the sketch than version (c).

The method and execution of this type of sketch in Thirtle's oeuvre much reminds one of Cotman's preliminary drawings.

1. P. Browne, *History of Norwich* 1814 p. 247.

2. Possibly that in Thomas Lound sale, Norwich, Spelman 6th March 1861 lot 100 *Quayside* bt. Titlow £3 and presumably that in the sale of Rev. Samuel Titlow, Norwich, Spelman Tues.–Fri., 13th–16th June 1871 first day lot 207 *Quayside, Norwich / a very fine Drawing*, bt. Hogarth $10\frac{1}{2}$ gns.

3. Possibly the drawing exhibited by James Reeve at the Crown Bank, Norwich in 1873 (2) *a sketch on the Quay Side, Norwich* (*Norwich Mercury* 1st Oct. 1873). No copy of the catalogue of this exhibition has yet been traced.

4. 1352.B1.235.951; CC MS vol. 2 p. 324 No. 136.

Works excluded from the Catalogue

The following drawings, which entered the collection as by John Thirtle, have been excluded from the catalogue because their attributions are either incorrect or under suspicion. They are arranged in the order in which they entered the collection. Three have been reattributed and are listed at the end.

Title	Medium	Museum No.
Portrait of James Thirtle	watercolour (miniature)	not registered
View of Norwich from the north east	watercolour	1143.76.94
The Broken Bridge	brown wash	1148.76.94
View of Norwich	watercolour	1156.76.94
View of the Cow Tower Norwich	watercolour	1157.76.94
View of Cromer	watercolour	1158.76.94
Church at Assumar, Portugal	pencil	1169.76.94
A Hall	pencil	1184.76.94
Landscape after Stark	watercolour	4.134.934
View from Hellesdon	watercolour	4.116.935
St. Benets Abbey	watercolour	115.936
Lakenham Mill	brown wash	60.155.938
An old House (Moreton Old Hall, Cheshire)	watercolour	30.940
Figure in fancy Costume	watercolour	1328.235.951
The Market Cart	watercolour	1329.235.951
Marine View	watercolour	1331.235.951
Studies of Boats	watercolour	1332.235.951
Shipping in Harbour	watercolour	1333.235.951
River Scene with Wherries	pencil	1335.235.951
Sailing Boats	pencil	1336.235.951
Near Norwich	watercolour	1337.235.951
Heath Scene	watercolour	1339.235.951
Bramerton Reach near Norwich	watercolour	1344.235.951
On the River Yare	brown wash	1349.235.951
Portraits of the Children of John Sell Cotman (See the entry for No. 129)	watercolour	1352.235.951
Quayside Norwich	watercolour	1352.B1.235.951
The Cow Tower on the Hospital Meadows	watercolour (faded)	1352.B33.235.951
Norwich Castle	watercolour	1352.B34.235.951
Tanyard, Norwich	watercolour	1352.B35.235.951
Gable end of House, Norwich	grey wash	1352.B40.235.951
View from Carrow	watercolour	1352.B55.235.951
Buckingham Ferry	grey wash	1352.B57.235.951
Trees at Framlingham	brown wash	2.1.957

Reattributed Works	Medium	Museum No.
Norwich Cathedral reattributed to James Pattison Cockburn (1778–1849)	watercolour	1134.76.94
A Loaded Wherry reattributed to James Stark (1794–1859)	watercolour	1347.235.951
Whitlingham Staithe reattributed to Thomas Lound (1802–1861)	watercolour	2.165.956

Watermarks

Includes all watermarks in papers of drawings in the Catalogue. The list is arranged in alphabetical order of paper maker; unidentified watermarks are given at the end.

Watermark	Churchill Ref.	Cat. Nos.
B.E & S / 18[?0]3 (indistinct)	—	107
BE & S / 1815	—	54
J BUDGEN / 1813	*1818 Budgen, J.* (p. 48)	131
E & P / 1801	*1801 Edmonds & Pine* (p. 50)	85
EDMEADS & PINE	,, ,,	22
A Strasburg Lily, of *KORFF & DEVRIES*	*1788* (p. 84, fig. 416)	5
PORTAL & BRIDGES / 1795	*1780 Portal, J. Lavestoke mill;* *1796 Portal & Co.* (p. 52)	1
PORTAL & BRIDGES	,, ,,	4
[*RUSE & TU*]*RNERS*	Records papers dated between 1805-45 with the watermark *Ruse and Turner,* with no *S* (p. 53); however a drawing in the collection, previously attributed to Thirtle (1335.235.951), bears the watermark *RUSE & TURNERS / 1823* which is not recorded by Churchill	94
S & A / 1828	*1816–54 Smith & Alnutt* (p. 53)	103, 120
SMITH & ALNUTT	,, ,,	121
J WHATMAN / 1809	*1760–1850 Whatman, James, Turkey Mill, Kent* (p. 54)	60
[*WH*]*ATMAN* [18] *10*	,, ,,	146
J WHATMAN / 1811	,, ,,	23, 47, 48, 104
[*W*]*HATMAN / 1811*	,, ,,	37
WHA[TMAN] / [18]*13*	,, ,,	168
J WHATMAN / 1828	,, ,,	111
J WHATMAN / 1830	,, ,,	122
J WHA[TMAN] *18 . .*	,, ,,	76, 99, 167
J WH[ATMAN]	,, ,,	96
[*WHA*]*TMAN . . . 8*	,, ,,	101
[? *WHATMA*]*N*	,, ,,	19
C/ 1815 (upper half only of digits visible)	—	56
? *P* (inverted, paper cut)	—	3
S & C	Records a watermark *1783 MARTEN SCHOUTEN & Co* where the name is shown as *MS & Co* (p. 69, fig. 94)	75
Strasburg Lily over *GR*	—	21
1818	—	84
Indistinct watermark (paper cut)	—	126

Norwich Castle Museum Catalogues—concordance

NCM n.d. [?1897]   *Catalogue of the Pictures, Drawings, Etchings and Bronzes in the Picture Gallery of the Norwich Castle Museum*, no date (1897. According to Geo. A. Stephen, "Norfolk Celebrities" II, *Norfolk Artists An Annotated Catalogue of the Books, Pamphlets and Articles Relating to Deceased Norfolk Artists in the Norwich Public Library*, published Norwich 1915 p. 6). Printed Jarrold & Sons, Norwich.

NCM n.d. [?1899]   —2nd Edition, no date (1899. According to Stephen *op. cit.*). Printed Edward Burgess & Sons Ltd., Norwich.

NCM 1904   —3rd Edition 1904. Printed Edward Burgess & Sons Ltd., Norwich.

NCM 1909   —4th Edition 1909. Printed "Norwich Mercury" Co. Ltd., Norwich. Illustrated.

NCM 1937   *Catalogue of the Norwich School and Other Pictures in the Art Galleries of the Norwich Castle Museum*, 1937. Printed A. E. Soman & Co. Ltd., Norwich. Illustrated.

Cat. nos.	1897	1899	1904	1909	1937
2	—	—	—	—	263
13	—	170	244	261	258
22	—	—	—	—	264
77	—	—	—	—	252
78	134	148	239	256	257
104	—	—	—	—	261
105	—	—	—	—	259
114	139	153	241	258	255
115	124	144	240	257	256
119	137	137	238	255	253
126	—	—	—	—	267
128	—	—	—	—	268
130	—	—	—	—	265
131	—	—	—	—	266

Colman Collection Catalogues—concordance

JJC — Typescript catalogue of pictures belonging to J. J. Colman, compiled by Mr. Clowes, Mr. Beecheno and Mr. Knights, no date.

Reeve Coll. MS — Manuscript catalogue of the James Reeve Collection, no date. Inscribed inside flyleaf 'Catalogue of drawings not sent to British Museum which afterwards were purchased by H. S. Theobald and subsequently to R. J. Colman'.

Card MS — James Reeve Manuscript Card Catalogue, no date, draft entries for the CC MS vols. 2 and 3.

CC Notebook — Manuscript Notebook of R. J. Colman containing draft entries for the CC MS vol. 2.

CC MS vols. 1 and 2 — Manuscript Catalogues based on the Card MS *op. cit.* Produced by R. J. Colman assisted by Percy Moore Turner and Frank Leney.

Vol. 1, 'Catalogue of Drawings in Watercolour and Black and White Chalk (unframed) by Norfolk and Norwich Artists in the Collection of Russell J. Colman', no date; last date mentioned, 1914. No photographs.

Vol. 2, 'Catalogue of Water Colour Drawings, (framed) by Norfolk and Norwich Artists, in the Collection of Russell J. Colman', no date; last date mentioned, 1916. Some photographs.

CC 1942 — *The Colman Collection*, 'A Catalogue of all the oil paintings, watercolour paintings, pencil drawings and chalk drawings by artists of the Norwich School and others in the collection at Crown Point Norwich with a monograph on the Norwich School of Painting with special reference to the Work of John Sell Cotman by Sydney D. Kitson and a Preface by Russell James Colman'. Printed privately for R. J. Colman, Oxford University Press, 1942. Some photographs.

Where two figures are given the page number is followed by the catalogue number. Figures in square brackets are manuscript additions to the catalogue. P indicates an accompanying photograph.

Cat. nos.	JJC	Reeve Coll. MS	Card MS	CC Notebook	CC MS vols. 1	CC MS vols. 2	CC 1942
1	—	—	454	—	119/454	—	—
5	[137]	—	137	137	—	324/137	—
6	—	—	—	—	117/441	—	1327
8	—	—	—	—	117/434	—	—
9	—	—	—	—	119/452	—	—
10	—	—	—	—	37/127	—	—
11	—	35/43	—	—	37/129	—	—
13	247	—	—	—	—	—	—
14	—	—	137e	137e	—	326/137e	—
15	—	—	—	—	121/462	—	—
21	—	—	—	—	117/444	—	—
24	251	—	125	125	—	318/125	—
25	—	—	—	—	37/123	—	—
26	—	—	—	—	117/435	—	—
27	249	—	131	131	—	322/131	—
28	[126a]	—	126a	126a	—	318/126a	—
31	—	—	—	—	121/462a	—	—
32	—	—	—	—	117/445	—	—
33	—	—	462b	—	119/462b	—	—
34	—	—	—	—	117/438	—	—
35	—	—	—	—	39/134	—	—
36	—	—	—	—	119/453	—	—
37	—	—	—	—	119/455	—	—
38	244	—	122	122	—	314/122P	—
39	—	—	—	—	119/458	—	—
40	—	—	—	—	39/137	—	1340
41	—	37/no no.	—	—	37/133	—	—
42	—	—	—	—	119/457	—	—
43	—	—	—	—	115/428	—	—
44	—	35/42	—	—	39/135	—	—

Cat. nos.	JJC	Reeve Coll. MS	Card MS	CC Notebook	CC MS vols. 1	CC MS vols. 2	CC 1942
45	—	—	—	—	117/440	—	—
46	—	—	—	—	121/460	—	—
48	—	—	—	—	39/136	—	1341
49	253	—	126	126	—	318/126P	1350
53	—	—	—	—	37/125	—	1330
54	246	—	133	133	—	322/133	—
55	—	35/41	—	—	39/140, 141	—	—
56	—	—	127a	—	—	320/127a	—
57	—	—	137f	137F	—	326/137f	—
58	252	—	124	124	—	316/124P	—
59	—	—	135	135	—	324/135	—
60	—	—	—	—	117/430	—	1343
61	—	—	—	—	117/429	—	1342
62	—	—	—	—	119/456	—	—
63	—	—	137d	137D	—	326/137d	—
64	—	—	—	—	119/450	—	1346
68	—	—	—	—	117/436	—	—
69	—	33/40	—	—	37/130	—	—
70	—	—	—	—	117/432	—	—
71	—	—	—	—	119/447	—	—
72	—	—	—	—	117/431	—	—
73	—	—	—	—	117/442	—	—
74	—	—	—	—	117/437	—	—
75	—	—	—	—	119/449	—	—
79	—	—	123	123	—	316/123P	—
80	—	—	—	—	39/138	—	—
82	—	81/no no.	137b	137B	—	326/137b	—
83	—	—	—	—	—	322/134a	1338
84	—	—	137 a.a.	137A	—	326/137 a.a.	—
87	—	—	—	—	35/120b	—	1334
103	—	—	—	—	117/443	—	1348
106	[132]	—	132	132	—	322/132	—
107	—	—	137h	—	—	325/137h	—
108	—	—	—	—	119/439	—	—
110	245	—	121	121	—	314/121P	—
111	—	—	137K	—	—	325/137k	—
112	—	—	128a	—	—	320/128a	—
116	[129]	—	129	129	—	320/129	—
117	—	—	128	128	—	320/128	—
118	[127], 250	—	127,130	127,130	—	320/127,130	1345
120	—	—	—	—	119/459	—	—
121	—	—	—	—	119/451	—	—
129	—	—	—	—	—	325/137i	1351

Concordance

Cat. nos.	Registration nos.	Cat. nos.	Registration nos.
1	1352.B39.235.951	52	99.937
2	9.21.21	53	1330.235.951
3	1352.B31.235.951	54	1352.B11.235.951
4	1352.B41.235.951	55	1352.B46.235.951
5	1352.B14.235.951	56	1352.B3.235.951
6	1327.235.951	57	1352.B6.235.951
7	1180.76.94	58	1352.B5.235.951
8	1352.B52.235.951	59	1352.B15.235.951
9	1352.B65.235.951	60	1343.235.951
10	1352.B59.235.951	61	1342.235.951
11	1352.B47.235.951	62	1352.B63.235.951
12	61.155.938	63	1352.B18.235.951
13	20.4.99	64	1346.235.951
14	1352.B27.235.951	65	7.134.934
15	1352.B58.235.951	66	116.959
16	1159.76.94	67	1.165.956
17	1144.76.94	68	1352.B37.235.951
18	1149.76.94	69	1352.B45.235.951
19	1145.76.94	70	1352.B62.235.951
20	1147.76.94	71	1352.B56.235.951
21	1352.B54.235.951	72	1352.B42.235.951
22	5.116.935	73	1352.B49.235.951
23	12.940	74	1352.B61.235.951
24	1352.B12.235.951	75	1352.B8.235.951
25	1352.B32.235.951	76	57.932
26	1352.B53.235.951	77	40.19
27	1352.B19.235.951	78	60.75.94
28	1352.B4.235.951	79	1352.B25.235.951
29	2.59.974	80	1352.B51.235.951
30	1.59.974	81	5.20.944
31	1352.B21.235.951	82	1352.B26.235.951
32	1352.B30.235.951	83	1338.235.951
33	1352.B13.235.951	84	1352.B67.235.951
34	1352.B38.235.951	85	1155.76.94
35	1352.B2.235.951	86	1154.76.94
36	1352.B44.235.951	87	1334.235.951
37	1352.B43.235.951	88	1153.76.94
38	1352.B16.951	89	59.155.938
39	1352.B36.235.951	90	1151.76.94
40	1340.235.951	91	1152.76.94
41	1352.B7.235.951	92	1150.76.94
42	1352.B10.235.951	93	1146.76.94
43	1352.B60.235.951	94	1135.76.94
44	1352.B48.235.951	95	1160.76.94
45	1352.B50.235.951	96	1137.76.94
46	1352.B68.235.951	97	1136.76.94
47	9.118.940	98	1142.76.94
48	1341.235.951	99	1141.76.94
49	1350.235.951	100	1139.76.94
50	99.937	101	1140.76.94
51	31.940	102	1138.76.94

Cat. nos.	Registration nos.	Cat. nos.	Registration nos.
103	1348.235.951	131	70.932
104	5.134.934	132	74.937
105	31.15	133	74.937
106	1352.B20.235.951	134	1170.76.94
107	1352.B22.235.951	135	1161.76.94
108	1352.B64.235.951	136	1163.76.94
109	89.942	137	1171.76.94
110	1352.B17.235.951	138	1173.76.94
111	1352.B23.235.951	139	1172.76.94
112	1352.B24.235.951	140	1164.76.94
113	360.957	141	1179.76.94
114	61.75.94	142	1178.76.94
115	62.75.94	143	1177.76.94
116	1352.B29.235.951	144	1176.76.94
117	1352.B28.235.951	145	1185.76.94
118	1345.235.951	146	1162.76.94
119	63.75.94	147	1167.76.94
120	1352.B9.235.951	148	1165.76.94
121	1352.B66.235.951	149–	
122	88.845	157	1183.76.94
123	54.932	158–	
124	66.30	164	1168.76.94
125	40.954	165	1182.76.94
126	55.932	166	1166.76.94
127	55a.932	167	1174.76.94
128	56.932	168	1181.76.94
129	1351.235.951	169	1175.76.94
130	70.932		

Previous collections and donors

This index includes all previous owners except auctioneers, and dealers buying at auctions for a known client. The index is arranged under surnames in alphabetical order. Where no source is given, information has been taken from standard works of reference, Art Dept. archives, local directories and newspapers.

Catalogue numbers are in bold type where the previous owner was also the donor.

Agnew, Thomas & Son.
The firm of art dealers, Bond Street, London, which was established in Manchester 1817 by Thomas Agnew (1794–1871) in partnership with Vittore Zanetti and which became Thomas Agnew & Son in 1851. 'You must all become Agnewsticks in art before the public will believe in you'—Robert Ross 1906.   23

Aldis, John Brown (?1833–1909)
Chester Place, Norwich.   112

Alston, Rev. A. E. (?1863–1927)
Rector of Framingham Earl for 40 years, 'voluminous writer and a man of striking intellectual gifts.'   77

Back, Philip (?1824–1900)
Eaton, Norwich.   56
Sheriff of Norwich in 1879.

Base, F.
Base & Son, pork butchers and sausage makers of Great Yarmouth, Norfolk, 1937.   132, 133

Beecheno, F. R. (?1855–1935)
92 Queens Road, Norwich.   **22,** (Bequest
Archaeologist and historian. Bequeathed collections of pictures, furniture, books and money.   Fund: 125)

Bircham, William (?1800–1886)
Sale: 'St. Ollands', Reepham, Norfolk, Spelman, 4th & 5th Oct. 1883.   13

Blyth, Dr. Ernest Egbert (1857–1934)
Heigham House, Norwich.   **65, 104**
Lawyer, author and educationalist. Had the distinction of being both the last Mayor and first Lord Mayor of Norwich; his portrait by Orpen is in the Civic Collection (No. 112). Bequeathed nineteen Norwich School pictures.

Boden, L. S. (fl. 1886)
London artist. The name does not appear in standard reference works.   54

Bolingbroke, Horatio, J. P. (?1799–1879)
Sale: Norwich, Spelman, 12th & 13th March 1879.   49
Member of the Committee of the Norfolk and Norwich Association for the Promotion of the Fine Arts.

Brightwell, Barron (?1813–1876)
Norwich.   59

Brightwell, Henry
Sale: Norwich, Spelman 26th Nov. 1890.   59
Of Flordon, Norfolk. Presumably descended from Thomas Brightwell whose collection of pictures was included in his sale, lots 69–150.

Brightwell, Thomas
Presumably Thomas Brightwell (?1787–1868) solicitor of Surrey Street, Norwich. Possibly   59
the Thomas Brightwell who was a member of the Norwich Art Conversazione in 1830.

Became a Fellow of the Linnaean Society in 1821, and presented his insect and other natural history collections to the museum. His son, Thomas Brightwell (1811–1879) was also a solicitor of Surrey Street, Norwich.

Brooke, W. A.

Spring House, Thetford. Died by 1944.　　　　　　　　　　　　　　　　　　　　　**81**
Collection of approximately thirty Norwich School pictures and miscellaneous prints.

Chambers, A. J.

Presumably Arthur John Chambers (fl. 1838–1893), artist, architect and surveyor of St.　　15
Giles Plain, Norwich. Painter and etcher of local subjects.

Chittock, A. T. (?1876–1953)

Sale: Norwich, J. R. E. Draper, 3rd. Feb. 1954.　　　　　　　　　　　　　　　　125
Solicitor of 12 Chapel Field North, Norwich, a collector of Norwich School pictures and a keen yachtsman. Awarded the MBE in 1943.

Clowes, Mrs.

Presumably Martha, Mrs. Francis Clowes (1816–1896) of Newmarket Road, Norwich.　　69

Colman, Jeremiah James, MP (1830–1898)

Carrow House, Norwich.　　　　　　　　　　　　　　　　　　　　　　　　1, 3–6, 8, 9, **13**, 15,
Founder of Colman's the mustard manufacturers and of the Colman Collection. Bequeathed,　24, 26–28, 32, 34,
in 1898, 20 Norwich School paintings. See also **Reeve.**　　　　　　　　　　　36–38, 43–46, 49,
　　　　　　　　　　　　　　　　　　　　　　　　　　　　　　　　　　　54, 57–64, 68, 70–
　　　　　　　　　　　　　　　　　　　　　　　　　　　　　　　　　　　75, 79, 84, 103, 106,
　　　　　　　　　　　　　　　　　　　　　　　　　　　　　　　　　　　108, 110, 116–118,
　　　　　　　　　　　　　　　　　　　　　　　　　　　　　　　　　　　121.

Colman, Russell James (1861–1946)

Crown Point, Norwich.　　　　　　　　　　　　　　　　　　　　　　　　**1, 3–6, 8–11, 14, 15,**
Son of J. J. Colman. Inherited and added to his father's collection which he bequeathed in　**24–28, 31–46, 48,**
1946 together with two galleries, opened in 1951, in which to house it. See also **Reeve** and　**49, 53, 55–64, 68–**
Theobald.　　　　　　　　　　　　　　　　　　　　　　　　　　　　　**75, 79, 80, 82–84, 87,**
　　　　　　　　　　　　　　　　　　　　　　　　　　　　　　　　　　　103, 106–108, 110–
　　　　　　　　　　　　　　　　　　　　　　　　　　　　　　　　　　　112, 116–118, 120,
　　　　　　　　　　　　　　　　　　　　　　　　　　　　　　　　　　　121, 129

Dalrymple

Presumably Arthur Dalrymple (d. 1868) of St. Giles Street, Norwich. A Clerk of the Peace　11, 57
from 1856, a Fellow of the Society of Antiquaries and collector of Norfolk portraits.

Davey, Miss

Presumably Miss Jane Davey (1815–1898) of 88 Upper St. Giles, Norwich.　　　　79

EAAS

In its first Annual Report 1880 the East Anglian Art Society stated that its object was "the　**78, 114, 115, 119**
acquisition and preservation of the pictures of the East Anglian Artists." In 1872 the first
President, John Brandram Morgan, with friends, began collecting funds for this purpose
which activity led to the formation of the Society. Its first meeting was held 17th March 1876
at Norwich Museum, then housed in the Haymarket. In 1893 the museum collections were
transferred to the Castle and the Society resolved at its 14th Annual Meeting, 24th April
1893, to offer its collection to Norwich Corporation. The gift was accepted by the City 19th
June 1894 and the collection transferred by Deed 27th February 1895.

Fitch, Robert, JP, FSA, FGA (1802–1895)

A Director of the Norwich Union; held many public offices. Member of the Norfolk and　**7, 16–20, 85–88, 90–**
Norwich Museum and honorary secretary of the Norfolk and Norwich Archaeological　**102, 134–169**
Society. Presented a large collection of antiquities, archaeological and geological material,　(Bequest Fund: 125)
manuscripts, books and etchings and drawings by Norwich School artists.

Geldart, Miss Alice M. (1868–1947)

2 Cotman Road, Norwich. 109

Sale: Norwich, Hanbury Williams, 14th July 1942.

Naturalist and egyptologist, Fellow of the Linnaean Society and President of the Norfolk and Norwich Naturalists' Society.

Hansell, Peter E. (1831–1921)

Wroxham House, Thorpe, Norwich. 78

Held many public offices. Member of Norwich Art Circle and Secretary of the Norfolk and Norwich Music Festival.

Holmes, Sir Henry Nicholas, JP (1869–1940)

Uplands, Upton Road, Norwich. **47**

Boot and shoe manufacturer. Twice Lord Mayor and also held other public offices. A catalogue of his collection was printed privately 1932. As well as bequests to local hospitals he left 14 of his Norwich School pictures to the museum.

Keith, T. H.

Son of F. T. Keith (?1829–1901), solicitor and member of Norwich Art Circle, whose sale, 14
held Norwich, Keith & Smith, 19th Feb. 1903, included several Norwich School pictures.

Kitson, Sydney D. (1871–1937)

Architect of Leeds. After the war Kitson retired prematurely through ill health and divided his **12, 89**
energies between the Honorary Secretaryship of the RIBA and his consuming interest in John Sell Cotman. His biography of Cotman was published just three months before his death. In his will he directed that the bulk of his Cotman drawings should go to the Leeds City Art Gallery and that selected drawings related to their own collections should go to the V & A and NCM. Sir Henry Hake had overall charge of the distribution.

Lound, Thomas (1802–1861)

Sale: Norwich, Spelman 6th March 1861. 39, 41, 42, 44, 46, 57,
Brewer by trade. A Norwich School artist, friend of Bright, Middleton and Leman. His sale 62, ?78, 120, ?122
included over 100 drawings by Thirtle in 23 lots.

Mills, James

Sale: Norwich, Spelman 12th–14th June 1865 11
Castle Meadow, Norwich. Formed a vast collection of antiquities, pottery and porcelain, objets d'art, gems, paintings, drawings and prints as well as a library of illustrated books. The collection was sold as 'Mr. James Mills' Museum' and the sale catalogue was compiled by James **Reeve,** then curator of the Norwich Museum.

Nutman, J. R.

Physician, Norwich. 47

O'Malley, L.

2 Temple Gardens, London. **130, 131**

Palmer, Wallace Morley (?1894–1970)

Mill House, Cringleford, Norwich. Retired in 1958 from his post as Clerk of the Markets, **50, 52**
Norwich. His collection of Norwich School pictures was shown at the museum in 1950.

Parr, Miss (fl. 1886)

Presumably a descendant of Catherine Burrell Parr (née Catherine Miles, b. 1791), Thirtle's 115
sister-in-law.

Parr, Mrs. Elizabeth (fl. 1894)

Daughter of William Miles Parr and ? presumably granddaughter of Catherine Burrell Parr 114, 115, 119
(née Catherine Miles, b. 1791) Thirtle's sister-in-law. Mother of William Henry Parr.

Parr, William Henry (?1863–1932)

7 Wood Street, Norwich.
Son of Mrs. Elizabeth Parr. Artist, composer and actor; his stage name was Henry Furnival.

76, 105, 111, 123, 126–128, 132, 133

Parr, William Miles (fl. 1842–1889)

Engineer. Nephew of Elizabeth Miles, Mrs. Thirtle and sole executor of her will. ?Presumably son of Catherine Burrell Parr (née Catherine Miles, b. 1791) Thirtle's sister-in-law. Father of Mrs. Elizabeth Parr.

105, 111, 114, 115, 119

Rae, Rev. C. T.

12 St. Leonard's Court, St. Leonard's Road, East Sheen, London, SW14.
Minister of Princes Street Congregational Church, Norwich, 1925–1941.

67

Reeve, James, FGS (1833–1920)

Officially connected with Norwich Museum for seventy-three years, curator from 1851–1910, consulting curator until his death. It was through Reeve's discernment and knowledge that the museum's Norwich School collection was formed. He was also a buyer for the Colman family. Reeve sold the major part of his own collection to the BM in 1902, but upwards of 100 watercolours and drawings by Cotman and the Norwich School artists were later bought by H. S. **Theobald** and sold subsequently to R. J. **Colman.**

2, 10, 11, 41, 44, 69, 82, 110

Root, Mr.

Thirtle's carver and gilder. Possibly the James Root given in *Chase's Norwich Directory* 1783 as 'Whitesmith' of '14 Red Lion Lane', and in *Peck* 1802 and *Berry* 1811 as of 'St. Saviours Church Lane'.

110

Russell, Benjamin (fl. 1811–?1905)

Clock and watchmaker of Magdalen Street, Norwich. Married Thirtle's sister Rachel, and was an executor of the will of Thirtle's father in 1826. Lent eight works to the Norwich Art Circle Thirtle exhibition 1886.

107

Sherlock, Rev. G. H. Kenneth

29, 30

Spelman, Clement Charles Rix (?1844–1899)

Eaton, Norwich.
Sale: Norwich, Spelman, 17th–19th March 1914.
Partner of Spelman auctioneers, collector of paintings, china, etc. Mayor of Norwich 1897–8.

3, 4, 31, 33, ?67, 129

Squire Gallery

London. The stock book of Percy Moore Turner (?1877–1950) records purchases from the gallery, including three other Thirtle watercolours, from 1935–1939.

51

Stone, Francis (1770–1835)

Norwich architect and County Surveyor. Member of the Norwich Society of Artists in 1806, 1809–1833, President in 1812 and 1822, Vice President in 1821. His original drawings for *The Norfolk Bridges,* lithographed by his son-in-law David Hodgson (1798–1864), are in the museum's collection.

?15

Theobald, Henry Studdy, KC, MA (1847–1934)

Sale: Sotheby's 13th May 1925.
Author of *Crome's Etchings,* London 1906, and collector of English watercolours. See **Reeve** and **Colman,** Russell James.

10, 11, 25, 35, 40, 41, 44, 48, 53, 55, 69, 80, 82, 87, 107

Thirkettle, Florence Catherine (d. 1957)

26 Mount Pleasant, Norwich.
Granddaughter of Thomas **Lound.** Bequeathed an album of watercolours and etchings by Lound and pictures by other Norwich School artists 1957.

113, 122

Thirtle, Mrs.

Elizabeth Miles (?1787–1882) wife of John Thirtle; see the entry for No. 131.
Sales: Norwich, St. George's Middle Street, c. 21st March 1840 (*Norwich Mercury*; the catalogue of this sale, if there was one, is untraced); Norwich, Spelman, 9th May 1882. Her sale included over 200 drawings by Thirtle in 58 lots as well as works by Clover and Bonington, engravings and etchings after Cotman, Prout, etc. and photographic apparatus. See **Parr,** William Miles.

1, 5, 6, 8, 9, 24, 26, 28, 32, 34, 36, 37, 43, 45, 60, 61, 63, 64, 68, 70–75, ?78, 84, 103, 106, 108, 110, 116–118, 121

Thompson, Charles

Possbily Charles Henry Thompson (?1864–1916) of Claremont Road. Managing Director of Chalk Hill Works, Norwich. Murdered on Rosary Road, Thorpe, 20th July 1916.

11, 58, 63, 84, 121

Turner, Charles (1789–1861)

Sheriff of Norwich in 1824 and Mayor in 1834. Father of Rev. Charles Turner.

77

Turner, Rev. Charles (d. 1890)

The Hall, Framingham Earl.
Son of Charles Turner. Held the living of St. Peter Mancroft, Norwich, 1848–78, later rector of Bixley and Framingham Earl.

77

Turner, Gertrude Mary (d. 1919)

Wife of Rev. Charles Turner.

77

Turner, Dawson (1775–1858)

Yarmouth banker, bibliophile, botanist and antiquarian. Patron of Crome and Cotman.

124

Turner, Percy Moore (?1877–1950)

Art dealer. b. Yorkshire. Lived in Norwich and became proprietor of the Independent Gallery, Grafton Street, London. Was a co-opted member of NCM committee. Turner's gifts to the Museum were crowned by his bequest of Rembrandt etchings in 1951. He also made gifts to the Louvre and was made by the French Government an Officer of the Legion of Honour.

23, **51,** 125

Walker, James William (1831–1898)

Died at The Grange, Brockdish, Norfolk. Artist and teacher. Presented a collection of pictures, ceramics etc. 1895–97 as well as bequeathing money.

?3
(Bequest Fund: 76, 105, 123, 126, 127, 128)

Weston, Miss

Sale: The Cottage, Mundesley, Spelman 11th Jan. 1889.

38

Woodrow, Miss

Presumably Maria Woodrow, daughter of Thomas and Maria Woodrow, she died 21st Jan. 1932 and is buried in the Rosary Cemetery, Norwich.

130, 131

Woolmer, Miss E. A. M.

Heath Cottage, Poringland.
Housekeeper to James **Reeve.** Died 11th March 1959.

66

Worthington, James

Sale Hall, near Manchester.

23

Worthington, Robert

Exeter (1943).

23

Exhibitions

This index contains details of exhibitions to which drawings in this catalogue were lent.

Abbreviation	Exhibition	Cat. nos.
Norwich Society of Artists 1809	Norwich, Sir Benjamin Wrenche's Court, *Fifth Exhibition by the Norwich Society of Artists, in oil and water colours.*	?13
Norwich Society of Artists 1810	Norwich, Sir Benjamin Wrenche's Court, *Sixth Exhibition of the Norwich Society of Artists, consisting of Paintings and Drawings.*	?15
Norwich Society of Artists 1812	Norwich, Sir Benjamin Wrenche's Court, *Eight Exhibition of the Norwich Society of Artists, consisting of Paintings and Drawings.*	?29
Norwich Society of Artists 1814	Norwich, Sir Benjamin Wrench'e Court, *Tenth Exhibition of the Norwich Society of Artists, consisting of Paintings and Drawings.*	?36
Norwich Society of Artists 1815	Norwich, Sir Benjamin Wrenche's Court, *Eleventh Exhibition of the Norwich Society of Artists, consisting of Paintings and Drawings.*	38
Norwich Society of Artists Secession 1816	Norwich, Threatre Plain, *Twelfth Exhibition of the Norfolk and Norwich Society of Artists, consisting of Paintings and Drawings.*	?47, ?130, ?131
Norwich Society of Artists Secession 1817	Norwich, Theatre Plain, *Thirteenth Exhibition of the Norfolk and Norwich Society of Artists, consisting of Paintings and Drawings.*	?30, 77
Norwich Society of Artists 1829	Norwich, Exchange Street, *Twenty-Third Exhibition of the Norfolk and Suffolk Institution for the Promotion of the Fine Arts, consisting of paintings, drawings, and engravings.*	?112, ?114
Norwich Society of Artists 1830	Norwich, Exchange Street, *Twenty-fourth Exhibition of the Norfolk and Suffolk Institution for the Promotion of the Fine Arts, consisting of paintings, drawings, and engravings.*	?115
Norwich, Fine Arts Association 1860	Norwich, Government School of Art, *Norfolk and Norwich Fine Arts Association.*	49, 77
Norwich 1867	Norwich, St. Andrew's Hall, *Norwich and Eastern Counties Working Classes Industrial Exhibition,* commencing 14th Aug.	78
Norwich 1873	Norwich, Crown Bank, *Works by Artists (Deceased),* the catalogue of this exhibition is untraced.	110
Norwich 1874	Norwich, St. Andrew's Hall, British Medical Association, *A Loan Collection of the Works of Norfolk and Suffolk Artists,* 12th Aug.	110
Norwich 1878	Norwich, St. Andrew's Hall, *Art Loan Exhibition in aid of the fund for the Restoration of St. Peter Mancroft Church,* 18th Nov.–7th Dec.	77
Norwich 1885	Norwich, St. Andrew's Hall, *Art Loan Exhibition in aid of the fund for the Restoration of St. Peter Mancroft Church,* 1st Jan. for one month.	13, 56

Norwich, Art Circle 1886	Norwich, Old Bank of England Chambers, Queen Street, *Norwich Art Circle Third Exhibition, John Thirtle,* July.	5, 13, 21, 24, 27, 28, 54, 57, 58, 59, 60, 63, 77, 84, 105, 106, 107, 110, 111, 112, 114, 115, 116, 117, 118, 119, 130, 131
Norwich, Art Circle 1889	Norwich, Old Bank of England Chambers, Queen Street, *Norwich Art Circle Twelfth Exhibition, Past and Present Norwich,* July.	32
Great Yarmouth 1889	Great Yarmouth, Town hall, *Art Loan Exhibition in aid of the Book Fund of the Free Library,* commencing 7th May.	115
RA Winter Exhibition 1892	London, Royal Academy, *Winter Exhibition.*	13, 38
Norwich 1894	Norwich, Agricultural Hall, *Loan Collection of Pictures by the Deceased Artists of the Norwich School,* 6th–10th Nov.	13, 110
London 1897	London, *The Victorian Era Exhibition.*	13, 38
Norwich, St. Andrew's Hall 1902	Norwich, St. Andrew's Hall, *Art Loan Exhibition in Aid of the Funds of St. George's Club for Working Girls,* 8th–26th April	38, 49, 69
Norwich 1903	Norwich, Castle Museum, *Loan Collection of Drawings in the New Picture Gallery.*	11, 24, 27, 38, 41, 58, 69, 79, 112
Tate 1922	London, National Gallery, Millbank, *Exhibition of Works by John Sell Cotman and some related painters of the Norwich School,* 7th April–9th July.	2, 13, 114, 117
Norwich 1927	Norwich, Castle Museum, *Norwich School of Painting,* 6th Oct.–5th Nov.	113, 122, 123, 125, 128, 132
Norwich 1932	Norwich, Castle Museum, *Exhibition of Sir Henry Holmes' collection of forty-two Norwich School pictures,* summer months.	47
RA 1934	London, Royal Academy, *Exhibition of British Art c. 1000–1860,* 6th Jan.–10th March.	28, 58
Norwich Boswell Centenary 1939	Norwich, St. Ethelbert's House, *Centenary of The House of Boswell 1839–1939 Exhibition of the Art of John Thirtle,* 16th June–1st July.	12, 51
Norwich, Thirtle Centenary 1939	Norwich, Castle Museum, *Thirtle Centenary Exhibition,* 19th July–4th Sept. (closed prematurely owing to the outbreak of war).	2, 13, 23, 33, 38, 40, 41, 42, 44, 47, 48, 50, 51, 52, 56, 64, 66, 67, 73, 75, 76, 77, 78, 89, 103, 105, 107, 110, 111, 113, 114, 115, 116, 122, 123, 126, 128 130, 131. 132
Norwich 1940	Norwich, Castle Museum, Nine drawings by John Thirtle were lent for exhibition by R. J. Colman in the hope of identifying some of the houses and bridges depicted, May.	62, 70, 71, 72, 74, 75
Arts Council 1947	Arts Council, *The Norwich School of Painting.*	13

Lowestoft 1948	Lowestoft, Art Centre, *Loan Exhibition of Water-colours of the Norwich School,* 12th–28th Feb.	2, 13, 50, 51, 81
Arts Council, Cambridge 1948	Cambridge, *Loan Exhibition of Watercolours of the Norwich School,* ?March.	51
Leeuwarden 1948	Holland, Leeuwarden, Friesch Museum, *Paintings and Watercolours of the Norwich School,* 10th–31st May.	2, 13, 50
Kettering 1952	Kettering, Alfred East Art Gallery, *Crome, Cotman and the Norwich Artists,* 13th Sept.–4th Oct.	2, 51, 89
Stoke-on-Trent 1953	Stoke-on-Trent, Hanley Museum and Art Gallery, *Norwich School Exhibition.*	2
Harrogate 1953	Harrogate, Public Library and Art Gallery, *Norwich School Paintings,* ? Aug.–13th Sept.	2, 23, 50, 51, 52, 89
Nottingham, Portsmouth & Bolton 1953–54	Art Exhibitions Bureau, Nottingham, Chapel Bar Art Gallery, 22nd Nov.–20th Dec. 1953; Portsmouth, Cumberland House Museum & Art Gallery, 9th Jan.–6th Feb. 1954; Bolton, The Museum, 13th Feb.–13th March 1954, *The Norwich School of Painting.*	2, 77
Kidderminster 1954	Kidderminster, Public Library, Museum and Art Gallery, *Watercolours of the Norwich School,* 1st–29th May.	2, 13, 51, 89, 122
Worthing 1957	Worthing Art Gallery, *Norwich School Paintings,* 27th July–31st Aug.	12, 23, 122
Derby and Nottingham 1959	Derby, Museum and Art Gallery, and Nottingham, University Art Gallery, *Paintings and Drawings of the Norwich School,* 3rd Jan.–1st Feb. and 18th Feb.–8th March.	13, 23, 113, 122
Wisbech 1960	Wisbech, The Wisbech Society, Peckover House, *Paintings of the Norwich School,* 19th July–2nd Aug.	89
Manchester, Whitworth 1961	Manchester, Whitworth Art Gallery, *The Norwich School Loan Exhibition of works by Crome and Cotman, and their followers,* 10th Feb.–11th March.	13, 122
China and Berlin 1963–64	China, Peking, Shanghai, Nanking, Chungking, Sian, Canton and Shenyang, *British watercolour painting during three centuries,* 2nd April–Oct. 1963; Berlin, National Gallery, *English watercolours,* 7th–31st Jan. 1964.	13
Norwich, University of East Anglia 1964	Norwich, University of East Anglia, *Loan Exhibition of Norwich School Pictures,* Oct.	12, 119
Bedford and Cambridge 1966	Bedford, Cecil Higgins Museum, and Cambridge, The Arts Council Gallery, *Norwich School Pictures,* April and 1st–22nd Oct.	12, 13, 48
USA 1967	USA: Jacksonville, Florida, Cummer Gallery of Art; Cheekwood, Nashville, Tennessee, Tennessee Fine Arts Center, and New Orleans, Louisiana, Isaac Delgado Museum of Art, *Landscapes of the Norwich School,* 22nd Feb.–11th June.	122
Rouen 1967	Rouen, Musée des Beaux-Arts, *Watercolours of the Norwich School,* 1st–30th Nov.	13, 16, 17, 19, 48, 92, 93

Norwich, Yare Valley 1968	Norwich, Castle Museum, *Yare Valley Exhibition,* May.	38
Kenwood 1969	London, Kenwood, The Iveagh Bequest, *Drawings of the Norwich School,* 1st–30th Nov.	13, 16, 19, 122
Colnaghi 1970	London, P. & D. Colnaghi & Co. Ltd., *A Loan Exhibition of Drawings and Watercolours by East Anglian Artists of the 18th and 19th Centuries,* 8th Sept.–2nd Oct.	28, 35, 41, 42, 56, 57, 58, 75, 120
Harlow 1976	Harlow, The Playhouse, *East Anglian Landscape,* 3rd June–2nd July.	41, 120
The Hague 1977	Holland, The Hague, Gemeentemuseum, *Romantic Watercolours of the Norwich School,* 25th March–8th May.	13, 43, 62, 122

Bibliography

This bibliography serves also as an index to abbreviations and is therefore arranged under authors' names in alphabetical order (or the title of the periodical when the author is anonymous). It contains only published sources to which reference is made in the text.

Baggs, A. P., 'Some notes on the history of cast iron in Norwich architecture', the *Handbook of the Norfolk and Norwich Association of Architects,* 1960–61.

Barnard, *The*
Studio Aug. 1947

Barnard, G. V., 'The Nation's Treasures: Norwich Castle Museum and Art Gallery', *The Studio,* Aug. 1947, vol. 134, No. 653.

Barnard

Barnard, G. V., *Paintings of the Norwich School,* Norwich n.d. c. 1950.

F. R. Beecheno
Notes on Carrow
Priory, 1886

Beecheno, F. R., *Notes on Carrow Priory, commonly called Carrow Abbey,* printed for private circulation 1886.

Ian Bennett,
The Connoisseur,
Jan. 1971

Bennett, Ian, 'Loan Exhibition of Drawings and Watercolours by East Anglian Artists of the 18th and 19th Centuries, P. & D. Colnaghi', *The Connoisseur,* vol. 176, no. 707, Jan. 1971.

Bol.

Bolingbroke, H., *Catalogue of the Etched and Engraved Work of Norwich Artists and Members of the Norwich School of Painting,* MS in Art Dept. archives.

Bolingbroke MS
(Thirtle)

Bolingbroke, L. G., *Manuscript list of works exhibited with the Norwich Society with annotations,* post 1909, in Art Dept. archives.

P. Browne,
History of Norwich,
1814

Browne, Philip, *The History of Norwich from the earliest records to the present time,* Bacon, Kinnebrooke and Co., Norwich, 1814.

Campbell, *Norwich*

Campbell, James, *Historic Towns, Norwich,* maps compiled by Johns, W. H., London, The Scholar Press, 1967.

Chambers, *Norfolk*
Tour, 1829

Chambers, John, *A General History of the County of Norfolk, intended to convey all the Information of a Norfolk Tour . . .* 2 vols., Norwich and London, 1829.

Churchill

Churchill, W. A., *Watermarks in Paper in Holland, England, France, etc. in the XVII and XVIII Centuries and their interconnection,* Amsterdam, Menno Hertzberger & Co., 1935.

Clifford

Clifford, Derek, *Watercolours of the Norwich School,* London, 1965.

Clifford, *OWCS,*
1966

Clifford, Derek, 'The Norwich School of Water-Colourists', *The Old Water-Colour Society's Club, The forty first annual volume,* ed. Adrian Bury, 1966.

Derek & Timothy
Clifford

Clifford, Derek & Timothy, *John Crome,* London, Faber & Faber, 1968.

Conisbee, Philip, *Claude Joseph Vernet 1714–1789,* catalogue of the exhibition held London, The Iveagh Bequest, Kenwood, 4th June–19th Sept. 1976.

Conrad, H. E., *England ein führer,* Munich, 1976.

Architectural
Antiquities of
Norfolk 1818

Cotman, John Sell, *A series of etchings illustrative of the Architectural Antiquities of Norfolk,* London, Norwich, Yarmouth Southtown, 1818.

Cotman and
Hawcroft

Cotman, Alec M., and **Hawcroft,** Francis W., *Old Norwich,* Norwich, 1961.

Cundall, *The Studio,*
1922

Cundall, H. M., 'The Cotman Exhibition at the Tate Gallery', *The Studio,* vol. 84, Aug. 1922.

Darvill, P. A., & **Stirling,** W. R., *Britain and the World Book 4,* Huddersfield, Schofield & Sons, 1973.

Day III   **Day,** Harold A. E., *East Anglian Painters*, Eastbourne, 1968, vol. III.

                                 De Mary, Eric, *Bridges of Britain*, London 1975.

Dickes   **Dickes,** W. F., *The Norwich School of Painting*, London and Norwich, 1905.

Excursions through   *Excursions in the County of Norfolk*, two vols., London, 1818, 1819.
Norfolk 1818

                                 Fawcett, Trevor, *The Rise of English Provincial Art*, Oxford Studies in the History of English
                                 Art & Architecture, Oxford 1974.

                                 Gage, John, *Colour in Turner Poetry and truth*, London, Studio Vista, 1969.

Hammelmann and   **Hammelmann,** Hans, edited and completed by Boase, T. S. R., *Book illustrators in*
     Boase 1975   *Eighteenth-Century England*, published for the Paul Mellon Centre for Studies in British Art
                                 (London) Ltd., by Yale University Press, New Haven and London, 1975.

Hardie vol. II   **Hardie,** Martin, *Water-colour Painting in Britain*, 3 vols., ed. Dudley Snelgrove, Jonathan
                                 Mayne and Basil Taylor, London, 1966–1968.

                                 Hayley, William, *Life of Cowper*, 3 vols., London, 1803–4.

Holmes Catalogue   **Holmes,** Henry N., *Catalogue of Oil Paintings and Water-Colour Drawings illustrative of the*
     1932   *Work of Artists of the Norwich School of Painting including John Crome and John Sell*
                                 Cotman, Norwich, 1932.

Kitson 1937   **Kitson,** Sydney D., *The Life of John Sell Cotman*, London, 1937.

Ladbrooke's   **Ladbrooke,** Robert, *Views of the Churches of Norfolk*, Drawn and Lithographed by Robert
     Churches   Ladbrooke, 5 vols., Norwich, Charles Muskett, 1843.

                                 Le Neve-Foster, Peter, *The Le Neves of Norfolk. A Family History*, privately printed 1969.

Mallalieu   **Mallalieu,** Huon, *The Norwich School, Crome, Cotman and their followers*, London and New
                                 York, 1974.

On View 1975   *On View, a guide to Museum and Gallery Acquisitions in Britain*, ed. Alan Osborne, London,
                                 Plaistow Publications, vol. 9, 1975 Edition.

                                 Parris, Leslie; **Williams,** Ian Fleming; **Shields,** Carol, *Constable Paintings, Watercolours and*
                                 Drawings, Tate Gallery, 1976.

                                 Penham, Hervey, *Once upon a tide*, London, 1955, revised 1971.

Pevsner   **Pevsner,** Nikolaus, *The Buildings of England*, vol. I, 'North-East Norfolk and Norwich',
                                 Middlesex, 1962.

Pevsner, *North-*   **Pevsner,** Nikolaus, *The Buildings of England*, 'North-West and South Norfolk', Middlesex,
     West and South   1962.
     Norfolk

                                 Press, Martin, H., 'The North Walsham and Dilham Canal', *The Edgar Allen News*, vol. 32,
                                 No. 368, Feb. 1953.

                                 Prout, Samuel, *Studies of Boats and Coast Scenery, 16 Plates of Picturesque Views in the Isle*
                                 of Wight, Deal, Brighton, Hastings, Eastbourne, The Thames, etc., pub. Ackerman's Reposi-
                                 tory, 1816.

                                 Prout, Samuel, *Easy lessons in Landscape Drawing contained in forty plates, arranged*
                                 progressively from the First Principles in the Chalk Manner to the Finished Landscape
                                 Colours, pub. Ackerman? 1819 (plates dated Feb.–Nov. 1819).

                                 Prout, Samuel, *Marine Sketches Drawn on Stone*, pub. Rowney & Forster, 1820.

Rajnai, Miklós, with the assistance of **Stevens,** Mary, *The Norwich Society of Artists 1805–1833 A dictionary of contributors and their work,* published for the Paul Mellon Centre for Studies in British Art (London) Ltd. by the Norfolk Museums Service, 1976.

Roget   **Roget,** John Lewis, *A History of the Old Water-colour Society,* 2 vols., London, 1891, reprinted Antique Collectors Club, Woodbridge, 1972.

J. W. Robberds, Stark's *Scenery of the Rivers of Norfolk*   **Stark,** James, and **Robberds,** J. W., *Scenery of the Rivers of Norfolk . . . from pictures painted by James Stark with historical and geological descriptions by J. W. Robberds, jun.,* Norwich and London, 1834.

Sillett, James, *Views of the Churches, Chapels and other Public Edifices in the City of Norwich by J. Sillett,* 59 plates 1828.

Singh, Duleep, *Portraits in Norfolk Houses,* ed. Rev. Edmund Farrer, 2 vols., Norwich, 1927.

Thistlethwaite 1974   **Thistlethwaite,** Jane, 'The etchings of E. T. Daniell', *Norfolk Archaeology,* vol. XXXVI, part 1 (1974).

Wallace Collection *Catalogue of Pictures and Drawings*   Wallace Collection Catalogues, *Pictures and Drawings* text, 16th Ed., London, 1968.

Whitley, William, T., 'Girtin's Panorama', *The Connoisseur,* May 1924, vol. LXIX, No. 273.

Williams, D. E., *Life of Lawrence,* 2 vols., London, 1831.

Williams, Iolo, *Early English Watercolours,* London, 1952.

Plate 1

15 View on the river near Cow's Tower, Norwich

30 Bishopsgate Bridge, Norwich—Evening 1813

35   Scene at Costessey, the Seat of Sir G. Jerningham

40 Riverside scene, near Norwich

41 Buxton Lamas, Norfolk

42 Cottage by the River at Thorpe, Norwich

75 Hoveton House, Norfolk

48 River Scene with Bridge

Plate 6

1 Whitlingham Church, Norfolk

2 Farm Buildings near Norwich

Plate 7

3   Gothic Barn, Castle Acre, Norfolk

4   Tudor House, Castle Acre, Norfolk

Plate 8

6 Two Wherries by a Wharf with a Figure unloading

7 Boat House on the River

Plate 9

5　Carrow Abbey, Norwich

8　Courtyard and Archway

Plate 10

10   Triforium, Norwich Cathedral

9   Interior of Binham Priory

Plate 11

12   The Devil's Tower, Norwich

11   View on the River Wensum, Norwich

Plate 12

14   Devil's Tower, Norwich

13   Devil's Tower near King Street Gates—Evening

Plate 13

26   Bishopgate Bridge and Cow Tower, Norwich

25   St. Benet's Abbey, Norfolk

Plate 14

22   St. Benedict's Abbey North Bure

21   St. Benets Abbey

Plate 15

24   St. Benet's Abbey, Norfolk

23   St. Benet's Abbey, Norfolk

Plate 16

19   River Scene

16   Castle on a Hill

Plate 17

20   Rainbow

17   A Castle

Plate 18

29 Boat Builder's Yard, near the Cow's Tower, Norwich

Plate 19

18   Sky Study with Trees and Rooftop

27   Lakenham Mills

Plate 20

34 Broken Ground in Thorpe

Plate 21

33   Kirby Bedon Church Tower, Norfolk

32   St. Ethelbert's Gate, Norwich Cathedral

31 Norwich Cathedral, South Transept and Cloister

Plate 23

37   St. Mary's Church, Wroxham, Norfolk

36   Catton Church—a Sketch

Plate 24

38   A view of Thorpe, with Steam Barge working up—Evening

39   Thorpe, Norwich

Plate 25

46   River Scene

43   The Abbot's Bridge, Bury St. Edmunds, Suffolk

Plate 26

45　Bridge over the Bure, Coltishall, Norfolk

44　Bridge over the Bure, Coltishall, Norfolk

Plate 27

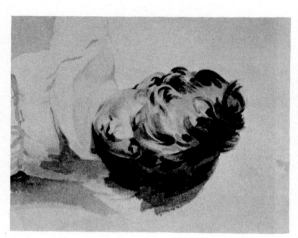

51   Head and Shoulders of a Child

50   Crossing the Brook—after Thomson

Plate 28

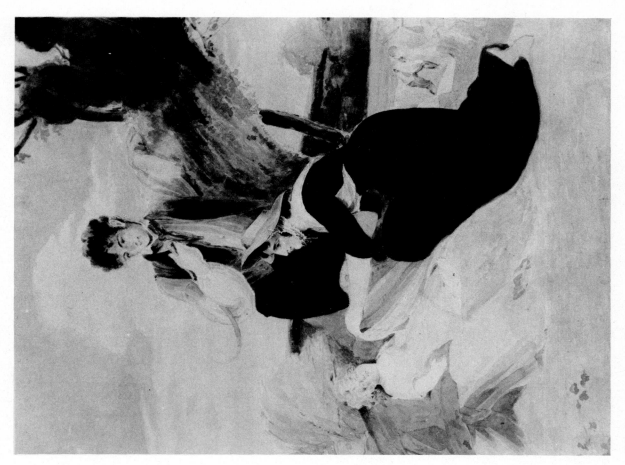

53 The Reaper's Child asleep, Harvest scene—after Westall

52 Dorothea—after Clarke

Plate 29

47   Evening River Scene with Bridge, Cows, Fisherman and Dog

49   Cattle on the River bank, Norwich Castle in the distance

Plate 30

59   St. Edmund's Church, Costessey, Norfolk 1816

56   Haymarket, Norwich

Plate 31

54   View of Norwich from the North-East

55   View of Norwich from Mousehold Heath

Plate 32

57   New Mills, Norwich

58   Fye Bridge, Norwich

Plate 33

61   Cottages, Cattle and Figure by a Broad

60   Hoveton Little Broad, Norfolk

Plate 34

63   Italianate Building

73   Caister Castle, Norfolk

Plate 35

64   Figures, standing beside Barrels, in a Square

65   Three Fishing Luggers and Two Figures on a Beach

Plate 36

66   Petch's Boat House opposite Cow Tower, Norwich

67   The Riverside, King Street, Norwich

Plate 37

74   Old Hall, Lakenham, Norwich

72   Burlingham House, Norfolk

Plate 38

70   Canal House, Ashwellthorpe, Norfolk

71   Stanfield Hall, Norfolk

Plate 39

68   Cluster of Houses by Water

62   A Norfolk Church

Plate 40

69   Lenwade Mill, Norfolk

80   Thorpe St. Andrew, Norwich

Plate 41

78   View on the river Wensum, King Street, Norwich

77   Rainbow Effect, on the River, King Street, Norwich 1817

Plate 42

76   Thorpe 1817

79   Thorpe Watering

Plate 43

83   Landscape with a Road to a Thatched Farmhouse

81   Putney Bridge, London 1819

Plate 44

84   Thorpe looking towards Whitlingham

82   Cottages and Trees beside the East End of Trowse Newton Church, Norfolk

Plate 45

87 Woman standing by a Font

100 Stranded Sailing Vessel

85 Lady sewing

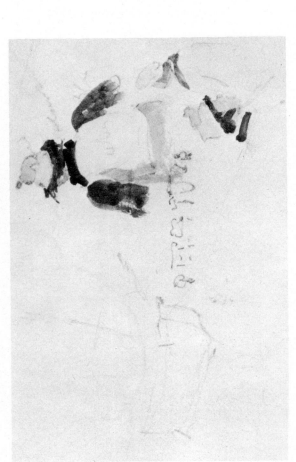

86 Study of a half length Figure, Two Heads and a Boat

Plate 46

95 River Scene with Wherries with Sketch of Boat in Sky

98 Riverside, Boats with Figures

97 Wherry with Sail lowered

96 Wherries and Figures

Plate 47

93   Wherry on River

101   Wherry and Sailing Boat

94   A Wherry

102   Wherry

Plate 48

99　A Sail, Sailing Boat with Figure, and a Figure

90　*Recto*, Riverside Scene with Wherry

103　River Scene with Billy Boy at Thorpe, Norwich

91　Old House with Foundry Bridge in the Distance

Plate 49

92   Duke's Palace Bridge, Norwich

108   The Devil's Tower and Carrow Bridge

Plate 50

106   The Devil's Tower, Norwich

107   The Devil's Tower and Carrow Bridge

Plate 51

104   *Verso*, Horstead Mill with two Cows

104   *Recto*, Beach Scene, Cromer with Sailing Ship and Figures

Plate 52

105　Buckenham Ferry, Norfolk 1827

114　Whitlingham Reach

Plate 53

113   River Scene with laden Wherries and Figures

112   Thorpe Staithe

Plate 54

109   *Recto*, Hilly landscape with a House and two Cows

109   *Verso*, Sunset Landscape with Windmill

Plate 55

111   Carrow Bridge, Norwich

110   Trowse near Norwich—after Vincent

Plate 56

121   *Recto*, Near Norwich, Trees and Figures on the right

120   Sunset Landscape with Thorpe Hospital, Norwich

Plate 57

116　Dilham Staithe

115　Dilham Staithe

Plate 58

118   Dilham Staithe, from the River

117   Dilham Staithe from the River

Plate 59

119   An East View of Norwich

122   Tombland, Norwich

Plate 60

88   Study of a Farm Cart

89   Two Horses between Shafts and Three Figures on the left

Plate 61

134 Church Porch with broken Cross in Foreground

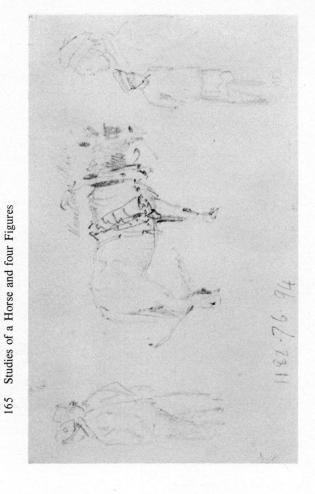

165 Studies of a Horse and four Figures

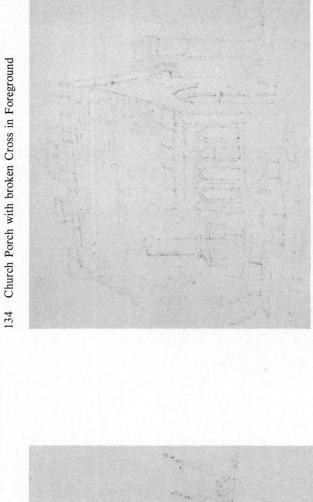

136 Building by Water with Boats and Figures

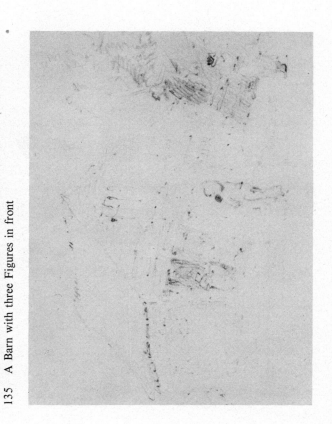

135 A Barn with three Figures in front

Plate 62

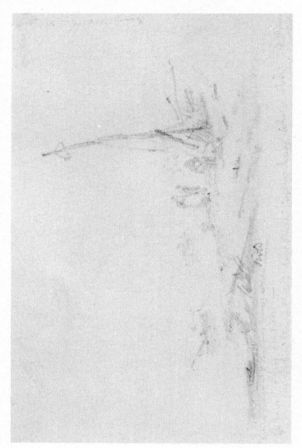

167 Beach Scene with Pole and Figures

168 Boats and Figures on a Beach

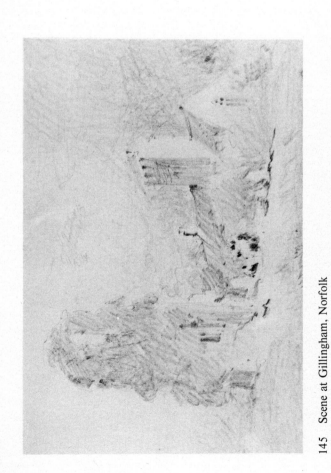

145 Scene at Gillingham, Norfolk

169 Quayside, Norwich

Plate 63

148   A Group of Five Sailors

146   Studies of Figures

Plate 64

147   Woman with a Jug beside and a Seated Man

166   Studies of Coaches

Plate 65

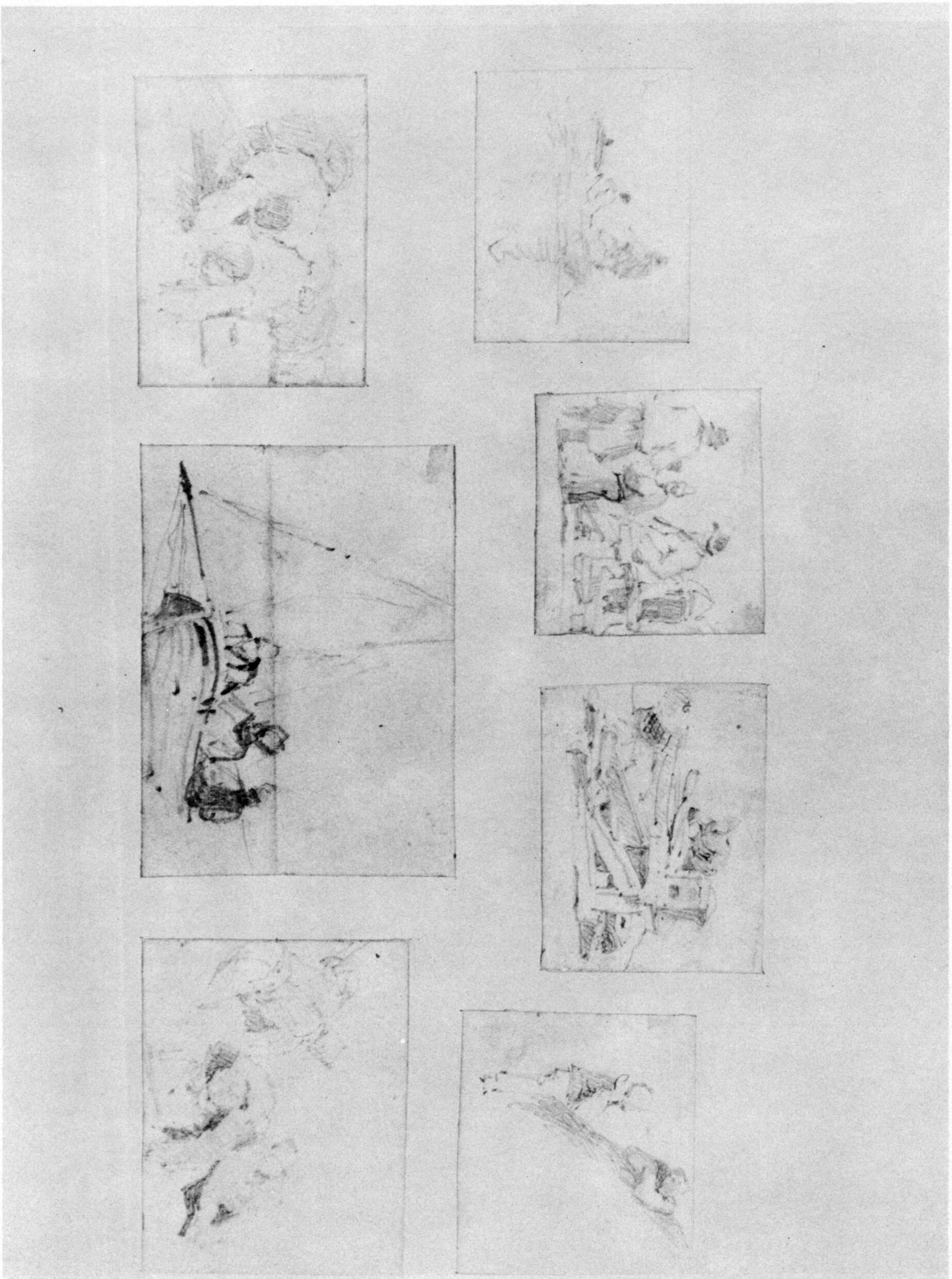

158–164 Sketches of Figures and Boats

Plate 66

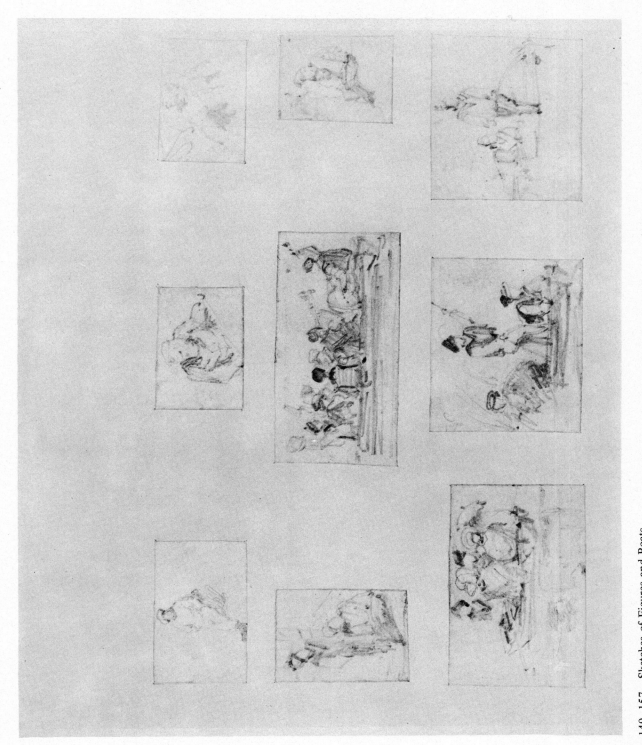

149–157 Sketches of Figures and Boats

142   A Country House with a female Figure in front

141   Burlingham St. Peter's Church, Norfolk

144   Two Figures and Trees with Pedimented Building

143   Two Figures by a ?Pump

Plate 68

137   Gateway of St. Benet's Abbey, Norfolk

138   Manor House in a Park

Plate 69

139   St. Margaret's Church, Felthorpe

140   Bishop Bridge, Norwich

Plate 70

123   Portrait of a Gentleman

124   William Cowper 1731–1800

Plate 71

127   Portrait of Miss Miles

125   Portrait of a Gentleman

126   Portrait of Miss Miles

128   Portrait of Mrs. Edmund Miles

Plate 72

132   Portrait of Catherine Miles on Cromer Beach

Plate 73

129 Portrait of a small Boy

133 Portrait of Catherine Miles

Plate 74

130 Self Portrait 1816

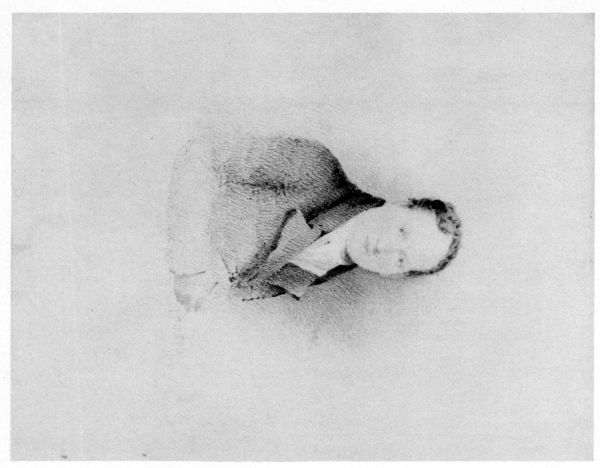

131 Portrait of the Artist's Wife, Elizabeth Miles 1816

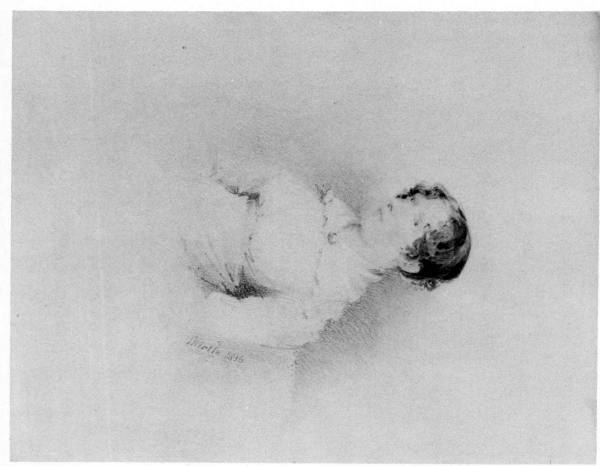